Experiencing Psychosis

Extensive sc ... g and learning
more about ... h the voice of
subjective ex ...)k, first-person
accounts are ... nt research to
suggest how ... understanding,
and therefor ...

Experienc ... who have either
experienced ... into the topic.
Chapters are ... personal and
research per ... hearing voices,
delusional b ... piritual issues.
Experts fror ... iis is a human
experience a ... ust have some
involvement ... ice.

This book ... onals involved
with psycho ... tories will also
attract servic ...

Jim Geekie ... osis Service at
St Luke's C ... Health Board
(ADHB), No ...

Patte Rand: ... ry at Buchanan
Rehabilitation ...

Debra Lampshire works for Auckland University and ADHB, New Zealand, leading the development in service-user involvement.

John Read is a Professor in Clinical Psychology at the University of Auckland, New Zealand and is Editor of the journal *Psychosis: Psychological, Social and Integrative Approaches*.

The International Society for the Psychological Treatments of Schizophrenias and Other Psychoses book series

Series editor: Brian Martindale

The ISPS (the International Society for the Psychological Treatments of the Schizophrenias and other Psychoses) has a history stretching back more than fifty years during which it has witnessed the relentless pursuit of biological explanations for psychosis. The tide is now turning again. There is a welcome international resurgence of interest in a range of psychological factors in psychosis that have considerable explanatory power and also distinct therapeutic possibilities. Governments, professional groups, users and carers are increasingly expecting interventions that involve more talking and listening. Many now regard skilled practitioners in the main psychotherapeutic modalities as important components of the care of the seriously mentally ill.

The ISPS is a global society. It is composed of an increasing number of groups of professionals, family members, those with vulnerability to psychosis and others, who are organised at national, regional and more local levels around the world. Such persons recognise the potential humanitarian and therapeutic potential of skilled psychological understanding and therapy in the field of psychosis. Our members cover a wide spectrum of approaches from psychodynamic, systemic, cognitive, and arts therapies to the need-adaptive approaches, group therapies and therapeutic institutions. We are most interested in establishing meaningful dialogue with those practitioners and researchers who are more familiar with biological based approaches. Our activities include regular international and national conferences, newsletters and email discussion groups in many countries across the world.

One of our activities is in the field of publication. Routledge has recognised the importance of our field, publishing the ISPS journal, *Psychosis: Psychological, Social and Integrative Approaches* (www.isps.org/journal.shtml). The journal complements Routledge's publishing of the ISPS book series, which started in 2004. The books aim to cover many topics within the spectrum of the psychological therapies of psychosis and their application in a variety of settings. The series is intended to inform and further educate a wide range of mental health professionals as well as those developing and implementing policy.

Some of the books will also promote the ideas of clinicians and researchers well known in some countries but not familiar in others. Our overall intention is to encourage the dissemination of existing knowledge and ideas, promote healthy debate, and encourage more research in a most important field whose secrets almost certainly do not all reside in the neurosciences.

For more information about the ISPS, email isps@isps.org or visit our website, www.isps.org

Other titles in the series

Models of Madness: Psychological, Social and Biological Approaches to Schizophrenia
Edited by John Read, Loren R. Mosher & Richard P. Bentall

Psychoses: An Integrative Perspective
Johan Cullberg

Evolving Psychosis: Different Stages, Different Treatments
Edited by Jan Olav Johanessen, Brian V. Martindale & Johan Cullberg

Family and Multi-Family work with Psychosis
Gerd-Ragna Bloch Thorsen, Trond Gronnestad & Anne Lise Oxenvad

Experiences of Mental Health In-Patient Care:
Narratives from Service Users, Carers and Professionals
Edited by Mark Hardcastle, David Kennard, Sheila Grandison & Leonard Fagin

Psychotherapies for the Psychoses: Theoretical, Cultural, and Clinical Integration
Edited by John Gleeson, Eión Killackey & Helen Krstev

Therapeutic Communities for Psychosis: Philosophy, History and Clinical Practice
Edited by John Gale, Alba Realpe & Enrico Pedriali

Beyond Medication: Therapeutic Engagement and the Recovery from Psychosis
Edited by David Garfield and Daniel Mackler

Making Sense of Madness: Contesting the Meaning of Schizophrenia
Jim Geekie and John Read

Psychotherapeutic Approaches to Schizophrenic Psychosis
Edited by Yrjö O. Alanen, Manuel González de Chávez, Ann-Louise S. Silver & Brian Martindale

Experiencing Psychosis

Personal and Professional Perspectives

Edited by Jim Geekie, Patte Randal, Debra Lampshire and John Read

Routledge
Taylor & Francis Group

LONDON AND NEW YORK

First published 2012
by Routledge
27 Church Road, Hove, East Sussex BN3 2FA

Simultaneously published in the USA and Canada
by Routledge
711 Third Avenue, New York NY 10017

Routledge is an imprint of the Taylor & Francis Group, an Informa business

British Library Cataloguing in Publication Data
A catalogue record for this book is available from the British Library

Library of Congress Cataloging-in-Publication Data
Experiencing psychosis: personal and professional perspectives/edited
by Jim Geekie . . . [et al.].
       p. cm.
   Includes bibliographical references and index.
   ISBN 978–0–415–58033–5 (hardback) — ISBN 978–0–415–58034–2
(pbk.)
   1. Psychoses. I. Geekie, Jim, 1961–
       RC512.E96 2011
       616.89—dc22

                                                                2011003757

ISBN: 978–0–415–58033–5 (hbk)
ISBN: 978–0–415–58034–2 (pbk)
ISBN: 978–0–203–80650–0 (ebk)

Typeset in Times New Roman by RefineCatch Limited, Bungay, Suffolk
Printed and bound in Great Britain by TJ International, Padstow,
Cornwall
Paperback cover design by Hybert Design

Contents

Tables and figures

Tables

Figures

List of contributors

Alan Barnard is a Senior Lecturer in the School of Nursing and Midwifery at Queensland University of Technology (QUT), Brisbane, Australia. He is a member of the QUT Institute for Health and Biomedical Innovation and is a Research Fellow at a major teaching hospital in Brisbane. He has qualifications in nursing, psychology, education and philosophy and has over 30 years' research, teaching, leadership and clinical experience. His research and scholarship interests relate to patient-focused care, chronic illness and interpretive qualitative research. He has been the recipient of research funding and has extensive publications in peer-reviewed journals. He is an experienced qualitative researcher and his recent research and publications include papers relating to the broad issue of the experience of person-focused care and health care delivery.

Vanessa Beavan is a Clinical Psychologist working in the Early Psychosis Service at St Luke's Community Mental Health Centre, Auckland, New Zealand. She is Co-Chair of the New Zealand Hearing Voices Network and Secretary of the International Society for the Psychological treatments of the Schizophenias and other Psychoses – New Zealand (ISPS-NZ).

Egan Bidois is a Mental Health (MH) Researcher and Liaison worker, and Cultural and Consumer Advisor to numerous bodies on national MH development from a Māori perspective. With constant lived experience of psychosis and paranoid schizophrenia, Egan maintains his wellness independent of MH services.

Wilma Boevink works as a researcher at Trimbos-institute in Utrecht, the Netherlands and as a professor of recovery in Hanze University in Groningen, the Netherlands. She is chair of Weerklank ('resonance'), the Dutch organization for voice hearers. She is a member of the supervisory board of The Netherlands Center for Chronic Early Childhood Traumatization (LCVT).

Rory Byrne is a researcher working for the NHS and the University of Manchester, UK, conducting research into Early Detection and Intervention for Psychosis, and the prevention or treatment of Psychosis using psychological therapies, rather than antipsychotic medication.

Dr. Michelle Campbell is a clinical psychologist currently working in an early detection team for psychosis in Leigh, UK. She has a particular interest in understanding psychosis and it was while working on her PhD that she recognized the value of exploring people's narratives of their experiences.

Dirk Corstens works as a psychiatrist and psychotherapist at RIAGG Maastricht in Maastricht, the Netherlands. He is chair of Intervoice, an international emancipatory organization for voice hearers.

Larry Davidson is Professor of Psychiatry at the Yale University School of Medicine, where he directs the Program for Recovery and Community Health. His research interests lie in processes of recovery in serious mental illness and promoting recovery-oriented care.

Jacqui Dillon is national Chair of the Hearing Voices Network in England, a Director of Intervoice and an Honorary Lecturer in Clinical Psychology at the University of East London. She has published numerous articles and papers and is co-editor of Living with Voices.

Jim Geekie is a Clinical Psychologist working in the Early Psychosis Service at St Luke's Community Mental Health Centre, Auckland, New Zealand. Along with John Read, he is co-author of *Making Sense of Madness* (Routledge, 2009).

Kate V. Hardy is a Clinical Psychologist working with the PREP program—a community-academic early psychosis service in the Bay Area, California and at the University of California, San Francisco.

Ingo Lambrecht is a Senior Clinical Psychologist for Psychotherapy Specialist Services, Auckland District Health Board, Auckland, New Zealand.

Debra Lampshire is an Experience-Based Expert. She has used her own lived experience of recovery as a voice hearer, incorporating this with experiences of consumers into clinical and educational settings. Debra currently works for Auckland District Health Board and Auckland University, leading the development in service-user involvement and psychological strategies.

Arnhild Lauveng is a clinical psychologist, currently doing a PhD at R & D Department, Mental Health Sevices, Akershus University Hospital, Norway. She is the author of three books. From 1988 to 1998 she was diagnosed with schizophrenia and spent most of this time in psychiatric wards. Today she is completely rehabilitated and off medications.

James Le Lievre has had a core interest in schizophrenia from the time a person well known to him was diagnosed. He has worked with diagnosed people voluntarily, at a clubhouse, in a private psychiatric hospital, and in his PhD studies on the subjective experience of emotional expression.

Eleanor Longden is a PhD student at the University of Leeds and part-time worker in the Bradford Early Intervention in Psychosis Service, UK. She is the coordinator for the Research Committee of Intervoice, the international network for training, education, and research into hearing voices.

David Lukoff is a Professor of Psychology at the Institute of Transpersonal Psychology and a licensed psychologist in California. He is author of 80 articles and chapters on spiritual issues and mental health and co-author of the DSM-IV category Religious or Spiritual Problems.

Paul H. Lysaker is a Clinical Psychologist at the Roudebush VA Medical Center in Indianapolis and Professor of Clinical Psychology in the Department of Psychiatry at the Indiana University School of Medicine, USA.

Lorenza Magliano is Associate Professor of Psychiatry at the Second University of Napoli, Italy. Her main research fields cover family burden in mental and physical illnesses, prejudices about persons with mental problems, and implementation of family interventions for schizophrenia in community-oriented mental health services.

Anthony P. Morrison is a Professor of Clinical Psychology at the University of Manchester and Associate Director for Early Intervention at Greater Manchester West NHS Trust, UK.

Jay Neugeboren is the author of 18 books, including award-winning books in fiction (*The Stolen Jew, Before My Life Began*) and non-fiction (*Imagining Robert, Transforming Madness*), along with three collections of prize-winning stories. His most recent novel is *1940*. A new collection of stories, *You Are My Heart and Other Stories*, was published in 2011.

Dr Patte Randal works as Medical Officer in Rehabilitation Psychiatry at Buchanan Rehabilitation Centre, ADHB, Auckland. She gained a DPhil from Sussex University, UK, has published research on recovery-focused multimodal therapy for people with treatment refractory psychosis, and is first author of the "Re-covery Model" (Randal *et al.* 2009). She teaches this model to postgraduates at Auckland University of Technology, to the ADHB and WDHB Key Workers and Care Coordinators and to Peer Support Workers. She is also involved in teaching psychiatry registrars as well as nursing students at Auckland University.

John Read is a Professor of Clinical Psychology at the University of Auckland, New Zealand. He was appointed to the programme in 1994 after twenty years working as a clinical psychologist, and service manager, primarily with people experiencing psychosis. He is on the Executive Committee of the International Society for the Psychological Treatments of Schizophenia (ISPS) and is the editor of the ISPS scientific journal *Psychosis: Psychological, Social and Integrative Approaches*. He is also the coordinating editor of *Models of Madness* (Routledge, 2004).

David Roe is an Associate Professor, clinical psychologist and chair of the Department of Community Mental Health, Faculty of Social Welfare and Health Sciences, University of Haifa, Israel.

Robert Schweitzer is an Associate Professor in Psychology in the School of Psychology and Counselling at Queensland University of Technology (QUT), Brisbane, Australia. He has a long-standing interest in phenomenology and psychopathology and established the clinical psychology training program at QUT. He also teaches clinical psychopathology and psychotherapy. His recent publications include papers relating to the broad issue of the experience of people entering Australia from refugee backgrounds. He is a member of the Northern Territory and Queensland Regional Board of the Psychology Board of Australia.

Dr. Melissa Taitimu (Te Rarawa) is a practising clinical psychologist. She conducted her PhD thesis, entitled '*Nga Whakaawhitnga*: Māori ways of understanding extra-ordinary experiences and schizophrenia' at the University of Auckland. Her research has focused upon indigenous psychologies, specifically Māori psychology.

John Wraphire is a former client of mental health services who experienced delusions. He is now fully recovered, hasn't used medications for many years and is a qualified teacher.

Preface
Comments by the editors

Working as a clinical psychologist in the area of early intervention for psychosis, I find the stories clients share with me to be profoundly moving and enlightening: it is through these stories that I have learnt most about the experience of psychosis. The notion that those who have first-hand lived experience of psychosis might be able to contribute to our understandings and approaches to these experiences seems to me to be so obviously true that it hardly merits stating. Yet, if we look at the literature on psychosis, it becomes clear that this notion does need to be stated. The voice of subjective experience has been sadly neglected. I believe that knowledge comes in many forms and that no single approach to knowledge and no single group of people have privileged claims to knowledge. The challenge we face is in integrating knowledge that comes from various sources or perspectives. The challenge in the area of psychosis is in bridging the gap that currently exists between the first-person perspective and other approaches to understanding. This book, by including both first-person and research perspectives, hopefully goes some way towards reducing this gap. I feel very fortunate to be living and working in New Zealand and to have colleagues like Patte Randal, Debra Lampshire and John Read, who share my commitment to the importance of subjective experience and my enthusiasm for this project, and each of whom promotes a way of thinking about and relating to mental health issues such as psychosis which sustains me in my work as a psychologist.

Jim Geekie

Jim asked me if I would be interested in co-editing and writing a chapter for a new book he was thinking about, exploring subjectivity. I responded with an immediate 'Yes!' We had previously co-authored the final chapter of a book and this had been a very enjoyable project. I had detailed aspects of my own subjective experience of episodes of psychosis, and the emergence of a spiritual understanding that became instrumental in my recovery. I had learned the value of talking about subjective experiences in this way from Debra. It had been my privilege to work alongside Debra in a little team which she led, developing an innovative way of helping people understand their voice-hearing experiences, and their distressing thoughts and beliefs. I had been encouraged by John's conviction that trauma was inextricably bound up with the inception of psychosis (which I intuitively knew was true). I remember being unable to stop crying with intense relief (and grief) when I first heard John speak publicly about the links between trauma and psychosis at the ISPS International Conference held in Melbourne in 2003. I felt so validated to hear his words. Working on the book with Jim, John and Debra has been an inspiration to me. My clinical practice has changed and I'm certain it is more effective as a result of reading and editing these chapters. I hope others will find the same healing resonance in these pages.

Patte Randal

For decades I waited, waited for the people who were allocated to help me, to listen. To listen with their hearts and minds, without preconceptions or judgement. To help unravel the mysteries of an inner world of which the code breaker can only be the person who has had the experiences. It did not happen. For decades I surrendered to a world of madness to survive both emotionally and psychologically. Slowly a new way of thinking has emerged. Enlightened professionals have had the audacity to embrace a simple concept: that if one is truly to be effective in assisting people to reclaim their lives, one needs to be authentic in listening to 'what has happened to people'. To explore life events we must listen with genuine curiosity to service users' narratives. This would seem self-evident. However, those of us whose lives have been devastated by madness have waited patiently for professionals to discover what has been so obvious to us: that those who experience distress need support and to become our own healers. Madness does not strip you of the basic human needs to be valued, treated with respect and regard, and 'loved'. It is through thoughtful relationships with family, friends and health professionals that we seek understanding and solace. This book is testament to those who actively work towards obtaining and sustaining mental well-being. The book acknowledges the courage service users have demonstrated to bring about changes in their own lives and invites professionals to do the same.

Debra Lampshire

In my 20 years working with people who hear voices or have unusual beliefs it has always seemed self-evident that the more I know about them and their lives, the better I can understand them, and, therefore, help a little. I was often surprised, at least in the early years, by the disinterest of many psychiatrists (and some other mental health professionals) in people's life stories and understandings of the causes of their difficulties. When I entered academia in 1994 I found, too, that most researchers in the field are more interested in dopamine receptors and chromosomes than in the actual lives and experiences, and needs, of the people they are studying. So I have really enjoyed working on this book with three people who share my interest in what people who actually experience 'psychosis' think and feel about it all. I believe that *Experiencing Psychosis* will turn out to be one of the most important books ever written about madness. It is just so much more interesting than most books on the topic – precisely *because* it places first-person accounts centre stage. I particularly valued writing the chapter on research about the experiences of family members. My clinical work, and my interest in the childhood trauma and abuse experienced by many people who experience psychosis as adults, has caused me to have to struggle not to have a rather stereotyped view of family members. Reading so many stories of love and caring, and of distress and hope, has helped me with that. I hope this book helps you question some of your own stereotypes about madness. We all have them.

John Read

Acknowledgements

The editors wish to acknowledge the wisdom and courage of those who agreed to share their stories for inclusion in this book, in the form of both first-person accounts and research looking at subjective experience. We hope these stories can inspire others, as indeed they have inspired us.

Chapter 1

Introduction

Jim Geekie, Patte Randal, John Read and Debra Lampshire

> If you do not know what is wrong with a person, ask him: he may tell you.
> George Kelly (1955: 322)

Among the defining characteristics of human beings is our great appetite for developing, reflecting upon and sharing with others our thoughts about the nature and meaning of our experiences. This quality permeates much, if not all, human behaviour and is, perhaps, most in evidence when we consider experiences that are deemed unusual or atypical. Run-of-the-mill everyday experiences may pass us by without attracting such scrutiny, but experiences which are out of the ordinary grab our attention and almost demand of us that we try to make sense of them. This is true, we contend, both of experiences in the world around us and of more intimate, private experiences – such as a dream, for example – that may be accessible only to the individual concerned.

Our concern in this book is how we go about the business of understanding and relating to a range of extra-ordinary human experiences. The particular experiences that concern us here are those that in clinical and scientific parlance tend to be referred to as phenomena that indicate psychosis and may be associated with diagnostic terms such as 'schizophrenia'. These might include experiences such as hearing voices that other people don't hear ('hallucinations'), or developing unusual, sometimes troubling, beliefs that don't seem to be supported by observable evidence ('delusions').

While the kinds of experiences we are talking about are, by and large, private in nature, in that they are immediately accessible only to the individual who actually has the experience, making sense of and deciding how to relate to these experiences commonly takes place in the interpersonal and social domain. Extensive scientific research has been conducted into understanding these experiences, although this research rarely takes account of subjective aspects of the experience. Widespread and well-established clinical and social services exist throughout the world to provide support to those who are troubled by these experiences, and this can, and is, sometimes provided in a compulsory manner, using powerful legislation which stipulates how these experiences should be understood and how they will be responded to (and this will commonly include enforced use of medication and/or admission to hospital). We mention these practices at this point not to disparage them, but to support our contention that making sense of psychosis takes place in the social arena and not purely within the mind of the individual who has these experiences, and that the sense we make can have major consequences in people's lives. We are well aware that experiences such as these and the behaviours that sometimes accompany them can be associated with considerable levels of confusion and distress for the individual concerned, for his or her family and friends, and sometimes for society at large, which may help explain why such practices have tended to occur.

However, given the nature of the phenomena we are referring to, it seems to us that the experience of the individual concerned must be central to any understanding of psychosis that we may develop. Sadly, if we look at the scientific research, we can see that this position is not shared by the vast majority of those who conduct research in this area, where the voice and perspective of the individual who experiences psychosis has been marginalized, occupying the position of what the French philosopher Foucault (1980) refers to as a 'subjugated knowledge'. One long-term advocate of recognising the importance of the subjective experience of those who experience psychosis, the American psychiatrist John Strauss (2008), recently lamented that – accurately we believe – 'There has been a major failure to consider adequately patients' subjective experiences in theory, research and practice.'

This neglect of the first-person perspective is, we believe, a tragedy of major proportions, for a number of reasons. Those who have such experiences feel 'silenced' and often subjected to the perspectives of others. Our understandings of psychoses are hampered by our failure to recognize the great contributions that can be made by those who are most intimately familiar with the phenomena. Opportunities for genuine collaboration between those who experience psychosis, and clinicians and researchers are lost. No doubt there are many other implications of this tendency to overlook the expertise of those with first-hand lived experience of psychosis. One of our aims in putting together this book is to help remedy this failure, by demonstrating the value of attending to the subjective experience of psychosis. Our hope is that this book will help shed some light on what it is like to have such experiences, encourage some consideration of how we might understand these experiences and develop some ideas around how we might relate to those experiences in ways which minimize any associated distress.

To achieve this goal, we invited a number of experts from around the world to contribute a chapter on the subjective experience of one particular aspect of what is referred to as psychosis. Following a discussion of the importance of personal understandings by David Roe and Paul Lysaker in the chapter following this introduction, the main body of this book consists of pairs of chapters on specific features of psychosis. The first chapter in each pair is a first-person account, given by an 'experience-based expert' (that is, someone who has first-hand lived experience of the phenomena being discussed). The second chapter in each pair is a discussion of scientific research into the subjective experience of the phenomena being considered. Our belief is that these chapters, though they were written entirely independently of each other, complement each other and demonstrate, first, that attending to subjective experience is an absolute requirement if we hope to develop adequate understandings of and clinical approaches to the experience of psychosis and, second, that the expertise of experience-based experts and researchers/clinicians (some of whom are themselves experience-based experts) in this field can – indeed *must* – be recognized for the unique contributions that each can make to the task of understanding the experience of psychosis. Genuine collaboration between the perspectives of first-hand lived experience and the research elaborating this, along with an acceptance of the differences and tensions between them, is a prerequisite if we are ever to make substantive progress towards understanding the all-too-human experience of temporarily losing one's bearings in the world. We must recognize that, first and foremost, psychosis is a human experience and as such is no different from a whole range of other human experiences. Understanding and appreciating the experience is enhanced by contributions from a range of perspectives, but can never be complete, never be even adequate, if the perspective of those who have first-hand knowledge of the experience concerned is excluded from the discussion of what the experience is, how best to understand it, and if and how we might respond to it.

At this point, we should stress that we are *not* arguing that subjective experience is somehow a royal road to some kind of infallible truth. We are arguing, simply, that subjective experience *must* be attended to, not that it is infallible. Here, we agree with the position of the British psychologist David Smail, who argues that: 'The subjective perspective needs to be evaluated intersubjectively (which brings it as near as possible to being objective) but there is still, ultimately, no authority beyond it' (Smail 2004: 33).

We agree with Smail that even personal accounts of experience are, and should be, subject to evaluation by others and that this evaluation is an essential consideration in gauging the contribution that these accounts make to our knowledge base. Sharing one's personal story, or one's research, in the public domain opens the way for such evaluation by others, where the reader can reflect upon the contribution the writer makes to our understandings of the experiences concerned. To encourage such considerations, as well as to establish some uniformity of structure in the book, we requested of contributors that, after discussion of their personal experience of or research into subjective experience, they should identify 'implications for understanding' and 'implications for practice' which emerge from their account.

As editors of this collection we have been moved tremendously by the generous, compassionate and perceptive accounts of the subjective experience of psychosis that the reader will encounter in this volume. We feel enormously privileged to have been entrusted with the stories shared in this book, and we would like to extend an invitation to the reader to listen to the diverse chorus of voices contained herein, each of which strives in its own unique way to express something about the nature of the human condition, something which often lies at the limits of what our language can sensibly convey, but which is ultimately the essence of what it is to be human: the experience which some call 'psychosis', some call 'madness' and others – as the reader will no doubt discover – argue we must recognize as an understandable response to intolerable, unbearable suffering.

References

Foucault, M. (1980) 'Body/power'. In C. Gordon (ed.) *Power/Knowledge: Selected Interviews and Other Writings, 1972–1977* (pp. 55–62). New York: Pantheon.

Kelly, G. A. (1955) *The Psychology of Personal Constructs, Volumes I and II*. New York: W.W. Norton & Co.

Smail, David (2004) *Power, Responsibility and Freedom*. Retrieved from: www.davidsmail.info/intpub.htm

Strauss, J. (2008) 'Prognosis in schizophrenia and the role of subjectivity', *Schizophrenia Bulletin, 34*: 201–203.

Chapter 2

The importance of personal narratives in recovery from psychosis

David Roe and Paul H. Lysaker

What we attend to is a matter of choice, a choice which is influenced by the context in which this choice is made. What we choose to attend to amongst the endless possibilities presented to us at any given moment is also a by-product of what we were taught, trained, encouraged and reinforced to view as valuable. A child may sit with his parents at a circus and be fascinated by a child his age sitting in the next row. His parents may actively encourage him to pay attention to the stage where the exciting show for which they bought expensive tickets is taking place.

At any given moment, a combination of internal and external forces, with various degrees of harmony or tension, influence what we end up choosing to attend to. For example, as clinical psychology interns at a community mental health clinic, we would, with great reverence, bring the raw data of the 'Bender' and 'Draw A Person' tests to supervision sessions with the chief psychologist who we simultaneously admired and feared. Our emerging clinical skills were primarily attuned to cues signifying what we should be attending to as well as its 'correct' interpretation. The size, proportion, intensity and location of the shapes and lines, so we learned, had profound meanings which we were taught to attend to and interpret in specific ways to complete a 'successful' assessment. At least successful enough so that the chief psychologist would approve our taking the licensing exam.

But what does a child sitting in a circus or a bunch of frightened clinical psychology interns have to do with the importance of narratives in recovery from psychosis? It is because, like the child or interns, when talking with a person who has experienced psychosis, as a listener one has to choose what to attend to when trying to understand and provide help. As Miller Mair (1989: 1) put it: 'We have not been encouraged to suppose that we are *choosing* to tell tales in particular ways, for particular *ends*, and for the approval of particular *audiences*.' In a recent first-person account of psychosis, Kean (2009: 1) writes: 'I was totally separated from myself, not knowing what action I was taking, let alone considering how to "communicate" . . . I was unaware of myself, and my psychiatrist was unaware of me.' In this chapter we will posit that a purpose for attending to the experience of persons with mental illness is to assist their 'personal recovery' (Slade 2009). If we are listening to people who have experienced psychosis in order to help them find the lives they are searching for, it would seem essential to carefully understand how they have made meaning of the story of their lives and their experience of psychosis. This process of developing 'enabling narratives' can occur without clinical assistance, and sometimes even despite clinical assistance, when those may undermine the narrators' roles as authors of their own experience. Debra Lampshire's account in this book is one such example.

But what do we know about the personal narratives of persons who have experienced psychosis? As we will see in the chapters which follow, many who have experienced psychosis are capable of constructing, and sharing, as they do in this book, their own unique narratives of their experiences and their varied ways of understanding, relating to and dealing with them. This chapter will focus on how we might listen to and understand the unique stories of unique persons who have experienced psychosis. It is divided into four sections. In the first we will explore what can be learned from first-person narrative accounts of mental illness. In the second and third we will explore qualitative and quantitative analyses of personal narratives. Finally, we will comment briefly on the theoretical and clinical implications of this work.

Researching personal narratives among people who have experienced psychosis

First-person accounts of mental illness

Modern descriptive psychiatry has tended to focus on what can be readily observed and measured. As such, much of our tradition involves persons in the position of expert drawing conclusions about the meanings of the experiences of others. Strauss (1989) was among the first to draw attention to how focusing narrowly on the effort to meet a particular conception of science has generated an unscientific tendency to ignore large amounts of important data simply because they are difficult to measure reliably using standard methodological tools. According to Strauss, essential information is lost in the process of systematically characterizing individuals' experiences on the basis of questionnaires or structured interviews. Frank and Frank (1993) point out, for example, that descriptive psychiatry's 'atheoretical' stance actually posits a theory in itself: that the meaning people attach to their experiences, their beliefs about and attitudes towards their experience of psychosis, and their social and historical context are all unimportant. Morstyn (1994) argues that many concepts lose their essential meaning in the process of operationalizing them so they can be reliably coded and subjected to statistical analysis. Chadwick (2006) accuses biomedical approaches in schizophrenia research of trapping clinicians in conceptual schemes which prevent them from listening to the experiences of their patients, leading to the alienation of healer and sufferer. Lysaker and Lysaker (2008) note that without a valuation of the life and experience of persons with any condition we hazard undermining the study of that disorder as a meaningful element of the human condition, amputating the person from the disorder.

One response to this criticism is an effort to understand psychosis from the 'inside' and explore the way it is experienced. Here we are referring to narrative characterizations of mental illness by persons who have experienced psychosis. Starting with pioneers such as Judi Chamberlin, Pat Deegan and Daniel Fisher, a growing number of people who had experienced mental illness and its aftermath began an international conversation about what it means to experience mental illness. A rapidly growing number of poignant first-person accounts began to be published in journals, books, and internet links, providing a much more rich, complex and personal perspective on having experienced psychosis, along with its social consequences. These first-person accounts helped the lay public as well as the professional community to realize that in order to understand the symptoms of mental illness it is not enough to just describe them. Instead, it is crucial to consider the personal context in which they take place, and the way they are experienced, perceived, interpreted and dealt with. It also became apparent that people who have 'been there' and 'lived through it' often acquire unique and valuable insights. For example, Chadwick (2006) draws from his experience as a psychologist, as a researcher and as someone who has experienced psychosis himself the importance of developing an attitude in which the person is the agent of his or her own beliefs and develops the ability to retain a critical reflective stance toward his or her own experiences. A powerful illustration of the profound challenge mental illness poses for one's sense of self is found in Kean's first-person account, which we will refer to again later.

> What lies behind the symptoms is a tormented self, a highly personal experience unchangeable and irreplaceable by any physical treatment ... Despite the 'usual' voices, alien thoughts and paranoia, what scared me the most was a sense that I had lost myself, a constant feeling that my self no longer belonged to me. This has nothing to do with the suspicious thoughts or voices; it is purely a distorted state of being. The clinical symptoms come and go, but this nothingness of the self is permanently there ... what scared me the most was a sense that I had lost myself, a constant feeling that my self no longer belonged to me. ... What he [the mental health professional] chose to see was nothing but the symptoms alone. I feel that my real self has left me, seeping through the fog toward a separate reality, which engulfs and dissolves this self ... the real 'me' is not here any more. I am disconnected, disintegrated, diminished ... Schizophrenia is ultimately a disorder of the self, a disturbance of one's subjective self-experience and the external or objective reality.
>
> (Kean 2009: 1)

Qualitative studies of personal narratives

In addition to influential first-person accounts there have been growing efforts to systematically study personal narratives. Adopting a narrative perspective helps us to understand how people create narrative identities, develop the capacity to make sense of and organize past experiences, seek to understand themselves as unique individuals and develop a sense of continuity across their lifespan (Raffard *et al.* 2010). Narrative research has helped us to better understand the recovery process of one's sense of self after experiencing psychosis. Focusing on narratives broadens the horizons concerning the range of factors that influence a person's understanding of, and response to, the onset of psychosis. Working from such a position, Estroff *et al.* (1991) referred to illness-identity work as the process through which a person learns about and incorporates psychiatric explanations once he or she comes into contact with mental healthcare or composes counter-claims about illness and self in reaction to a biomedical explanation. In their view, this process generates two main types of talk about self and illness: normalizing talk, which disputes the assignation of illness and reauthorizes either the condition as commonly occurring or the person as not sick, and illness identity statements, which include self-representations that incorporate illness. Roe and Ben-Yishai (1999) identified five distinct categories that speak to different relationships that emerge in this process. In the first category, participants separated their 'healthy' self from their 'ill' self. This separation occurred at the narrative level, in the story the participants told, which revealed various stages of perception of self in relation to their illness, shifting from a 'split' between the two to a fuller and more integrative story which included various aspects of self and illness over time in which the self was protagonist. This sort of stand is in line with a shift along the theoretical construct from invalidation to validation (Geekie & Read 2009), during which one's authority over the interpretation moves from being under-mined to being validated.

In addition to the contribution of narratives to developing a better understanding of important changes in the experience of self and self in relation to illness, other studies have provided useful insights into the process of recovery and helped to identify distinct stages. Ridgway (2001) published first-person accounts of recovery and identified broad common themes including moving from despair to hope, from withdrawal to engagement, from passive adjustment to active coping, and reclaiming a positive sense of self, meaning and purpose. In another study, Jacobson (2001) analyzed published narratives of recovery using a dimensional analysis and identified component processes which corresponded to four central dimensions: recognizing the problem, transforming the self, reconciling the system and reaching out to others. Based on a select sample of the recovery literature, Andresen *et al.* (2003) proposed a five-stage model which included a shift from a moratorium characterized by denial towards rebuilding a positive identity and experiencing growth.

Finally, qualitative research has emphasized the potentially powerful healing value of narratives. Stories are a way of curing the wounds that illnesses often create, helping to make sense, redraw maps and find new destinations (Gold 2007; Roe & Davidson 2005). Narratives provide an important tool to search for and create a personally meaningful way of making sense of psychosis and its aftermath (Larsen 2004), to find meaning (Wagner & King 2005), and to communicate and earn the respect and validation of others (Geekie & Read 2009).

Stories provide narrators with the opportunity to renegotiate the meaning, sequence and connection between past and present life events and accept themselves and their personal histories. Narratives also provide a fundamental tool to help communicate with others as stories are comforting and help bond people together (Gold 2007).

Quantitative studies of personal narrative

In contrast to work which has sought to discern the common themes and qualities of personal narratives of persons who have experienced psychosis, more recent literature has sought to quantify in some manner the degree to which personal narratives cohere or fail to cohere in an adaptive manner. This literature has sought to determine to what extent the relative absence vs. presence of certain aspects of a personal narrative can be objectively observed and to what extent their presence is predictive of various outcomes. What are the ways in which personal narratives differ from one another and how are such differences related to wellness?

In one of the first attempts to quantitatively study personal narratives, Lysaker *et al.* (2006a; 2006b), developed the Scale to Assess Narrative Development (STAND). The STAND was constructed on the basis of narrative theory which stresses that a sense of self can vary from a state of more to less coherence according to how it is constituted with a past and present as embodied within the stories one tells oneself and others. The STAND contains four Likert scales which can be applied to rate speech samples in which persons give a narrative account of their lives. The four subscales assess the extent to which individuals portray themselves within their own life stories as having:

i   Illness Conception, or realistic life challenges
ii   Agency, or a sense of being as an active agent in their own lives
iii   Alienation, or meaningful bonds with others, and
iv   Social Worth, or value in their community.

In the first empirical study of the STAND (Lysaker *et al.* 2006a), narratives of 34 participants with a diagnosis of schizophrenia spectrum disorders were analyzed. An acceptable degree of inter-rater reliability was established and higher scores on the STAND were found to be associated with greater levels of self-esteem and greater overall readiness for change. Specifically, greater levels of readiness for change were linked with greater Illness Conception and greater self-esteem was linked to higher levels of Social Worth and Agency. In the second study (Lysaker *et al.* 2006b), with a sample of 65 persons with a schizophrenia spectrum disorder diagnosis, higher STAND scores were linked to higher levels of hope and social function, and lower levels of positive and disorganization symptoms. In subsequent studies lower STAND scores were found to be linked to higher levels of self-stigma (Lysaker *et al.* 2008). Finally, higher STAND ratings have been found to be correlated with greater levels of quality and quantity of social relatedness independent of the effects of related constructs such as hope and self-esteem (Lysaker *et al.* 2010a).

From a different angle, Saavedra alone (2009) and with colleagues (2009) has analyzed the narratives of adults with a diagnosis of schizophrenia. It is reported that it is possible to distinguish narratives in terms of the extent to which persons define themselves as a patient, the degree of agency they perceived in their lives and the extent to which highly implausible accounts of life experiences obscure underlying meaning. These different dimensions were linked with differing degrees of health and well-being.

Investigating where personal narratives may break down in terms of narrative content, Gruber and Kring (2008) have explored the degree to which the emotional quality of a life event affects how it is narrated. In comparison with persons who do not experience any mental illness, they note that persons with a diagnosis of schizophrenia tend to tell less coherent narratives in terms of temporality and appropriateness of content when strong emotions are at play. Raffard *et al.* (2010) confirmed that persons with a diagnosis of schizophrenia tend to have greater difficulties constructing coherent narrative accounts of their lives. They noted that greater duration of illness predicted greater difficulties in narratizing life events and that higher levels of negative symptoms predicted fewer connections between persons and the events of their lives and fewer meaningful details about those events. These findings may possibly reflect having been more exposed to the dominant medical paradigm within mental health care, a framework which tends to promote the notion that there isn't any meaning in the person's experience, and that it is not related to life events and context.

Implications for theory and practice

Personal narratives as a crucial domain of recovery

One implication from the material presented above is that personal narrative, or the meaning persons make of their lives in a storied manner, may stand as a unique dimension of recovery. As suggested above and elsewhere (Lysaker *et al.* 2010b; White & Epston 1990), the story one tells about one's life, including the experiences of illness, may be related to symptom severity and the achievement of milestones, but it is not reducible to those events. To have or not have symptoms and to have or not have a job are not the same as to have or not have a rich story of one's life. Similarly, to have hope for the future or a view of oneself as capable or likable would also seem to be related to the kind of story one tells of one's life. A personal narrative, its richness and adaptiveness, cannot be reduced to a matter of possessing a certain degree of hope or self-esteem. Certainly, there could be very rich narratives in which hope is slim and there is an articulate expression of marginalization. It is also possible that a disconnected narrative could serve a protective function as well.

As an illustration, we suggest that in Kean's (2009) narrative described above, we can find an individual who speaks with a coherent authenticity. This authenticity, importantly, is not just a matter of hope, symptom remission or empowerment. She is actively making meaning of her own life, in her own voice. The meanings she makes possess consensual validity but she is not reading from a script or endorsing beliefs that might be found in a recovery questionnaire. Accordingly her life is her own, no matter how painful, and as such she is capable of making her own sense of her dilemma and deciding what to do. Her narrative – because it is her own – allows her to possess some ownership over her life, to function as an agent in the world, no matter how painful that world is at the moment.

It may be essential for future studies of recovery to take into account the stories of people seeking to move towards recovery. It may be that to fail to take these into account would mean missing an important way in which a person has achieved or is still struggling to achieve a degree of health. Longitudinal studies of narrative and other objective and subjective aspects of recovery may furthermore allow for the discovery of answers to a range of important questions. For instance, how often do changes in narrative precede or follow changes in other facets of recovery such as the development of hope, success in work or symptom remission? What sorts of experiences are linked to the development of a rich personal narrative for persons who previously had lost the thread of their life story? As persons recover, how important is it that the trauma of psychotic experience itself is processed and understood?

The systematic consideration of personal narratives, both in a qualitative and a quantitative sense, would seem to promise some answers to these questions and also helps us to keep alive an awareness of the individual person who not only experiences a range of challenges but also actively makes meaning of them.

Personal narratives as a means to facilitate recovery

If we accept personal narratives as a unique element of recovery, it seems natural that they be considered in discussions of both existing and evolving treatments, rehabilitation and system change.

One place to think about this issue in terms of current treatments (e.g. Acceptance and Commitment Therapy and supported employment) is to begin with the consideration that during those treatments there are often lengthy conversations between persons with mental illness and their clinicians or rehabilitation specialists. While those conversations may often be problem-focused, these conversations may also involve how persons understand their life. Many conversations in interventions such as these likely include discussions in which clients clarify what in the course of their life has gone wrong, what has not gone wrong, and what they hope for, grieve and plan to do about it. These sorts of conversations may also help to identify the narratives clinicians use in making sense of psychosis and help them to focus on enabling narratives rather than imposing information.

If narratives grow through the telling and retelling of one's story then there should be room within these interventions for persons to be afforded a place to decide how they choose to understand their current challenges in light of what they believe has transpired over the course of their life. Assisting with this may require treaters and rehabilitation specialists to speak with clients in a consultative, non-hierarchical way, one that does not authoritatively usurp a person's right to make their own sense of their needs and hopes. It may, though, be essential at times to also invite clients to pursue opportunities to decide what they believe. In this way, it may be useful to conceptualize services and interventions as processes that are more than treatments for problems. Interventions could be seen as offering consultation regarding the different ways the recovering person is telling their story of the experiences of living with a mental illness and its aftermath. Indeed, it is possible that this is a non-specific factor already at work within the practice of many of these interventions. Such possibilities are consistent with developments in recovery-oriented psychotherapy as discussed elsewhere (Lysaker *et al.* 2010a).

With respect to the development of new services, the work reviewed above also seems to point to the possibility of interventions which might focus specifically on personal narrative in the context of other issues. One illustration is a structured group intervention we have recently developed with the goal to decrease self-stigma among people who have experienced psychosis (Yanos *et al.* in press). The intervention, which we entitled Narrative Enhancement/Cognitive Therapy (NECT) features a guide for the practitioner aimed to help explain the rationale, tone and technique, as well as handouts that can be used to guide group discussions. In addition, the manual includes worksheets that can be used to help group members to learn and practice skills for coping with internalized stigma by identifying cognitive distortions or dysfunctional attitudes related to having a mental illness. Finally, and most directly related to the topic of this chapter, the intervention focuses on offering participants the opportunity to tell their own unique stories and provide constructive feedback to the stories of other participants.

Overall, the work reviewed above seems to us to point to a wide range of possibilities for professionals to develop new ways to directly seek to facilitate the process of constructing and telling stories. In formal and informal consultation, in individual, group, family and community settings, we see the promise of helping persons who have experienced psychosis to find their own consensually valid ways of framing the past, seeing themselves as not just defined by illness, feeling a sense of control over illness and that life gives meaning to particular events in the present, as well as communicating with others. Perhaps most important is that by refining and developing new interventions we can support persons becoming the authors of their own life story and an active agent, a self, authoring a new story. The following chapters provide a rich and diverse source to help move along this important path.

References

Andresen, R., Oades, L. and Caputi, P. (2003) 'The experience of recovery from schizophrenia: Towards an empirically validated stage model', *Australian and New Zealand Journal of Psychiatry*, 37: 586–594.

Chadwick, P. (2006) *Person-based Cognitive Therapy for Distressing Psychosis*. New York: Wiley.

Estroff, S. E., Lachicotte, W. S., Illingworth, L. C., and Johnson, A. (1991) 'Everybody's got a little mental illness: Accounts of illness and self among people with severe, persistent mental illness', *Medical Anthropology Quarterly*, 5: 331–369.

Frank, J. D. and Frank, J. B. (1993) *Persuasion and Healing: A Comparative Study of Psychotherapy* (3rd ed.). Baltimore, ML: The Johns Hopkins University Press.

Geekie, J. and Read, J. (2009) *Making Sense of Madness: Contesting the Meaning of Schizophrenia*. Hove, England: Routledge.

Gold, E. (2007) 'From narrative wreckage to islands of clarity. Stories of recovery from psychosis', *Canadian Family Physician*, 53: 1271–1275.

Gruber, J. and Kring, A. M. (2008) 'Narrating emotional events in schizophrenia', *Journal of Abnormal Psychology*, 117: 520–533.

Jacobson, N. (2001) 'Experiencing recovery: A dimensional analysis of recovery narratives', *Psychiatric Rehabilitation Journal*, 24: 248–256.

Kean, K. (2009) 'Silencing the self: Schizophrenia as a self-disturbance', *Schizophrenia Bulletin*, 35: 1034–1036.

Larsen, J. A. (2004) 'Finding meaning in first-episode psychosis: Experience, agency, and the cultural repertoire', *Medical Anthropology Quarterly*, 18: 447–471.

Lysaker, P. H. and Lysaker, J. T (2008) *Schizophrenia and the Fate of the Self*. Oxford: Oxford University Press.

Lysaker, P. H., Taylor, A., Miller, A., Beattie, N., Strasburger, A. and Davis, L. W. (2006a) 'The Scale to Assess Narrative Development: Associations with other measures of self and readiness for recovery in schizophrenia spectrum disorders', *Journal of Nervous and Mental Disease*, 27: 233–247.

Lysaker, P. H., Buck, K. D., Hammoud, K., Taylor, A. C. and Roe, D. (2006b) 'Associations of symptom remission, psychosocial function and hope with qualities of self experience in schizophrenia: Comparisons of objective and subjective indicators of recovery', *Schizophrenia Research*, 82: 241–249.

Lysaker, P. H., Buck, K. D., Taylor, A. C. and Roe, D. (2008) 'Associations of metacognition, self stigma and insight with qualities of self experience in schizophrenia', *Psychiatry Research*, 157: 31–38.

Lysaker, P. H., Glynn, S. M., Wilkness, S. M. and Silverstein, S. M. (2010a) 'Psychotherapy and recovery from schizophrenia: A review of potential application and need for future study', *Psychological Services*, 7: 75–91.

Lysaker, P. H., Roe, D. and Buck, K. (2010b) 'Recovery and wellness amidst schizophrenia: Definitions, evidence and the implications for clinical practice', *Journal of the American Psychiatric Nurses Association*, 16: 36–42.

Mair, M. (1989) 'Kelly, Bannister and a storytelling psychology', *Journal of Constructivist Psychology*, 2: 1–14.

Morstyn, R. (1994) 'Clinical practice beyond science', *Australian and New Zealand Journal of Psychiatry*, 28: 352–354.

Raffard, S., D'Argembeau, A., Lardi, C., Bayard, S., Boulenger, J. P. and Linden, M. V. (2010) 'Narrative identity in schizophrenia', *Consciousness and Cognition, 19*: 328–340.

Ridgway, P. (2001) 'Restoring psychiatric disability: Learning from first-person recovery narratives', *Psychiatric Rehabilitation Journal, 24*: 335–343.

Roe, D. and Ben-Yishai, A. (1999) 'Exploring the relationship between the person and the disorder among individuals hospitalized for psychosis', *Psychiatry, 62*: 370–380.

Roe, D. and Davidson, L. (2005) 'Self and narrative in schizophrenia: Time to author a new story', *Journal of Medical Humanities, 31*: 89–94.

Saavedra, J. (2009) 'Schizophrenia, narrative and change: Andalusian care homes as novel sociocultural context', *Culture, Medicine and Psychiatry, 33*: 163–184.

Saavedra, J., Cubero, M. and Crawford, P. (2009) 'Incomprehensibility in the narratives of individuals with a diagnosis of schizophrenia', *Qualitative Health Research, 19*: 1548–1558.

Slade, M. (2009) *Personal Recovery and Mental Illness. A Guide for Mental Health Professionals*. Cambridge: Cambridge University Press.

Strauss, J. S. (1989) 'Subjective experience in schizophrenia: Towards a new dynamic psychiatry', *Schizophrenia Bulletin, 15*: 179–187.

Wagner, L. C. and King, M. (2005) 'Existential needs of people with psychotic disorders in Pôrto Alegre, Brazil', *British Journal of Psychiatry, 186*: 141–145.

White, M. and Epston, D. (1990) *Narrative Means to Therapeutic Ends*. New York: W.W. Norton.

Yanos, P. T., Roe, D. and Lysaker, P. H. (in press) 'Narrative enhancement and cognitive therapy: A new group-based treatment for internalized stigma among persons with severe mental illness', *Journal of Group Psychotherapy*.

Part I

Recovery

We begin our pairs of chapters, intentionally, with a focus on the process of recovering from the experience of psychosis. We place these chapters at the beginning of this section to stress our belief that those who experience psychosis can, and do, recover.

In the first of the two chapters, Jacqui Dillon shares her moving story and challenges us to view her unusual experiences not as evidence of 'psychosis', but as normal reactions to the extreme events of her childhood. Larry Davidson provides us with an overview of his research into the experience of recovery, drawing our attention to the importance of attending to doing ordinary, everyday activities and introduces the helpful concept of 'hurrying slowly'.

What we have our attention drawn to in both chapters is the vital importance of one's sense of self in the recovery process. We see how making sense of the experience in a personally meaningful and enabling way, and having this sense making validated by an 'empathic witness', can be central components of the process of recovery. On the other hand, we see also how denial of the individual's subjectivity can exacerbate feelings of helplessness. Making sense of the experience nurtures and enhances the development of a sense of agency and control over important aspects of one's life, and, associated with this, facilitates the individual in getting on with the business of living.

Chapter 3

Recovery from 'psychosis'

Jacqui Dillon

From my subjective experience it would have made more sense to me if I were writing about recovering from child abuse rather than recovering from 'psychosis'. As Lucy Johnstone has said:

> The main point of the research of Read and others is that there is growing evidence that unusual beliefs, distressing voices and so on are, often, a reaction to the abuses that service users have been subjected to. There is the abuse, and there are the responses to the abuse. There is no additional 'psychosis' that needs explaining.
>
> (Johnstone 2009: 187)

My experiences of hearing voices, seeing visions, tactile sensations, feeling suspicious and paranoid, having a different experience of reality to others and so on, have been deemed by others as 'psychosis' or a form of serious mental illness. For me, these experiences are all a natural and human consequence of the extreme experiences that I survived as a child and make total sense within that context, although I didn't always know that.

My early years were filled with many terrifying and overwhelming experiences which literally drove me mad. As a small child, I experienced physical, emotional and sexual abuse combined with emotional neglect at the hands of those adults who were meant to be protecting me. The consequence of such extreme abuse and profound betrayal is absolutely devastating and has shaped every aspect of my experience – both my internal and external worlds.

The denial endemic within and surrounding abusive families only served to compound my sense of feeling crazy and consequently I grew up with a sense of there being two realities. In one version of reality, I and everyone else pretended that I was fine, everything was normal and that all was ok in the world. In the other reality, the world was filled with inescapable, arbitrary cruelty. My abusers were apparently omnipotent with the freedom to commit atrocious acts with impunity. As a small child I was told that insects worked for them and would report back to them if I ever spoke about the abuse.

These two realities co-existed throughout my childhood and into adulthood with some degree of success. I was able to develop a successful career and to live independently and give the appearance of living a functional life although I was still hearing voices, self-harming and having major issues with my eating throughout this time. That was until things came full circle and I became a mother myself. With primary responsibility for protecting my tiny, vulnerable child, the two worlds finally, spectacularly, collided and in the aftermath, there was only one reality: a world filled with terror, horror and desolation. My voices multiplied and said things which frightened and disturbed me. I became intensely paranoid, scared to leave the house in case someone tried to hurt me or my baby. I would be changing my baby's nappy when suddenly I would look at her and she would be covered in blood. I would blink and the blood would disappear. I was tormented by terrifying night terrors. My self harm spiralled out of control and my attempts to recreate the pretend world failed at every attempt until I had to concede defeat. It was then that I turned to statutory mental health services for help.

When I attempted to disclose the horrendous abuse that I had experienced as a child to the mental health professionals in charge of my care, I was told that these experiences hadn't really happened to me, but that they were, in fact, delusions, one of the primary symptoms of my mental illness. When I became upset and angry at having my experiences denied I was told that this was also a symptom of my illness. When I began to bang my head against the wall in utter frustration and despair, this too was considered a consequence of my illness. Throughout my experiences of madness and recovery, being told by others that I lacked insight and observing their attempts to render my experiences as a biomedical illness which had no subjective or objective reality or validity is what has seemed most crazy to me. I once naively believed that psychiatric services provided sanctuary for those in deep distress. What I discovered was that they would only add insult to injury and do more harm.

In order to escape this crazy-making world, I temporarily returned to the dual world where there were two realities and I was normal and everything was ok. Growing up, I had become adept at inhabiting different realties and at keeping secrets locked inside of me, so I returned to a familiar world of lies, pretence, and smiling when I felt I was dying inside. I told the staff that I felt much better after a rest in hospital, appeared calm and well behaved and stopped mentioning abuse. This facade is what enabled my safe exit from psychiatric services and this is when my recovery began.

I was fortunate enough to find and work with a number of therapists, both male and female, who did believe me. For the sake of simplicity here, I will refer to a single therapist, though in reality this work was conducted over a number of years with different therapists. My therapist believed that some adults do terrible things to children and he also believed that I was more than the sum total of the bad things that had happened to me. Critically, he also understood that all of my so-called symptoms were in fact creative, life saving survival strategies that made absolute sense within the extreme conditions in which they had developed. This knowledge underpinned and became the guiding principle of our work together.

Early on in my recovery journey my therapist and I came across the work of the eminent psychiatrist Judith Herman (1992) in *Trauma and Recovery* and reading that book changed my life. In placing my own experiences of abuse and the subsequent denial I had faced within wider political issues of power, trauma, and oppression, awareness that the personal is political emerged for me (Dillon 2010). In proposing potential solutions via a process of recovery which favours a humane and honouring journey of reintegration, *Trauma and Recovery* became my bible and I am not a religious person. My therapists and I used the model that Herman proposes – of establishing safety, in order to approach the work of remembering and mourning the trauma and finally moving onto reconnection, to guide our work together. Knowledge is power and so began my self-education. I began to read a vast amount of material on an array of subjects that helped me to make better sense of my experiences, and to develop my own paradigm that helped me to make better sense of my world. I was particularly drawn to psychoanalysis, attachment theory, dissociation, feminism, philosophy, existentialism, Zen Buddhism, prose, poetry and the work of other survivors and visionaries who inspired, enlightened and sustained me.

My therapists were very clear that I was in charge of the process – too many things had already happened to me outside of my control which had left me feeling terrified and overwhelmed, so they entrusted me to lead the journey, with them at my side. Their faith in me proved to be a real gift as I began to develop more confidence in my own ability to know what I needed, which fed my burgeoning awareness of making sense to myself and to others. In sessions I would say things, during a stream of consciousness, which felt disconnected and confused but when I would ask my therapist/s, 'do you understand me?' they would always reply, 'what you are saying makes perfect sense to me.' Hearing those words often surprised me but always brought a tremendous sense of relief often followed by many tears. Even though I was in charge of the process, I could not have undertaken the work without my therapists. Having an empathic witness who was willing to hear and see my suffering made me feel real and, for the first time, as if I mattered. Their love and faith in me sustained me during those times when I felt lost, ruined and despairing.

Our therapeutic alliance was the key thing that enabled me to transform my subjective reality of a terrifying internal and external world. The outside world seemed a terrible and dangerous place filled with barely concealed threats and sinister people and I lived with an eternal sense of impending dread. I was scared to close my eyes, scared of what images I would see and the screams that resounded all around me. I began to be able to distinguish between the past and the present, from what was inside of me and what was outside of me, to know what was real, in the here and now. The therapy room was the first place where I began to have some inkling of feeling safe. Although in the early days I was having three sessions of therapy a week in an attempt to process and contain all of the traumatic memories which were surfacing, I still had to develop other ways of keeping safe outside of therapy. As I used to say to my therapist – I have to live this 24/7. The use of transitional objects (Winnicott 1947) proved helpful. At critical times I was given a special stone, a teddy, a blanket, which all helped me to hold onto the safety that I felt in the therapy room and to the knowledge that I wasn't alone. I was engaged in a meaningful process of transformation and recovery and someone believed in me and cared about me.

The realization that ultimately no one could save me but myself was both terrifying and clarifying. I knew that it was not an option to return to mental health services and although I frequently felt acutely suicidal I realized that if I was going to make it, I needed to become active in creating the best chances of survival for myself. So, I created a safe place in my house with cushions, blankets and soft toys, where I could retreat to when I felt terrified. I wrote a list of 20 things to do when desperate to remind myself of how to keep safe when my voices were ordering me to jump out of the window or to slit my wrists. I also used a number of self-hypnotic techniques to help myself feel safe (Dolan 1998) and to deal with intrusive traumatic memories. I stopped having contact with people who undermined me and my healing and slowly developed relationships with people who understood and accepted me. In essence, I created a sanctuary for myself which allowed me to safely work through the traumas that I had experienced. I fought for my own life and my right to the best life that I could have. My sense of outrage at both my abusers and at a world that had systematically failed me actually motivated me to keep going through the darkest times. The old adage living well is the best revenge became my mantra. I was a woman on a mission. One day I would show them all.

The biggest turning point in my whole journey was when I began working directly with my voices. Up until that point I was still largely terrified of them, as they said and did things that disturbed and frightened me and appeared enormously powerful, as if they were omnipotent. They had the power to create physical pain which sometimes appeared as real marks and bruises on my skin, intense paranoid fantasies and night terrors, and to torment me in any number of ways. I hated them and blamed them for my distress. It was only when I began to understand what they said and did within the context in which they had originally emerged that my attitude towards them started to change.

This shift began when I started to ask them direct questions and their answers enabled me to see that they were really suffering. The voices that were telling me to jump out of the window weren't intentionally trying to torment me but only expressing the very real desperation that they contained. By listening to their despair it didn't make matters worse as I had initially feared, but actually helped them and me to feel calmer, less alone and less suicidal. Over time, I discovered that the most abusive voices had actually experienced the most abuse and rather than me silencing or punishing them further what they really needed was my love and understanding. This shift in attitude brought about the most profound healing and transformation. Everything made sense. All of my voices were in fact disowned selves, each a part of the whole of me. Rather than each living in its own conflicted and isolated reality, we began working collaboratively towards a mutually satisfying life.

I once felt deeply ashamed and saw myself as a freak of nature. I now feel enormously proud of my survival and grateful that I had the creativity and internal resources required to get me through. I also feel deeply grateful to have been able to work with such wonderful and committed therapists. Having survived such extreme experiences has taken me to the outer edges of human experience and has given me capacities that others never have the need to discover. I no longer see myself as having deficits but rather as being gifted. I am highly creative, sensitive and intuitive, and live my life to the full. My voices help me to feel less alone, they comfort me, make me laugh, provide me with inspiration. I often sit down to write a paper and they have already done most of the work for me, so I just transcribe what they have already composed. When I gave birth to my second child at home, the two lovely midwives who cared for me were both astonished at how calmly, quietly and effortlessly I gave birth. They asked me what my secret was. I replied, 'dissociation.' I explained that because of the abuse I had experienced and the work I had done in making sense of it, I could sometimes switch into an altered state of consciousness when I needed to, for example to bear physical pain. They were highly impressed.

I still sometimes hear the different selves having a debate about the best course of action in a particular situation and the overriding decision is always to 'do it for Jac – she deserves the best life she can have after all we've been through.' This illusion, that we are different people, has become less confusing and problematic the more conscious of it I have become, and has proved to be enormously useful. I have developed a greater appreciation of its benefits. It has enabled me to survive horrendous abuse, to lead a high functioning life, to use my own negative experiences to create positive change in the world and, most importantly, to be a loving mother to my own children despite my early experiences. Being me isn't always easy. I have disrupted nights because my voices never sleep at the same time and I am still inhabited by a cast of characters – a loving mother, a cockney bloke, screaming babies, rebellious teenagers, philosophers and visionaries to name but a few, but it adds up to an interesting and rewarding life. Fortunately, I have risen to the challenge and adapted accordingly. I live my life authentically, in the way that makes sense to me and works for me and my life just seems to get better and better. I have grown to love each and every part of myself and feel such deep gratitude to all of the selves that have enabled me to come this far and to live the privileged life that I do.

Implications for understanding

In making sense of what has been deemed 'psychosis' it is essential that we see so-called symptoms as profoundly meaningful attempts to survive overwhelming and distressing life experiences. There is inherent meaning in madness which is inextricably bound up in unresolved, traumatic experiences. These meanings may be communicated in a number of highly symbolic, metaphorical and literal ways and need to be untangled, teased out and examined within the context of the person's life history. Each voice is an echo of the person's experience so an attitude of curiosity, understanding and compassion towards all voices is the best stance as it will encourage and support internal communication and, ultimately, self acceptance.

This work demands seeing the world and human experience in new ways including an understanding that reality is shaped by experience. This, combined with a willingness to view life through the lens of the person's subjective experience, enables the co-creation of a shared meaning, deepening mutual understanding and leading to increasing acceptance of self and other. To support and nurture healing from 'psychosis', faith in the possibility of recovery is vital.

Implications for practice

In supporting people experiencing 'psychosis' it is essential that individuals are offered long-term, respectful, therapeutic relationships and that safety is established before exploring painful or traumatic experiences in any depth. Building trust takes time and allowing the person to feel in control of the pace will help to establish safety and an increasing sense of self and agency. A willingness to be flexible, creative and open to different approaches is helpful as different things will be needed at different times. As Winnicott (1947: 196) said, 'if we are to become able to be the analysts of psychotic patients we must have reached down to very primitive things in ourselves', so only those with substantial self-awareness, compassion, curiosity and courage need apply.

References

Dillon, J. (2010) 'The Personal is Political'. In *Telling Stories? Attachment Based Approaches to the Treatment of Psychosis* (Monograph). London: Karnac.

Dolan, Y. (1998) *Beyond Survival: Living Well is the Best Revenge*. London: BT Press.

Herman, J. (1992). *Trauma and Recovery. The Aftermath of Violence – From Domestic Abuse to Political Terror*. New York: Basic Books.

Johnstone, L. (2009) 'Controversial issues in trauma and psychosis', *Psychosis*, 1: 185–190.

Winnicott, D. W. (1947) 'Hate in the Countertransference'. In *Through Paediatrics to Psycho-Analysis*. London: Hogarth Press (1975) (pp.194–203).

Chapter 4

Hurrying slowly

Initial steps towards recovering from psychosis

Larry Davidson

> I have learned to *hurry slowly*
> (Woman recovering from psychosis speaking to interviewer)

There are many ways to approach the topic of qualitative research on the subjective processes involved in recovering from psychosis. Given the tenor of many first-person accounts, it seemed to me that focusing on the earliest steps of rebuilding a coherent sense of self provides the best place to start. It also has been my experience that these are the steps most often overlooked by practitioners and family members; an assessment confirmed by findings of a multi-national qualitative study on recovery conducted a number of years ago, in which one participant suggested that: 'People take for granted that you just do things' (Davidson *et al.* 2005). These early steps typically involve the kind of 'things' that many people do, indeed, take for granted: the small, mundane, barely detectable – if not altogether invisible – activities that the rest of us do, as it were, on autopilot. But for people emerging from the kinds of horrors that many who experience psychosis describe, including experiences such as thought insertion, ideas of reference, and delusions, very few vestiges of such automatic activities may survive the ravages of the trauma and psychosis. For people who are struggling to stick their heads up and out of these turbulent waters, who are working hard just to catch their breath, many of these seemingly trivial activities need to be relearned, if not, in some cases, learned for the first time. Practitioners and family members who are looking for the person to swim may miss the effort, energy, and focus needed for the person simply to resume breathing under these circumstances, even though breathing is an obvious and necessary prerequisite to learning to swim.

It was in reference to just this kind of basic activity that the woman quoted above had commented that she had learned to 'hurry slowly.' Hurrying slowly, or, in the original Latin, *festina lente*, was a popular phrase in the Middle Ages attributed to Erasmus and adopted as a motto by Aldus Manutius, the Venetian who is credited with inventing the art of publishing. For both men, hurrying slowly captured the simultaneous need to act with urgency while also taking the time and care to be deliberate, thoughtful, and reflective. It is at times important to act, rather than to wait until one has all the facts, has considered all the options, or is sure of one's decision, etc., but it is equally important to remain open to learning from one's mistakes, making mid-course corrections, and adjusting to new realities and contingencies that simply could not have been anticipated, no matter how long the eventual actions were delayed. While the woman quoted above may have been unusual in some ways for a participant in a qualitative study of recovery from psychosis – for example, she was exceptionally well-read and extremely articulate – the experiences she describes, and the lessons she has learned, are anything but unusual. In fact, they are so usual that they are, as I suggested above, most often overlooked by people who are not themselves struggling with some kind of adversity, whether it be psychosis, abuse, rape, torture, and/or imprisonment. These experiences and lessons remain nonetheless crucial to establishing a foundation for recovering from psychosis.

This chapter will be primarily concerned with these 'taken for granted' aspects of experience which, unfortunately, often can*not* be taken for granted in the lives of persons with psychotic disorders, who therefore must acquire them by hurrying slowly. These aspects include an implicit belief in one's own agency and efficacy, a sense of control over some aspects of one's life, an appreciation of the present as following after a discernible past and flowing into an uncertain future, and confidence in the continuity between past, present, and future that allows for a sense of predictability and coherence in one's experience (see the 'existential' chapters in the present volume for further discussion of these issues). Many of these aspects come together in the occupational science literature as constituting the concept of 'habit'. In this case, however, it is not a specific habit that is being taken for granted, such as brushing one's teeth or washing one's hair, but rather the very possibility of there being habits to begin with. Habits cannot be formed in the absence of continuity and predictability, nor can they be formed by a person who sees him or herself as having no say in his or her own behaviour or awareness. Forming a habit requires confidence, both in oneself and in the continuity and coherence of the world. Both of these forms of confidence can be severely diminished by psychosis, and both need to be restored as the basis for battling, compensating for, and overcoming the condition.

Losing confidence in oneself and the world

Before turning to processes of recovery, it may be necessary to explain how psychosis undermines such confidence in the first place. These processes have been described in detail in numerous first-person accounts and analyses (e.g. Davidson 2002, 2003; Wiggins *et al.* 1990), and new light undoubtedly will be shed on them by the recent interest in qualitative research on experiences in the prodromal and earlier stages of psychosis. For our purposes, these processes have been described both succinctly and recently by Elyn Saks in her 2007 auto-biography, *The Center Cannot Hold*. Saks describes having psychotic symptoms as early as elementary school and being diagnosed with schizophrenia in college, a condition she then carried with her through graduate school at Oxford, law school at Yale, and up to her current position as Associate Dean of the Law School and Professor of Law and Mental Health at the University of Southern California. Once she received tenure, she felt it was possible and important to make her story public to inspire hope in others, as she – like most people of her generation and many up to the present day – was told that she would never work, never finish school, never get married, and, basically, never have a life. She wanted others with this condition to know that recovery was possible.

As Saks describes, it was experiences of cognitive impairments and anomalies that initially robbed her of her sense of being an autonomous agent in a predictable world. She writes:

> And then something odd happens. My awareness . . . instantly grows fuzzy. Or wobbly. I think I am dissolving. I feel – my mind feels – like a sand castle with all the sand sliding away in the receding surf. . . This experience is much harder, and weirder, to describe than extreme fear or terror . . . Explaining what I've come to call 'disorganization' is a different challenge altogether. Consciousness gradually loses its coherence. One's center gives way. The center cannot hold. The 'me' becomes a haze, and the solid center from which one experiences reality breaks up like a bad radio signal. There is no longer a sturdy vantage point from which to look out, take things in, assess what's happening. No core holds things together, providing the lens through which to see the world, to make judgments and comprehend risk. Random moments of time follow one another. Sights, sounds, thoughts, and feelings don't go together. No organizing principle takes successive moments in time and puts them together in a coherent way from which sense can be made. And it's all taking place in slow motion.
>
> (Saks 2007: 46–47)

Regaining confidence in oneself and the world

How, then, does one go about rebuilding or reclaiming a 'sturdy vantage point', a 'core', from which to 'look out' and 'take things in', to experience reality, to assess what's happening and make judgments, and from which to gain a sense of temporal perspective? There are several interrelated steps in this process which do not follow neatly one after another, but which appear to unfold in interwoven ways, each requiring and yet also making each other possible in a reciprocal fashion. As we have to begin our description with some specific element, though, we will begin with the issue of temporality and work our way, as it were, backwards to the reconstruction of self as the sturdy vantage point of experience. For hurrying slowly appears to require the person to re-ground him or herself in the present moment as a way of making sense of both past and future.

This re-grounding in the present was described by a female Swedish participant in the aforementioned multi-national study of recovery as follows:

Before . . . everything was in the long term . . . Instead, having to hang on, to find strength, I live small moments more intensely. Now we're here, you and I, and my whole life is all here, only here. It doesn't matter what else happens . . . This moment here is more important than anything that might happen tomorrow. This was definitely decisive for me, this fact of living intensely what I'm doing instead of worrying about the future or other things was a real support, a cornerstone for everything . . . a very difficult awareness, a difficult position to take, but living intensely whatever I'm doing, being very concentrated, for me personally . . . I did this and no one told me to do it. I did it on my own and it works. For me.

(Davidson *et al.* 2005: 9)

In order to appreciate the value of such experiences, it is important to keep in mind that people struggling to emerge from active psychosis, like Saks, may have lost any sense of an anchor point amidst the cacophony of sounds and kaleidoscope of visual sensations bombarding them from every direction. What they are seeking, while being tossed to and fro on the waves of this turbulent ocean of stimulation, is any firm footing that will allow them to regain a sense of orientation. That orientation can come, as it did for the doubting Descartes through his *cogito ergo sum*, by catching oneself in the present moment: 'I am here, right now.'

In addition to describing the importance of regaining the moment in its concrete and immediate presence (a strategy that is also useful, in perhaps a slightly different way, for people with experiences of dissociation), the woman quoted above points to another of the benefits that regaining the moment can generate for the person in recovery: namely, reclaiming the sense of agency that emerges with the taking of initiative or decision-making that it makes possible. It is not possible to set one's own course or make one's own decisions while being buffeted about by the waves. But once one has regained one's footing, it becomes possible to decide what steps one might take to escape one's predicament or to find one's way to firmer ground. Doing so then allows the person to see him or herself once again as an agent, an actor, in his or her own life. As long as everything is being decided by forces outside my own control, whether these be forces of nature or the actions of others, it will be difficult for me to see myself as anything more than an object (e.g. a machine, a robot, a computer). It is in taking the initiative to act and in making decisions, even if these are initially only decisions about where I will direct my gaze, that I discover, or in this case rediscover, that I am fully a person, an autonomous subject (Davidson 2002).

A few examples of the kind of concrete, if seemingly trivial, steps that can be taken to regain such a sense of agency were provided by an American woman who participated in a study of recovery in the early 1990s. You will note that the language she used in describing the value of rediscovering her ability to regulate her own access to the music she loved, the emphasis she placed on these actions being both for and by her, is strikingly similar to the Swedish woman quoted above, who was interviewed 15 years later. She said:

It is being active, and I take pride and I'm independent to a certain extent . . . like in my jazz music, like I'll turn on my jazz radio, and I'll love it . . . it's my interest. I turn the radio on myself, no one had it going to nourish *them*selves, to entertain *them*selves, like parents would at a house. *I* turn it on, *I*'m responsible, *I* enjoy the music, *I* make notes and draw while I'm hearing it . . . Then I turn it off, then I have some evidence, I've got something done, I've been productive, I have the drawings to look at . . . It was for me and by me. My own nurturing. So I'm proud of this effort.

(Davidson & Strauss 1992: 137)

Efficacy and a sense of control

With the reclamation of a sense of agency, a further challenge becomes viewing oneself as having some modicum of control over what happens in one's life. It is certainly possible to view oneself as having a sense of agency without viewing that agency as being effective in the world. I can make all kinds of decisions, and take all kinds of initiative, without any of those actions being successful. Once my confidence in my ability to make such decisions is restored, the questions of efficacy, and of control, thus naturally come to the fore. Am I able to complete what I begin, will I be able to follow through with a plan or intention, can my internal sense of agency become manifest in the world outside of my own awareness? I have known for many years a woman diagnosed with schizophrenia who had previously been a promising young actor and director at the Yale School of Drama. At one point, when she was still struggling mightily with this condition, I asked her if she would be interested in beginning to work a few hours a week with a community theatre company as a way of breaking out of her boredom and apathy. Her response was: 'I know myself well enough to know that even if I tell you yes today, when the time comes for me to go I probably won't be able to. And I don't want to make you any promises I won't be able to keep.' Regaining a sense of control over one's own behaviour may thus be no small matter for someone with a prolonged psychiatric condition.

Even for those people whose sense of self may have been re-established more firmly, regaining a sense of control also involves doing battle with the condition and with other aspects of life – such as discrimination – that undermine any confidence that may have been restored. As one woman described:

There is this wicked side of me that can stop me. Just like when I'm looking for a job and see a job that would suit me, there is a voice that says, 'Ah, that's no job for you', and stuff like that. And so I have to work a lot with that voice, 'Oh, shut up, I'm going to apply for that job anyway.' It's a struggle going on inside me all the time.

Others described similar struggles with the decision of whether or not to get out of bed in the morning, whether or not to leave their apartment and venture out into the social arena, and whether or not to place their trust in another person. These are the kinds of accomplishments that allow people with psychosis to begin to feel that they can once again trust themselves as well.

With some sense of effectiveness and control re-established, no matter how tenuously, it then becomes possible for the person to begin to make plans, to succeed at personally chosen tasks, and to view him or herself as more and more capable over time. It is at this point that habits can be re-established to provide a sense of coherence and predictability to the person's life. Once again, for people whose lives have been turned upside down and inside out by trauma and/or psychosis, and who have recently emerged from such chaos, just having a sense of coherence and predictability in one's daily life can represent a major accomplishment, and one that may need to be cherished for a while before the person feels ready to take new risks. As another participant in the multi-national study (Davidson *et al.* 2005) described:

> My way is to simply see to it that I have something to do, to take a walk, light a cigarette, drink a cup of coffee, eat an apple, watch TV and be on the go. Like, I can't just sit around or lie down and sleep all day, I can't do that. It's just not something I can do . . . I feel well enough now that I want to do something, I want to be active, creative, have some company around me. I want to make something positive of the day, meet people, I want to talk. I'm pretty keen on having company and I don't just lie in bed and sleep all day . . . I can't understand how you could waste your days when you only have one life. And so you have to make something of it.

In order to 'make something of it,' the person can then 'hurry slowly' in the pursuit of a richer and more gratifying life based on his or her own values and preferences. The woman quoted at the opening of this chapter went on to describe what this process looked like for her:

> So I take it step by step. I have learned to *hurry slowly* and do it in stages and set partial goals when I have discovered that it makes sense . . . doing it by partial goals and making it manageable, then you get positive feedback that it's going okay and then you don't hit the wall. That's my strategy, the strategy for success: partial goals and sensible goals and attainable goals, and that's something I've learned to do in order to achieve things. When I have been able to deal with something that's been a struggle and feel secure, I move on. Step by step, put things behind me.

Fortunately, as this process progresses, the psychosis itself becomes one of the 'things' people can begin to put 'behind' them. It is at this point that medication and psychosocial treatments and interventions, such as cognitive behavioural psychotherapy and psychiatric rehabilitation, can be used most effectively as tools in reducing and managing the remaining symptoms and in building a life in the presence of, or beyond, the disorder. It also is at this point that people begin to feel capable of giving back and helping others through use of their own experiences, feeling increasingly worthwhile and competent as their contributions are valued by others.

Implications for understanding

The findings described above reinforce the argument that qualitative research provides a unique avenue of access to extremely important, but often overlooked, aspects of both mental illnesses and recovery (e.g. Davidson 2003; Davidson *et al.* 2008a, 2008b). In this case, the most important implication that these data have for understanding psychosis and recovery is that there is a considerable amount of work – much of which remains below the interpersonal radar, and undetectable by objective means – involved in simply surviving and re-emerging from the chaos of an active psychosis. Prior to starting a job, returning to school, exploring new relationships, or even pursuing a hobby, a person with psychosis might first have to re-establish and secure a sense of self as an active, volitional agent and a sense of the world as a coherent and somewhat predictable place (e.g. if I open this door I will still find that it opens out onto my front yard). One of the challenges that such people may face in the process, however, is that there is no way to re-establish and secure such a sense of confidence in oneself and in the world except by making decisions, acting in the world, and seeing the fruits of one's labours. Fortunately, smaller actions can build on each other over time into larger actions, such as in the case of the Swedish participant, who said:

> My first step after getting out of bed was to come here (to the centre); I'd come here even if it were only for 5 or 10 minutes a day. And those 5, 10 minutes turned into hours, weeks and finally I became the secretary and district representative, and now I write for Revansch! [magazine] and the local newspaper.
>
> (Davidson *et al.* 2005: 13)

Over the last 50 years, the mental health system has certainly erred more by expecting too little of individuals with serious mental illnesses than by expecting too much. As a result, many people with psychosis feel they must wait for their conditions to abate or for their impairments to be remediated before they can return to school, get a job, date, or pursue their social and leisure interests. While it certainly can be extremely difficult, if not impossible, to go from simply surviving day-to-day to functioning adequately in any of these demanding social roles, it may not be the condition itself that poses the most formidable obstacle to recovery. Rather, an equally important – if not even more substantial – factor may be the damage that the condition has done to the person's sense of self and confidence in the world and his or her ability to function within it. These sequelae are not directly responsive to medication, and can only be reversed through the person's own active efforts to emerge from, to stick his or her head out of, the turbulent waters. Rather than waiting for the condition to go away, the steps described above of reclaiming one's self from out of this chaos represent a significant part of the early work of recovery that are worthy of attention.

Implications for practice

It follows from the section above that the focus for interventions early in the course of a person's recovery should include the impact of the psychosis on the person's sense of self and world as well as on the condition itself. Addressing the destructive impact of these experiences might require enhancing the person's access to opportunities, or creating new opportunities, for him or her to regain firm footing in the present, to take initiative and make decisions, and to see him or herself as an effective agent in the world. As these are aspects of everyday life that most people take for granted in their own lives, there may be a need for clinicians to develop a better or deeper appreciation of the importance of the so-called 'obvious' in their patients' lives, as these aspects may be far from obvious to their patients (Davidson 2003). One particularly promising method for cultivating such an appreciation on the part of clinicians is to adapt the approach of 'activity analysis' which is utilized in occupational therapy primarily for the functional impairments of people with physical disabilities (e.g. the steps involved in making a phone call) for the additional social, interpersonal, emotional, and cognitive impairments or challenges associated with serious mental illnesses – e.g. the steps involved in purchasing the ingredients for and cooking for oneself a dinner of spaghetti and meatballs (Davidson *et al.* 2010).

Naturally intuitive staff, staff with training in rehabilitation and/or occupational science, and some peer support staff who have first-hand experiences of these same challenges, may already practice in this way, albeit in an implicit or invisible way. What remains to be developed is more comprehensive knowledge of how the processes described above unfold and how they can be promoted and facilitated. Once this knowledge is amassed, it will then be possible to develop training curricula and to teach clinicians these same skills in a more systematic and explicit fashion.

References

Davidson, L. (2002) 'Intentionality, identity, and delusions of control in schizophrenia: A Husserlian perspective', *Journal of Phenomenological Psychology*, *33*: 39–58.

Davidson, L. (2003) *Living Outside Mental Illness: Qualitative Studies of Recovery in Schizophrenia*. New York: New York University Press.

Davidson, L. and Strauss, J. S. (1992) 'Sense of self in recovery from severe mental illness', *British Journal of Medical Psychology*, *65*: 131–145.

Davidson, L., Borg, M., Marin, I., Topor, A., Mezzina, R. and Sells, D. (2005) 'Processes of recovery in psychosis: Findings from a multi-national study', *American Journal of Psychiatric Rehabilitation*, *8*: 177–201.

Davidson, L., Ridgway, P., Kidd, S., Topor, A. and Borg, M. (2008a) 'Using qualitative research to inform mental health policy', *Canadian Journal of Psychiatry*, *53*: 137–144.

Davidson, L., Wieland, M., Flanagan, E. and Sells, D. (2008b) 'Using qualitative methods in clinical research'. In D. McKay (ed.) *Handbook of Research Methods in Abnormal and Clinical Psychology*. Thousand Oaks, CA: Sage.

Davidson, L., Rakfeldt, J., and Strauss, J. S. (2010) *The Roots of the Recovery Movement in Psychiatry: Lessons Learned*. London: Wiley-Blackwell.

Saks, E. (2007) *The Center Cannot Hold: My Journey Through Madness*. New York, NY: Hyperion.

Wiggins, O. P., Schwartz, M. A. and Northoff, G. (1990) 'Toward a Husserlian phenomenology of initial stages of schizophrenia'. In M. Spitzer and B. A. Maher (eds) *Philosophy and Psychopathology*. New York, NY: Springer.

Part II

Cultural perspectives

The following two chapters consist of contributions by authors invited to submit chapters emphasizing the role of culture in the subjective experience of psychosis. Reflecting the specific context within which this book was developed (in New Zealand) particular attention is given to Māori cultural perspectives, as Egan Bidois shares his personal experience, while Ingo Lambrecht and Melissa Taitimu discuss research into the subjective experience of psychosis. Though this focus in these chapters reflects a local cultural perspective in New Zealand, the issues raised have universal implications.

In his personal account, Egan Bidois invites us in to consider how his experience can be construed within a Māori perspective, acknowledging explicitly that this is but one of a multitude of views available to Māori, and, as in Jacqui Dillon's chapter earlier, he questions the utility of describing his experience as 'psychosis'. Ingo Lambrecht and Melissa Taitimu share with us their research into Māori understandings of extra-ordinary experiences and Shamanic trance states in South Africa and remind us that the notion of 'subjectivity' itself exists within historical, political and cultural contexts.

What these chapters share is an emphasis on the role of meaning and meaning-making in determining how an individual, or a particular culture, will think and respond to the experiences that within a Western psychiatric perspective are referred to as 'psychosis'. Both chapters recognize that how we understand experience determines what the experience means to us and how we relate to it and, importantly, that this process of developing an understanding of experience always takes place within specific cultural contexts. Both chapters suggest that for the individual, developing an understanding that is congruent with his or her own life views, experience and cultural orientation is important in finding a helpful way of relating to the experience. The challenge for mental health services is to develop ways of recognizing this and responding appropriately.

Chapter 5

A cultural and personal perspective of psychosis

Egan Bidois

> *Ko Takitimu, ko Te Arawa oku Waka*
> (Takitimu and Te Arawa are my Canoes)
> *Ko Ngati Ranginui, ko Ngaiterangi, ko Te Arawa oku Iwi*
> (Ngati Ranginui, Ngaiterangi and Te Arawa are my Tribes)
> *Ko Pirirakau, ko Ngati Pikiao, ko Ngati Whakaue oku Hapu*
> (Pirirakau, Ngati Pikiao and Ngati Whakaue are my Sub-tribes)
> *Ko Poututerangi, ko Rakeiao, ko Te Takinga oku Marae*
> (Poututerangi, Rakeiao, and Te Takinga are my ancestral meeting houses/sites)
> *Ko Egan Bidois ahau*
> (I am Egan Bidois)

I have been invited to contribute a personal and cultural perspective of my experiences of psychosis. I guess there is no other perspective I can write from. I am a voice-hearer, I am a seer, I have been previously diagnosed with psychosis – and I am Māori (Native people of New Zealand). As such, my culture influences my understandings of the experience. That said, while my perspectives may be seen in a cultural mindset, I am deeply cognizant that what constitutes a 'Māori perspective' varies from *Iwi* (tribe) to *Iwi, Hapu* (sub-tribe) to *Hapu, Whanau* (family) to *Whanau*, person to person. So I wish to acknowledge the multitude of viewpoints and understandings held by others regarding our culture. I also encourage you to reflect upon how your own culture makes sense of the experiences described below. How do your upbringing, learnings and understandings influence your own perspectives regarding such experiences? This is just my understanding as I have learnt it, processed it, and embedded it within myself along the journey of recovery and the perhaps deeper journey of self-re-discovery.

My first memory of seeing something 'different' was around four years old. I woke one night and saw a pillar of white/gold light standing at the foot of my bed. I say standing, as the impression I got was this light pillar was actually a *someone*, an embodiment of light. It stood six and a half feet tall easily, had a male feel to it and was facing me. There was no discernable face to it; I just felt it was facing me as it stood there. It didn't scare me – apart from my somewhat startled response to seeing it, given that a tall pillar of glowing white/gold light isn't what you'd normally expect to see at the foot of your bed. This pillar of light wasn't present every night – just occasionally, and sometimes it'd be there for a few consecutive nights. Always standing there, facing me, unmoving and unspeaking.

One night I woke and it had a companion. There was another pillar of brilliant white/golden light. This one felt female. This time they were both facing away from me, towards my bedroom window. It was then I felt something else – something ominous approaching. I didn't see it, I just had an overwhelming feeling *something evil* was coming. I felt this *something* stop outside my bedroom window. At that point the two pillars of light came together, merged into a much larger sphere of light and flew out through my bedroom window towards this *something*. The *something* vanished with them, and the ominous feeling ceased. From a Māori cultural perspective they might be seen as *kaitiaki* (guardians) or *apa* (angels).

I saw the male *apa* again last year. My wife and I have a five-month-old boy – our first child. He has (fortunately or unfortunately depending on your perspective) been born with my eyes. Physically and spiritually. He sits and stares at *things* that I'm also aware of, often engages with them as well. Such is another facet of cultural understanding regarding such experiences – *Whakapapa*. Heritage, inheritance, ancestry.

Our boy went through a phase of being bothered by unsavoury spiritual visitors while in his cot. He would scream the most terrified scream and when I'd enter the room I'd feel *something* had been there. Dark. Heavy. Ominous. I did *karakia* (prayer) for him regularly, attempting to intervene in those experiences. My motivation for doing so was based on my focus of protecting him but also very much a focus of 'You spooks want to harass *my* son! I'll waste every last one of you!' The *Tohunga* (healers in this usage) I spoke with all said I was making it personal and needed to 'hand it over' to God, to *tipuna* (ancestors), to call them in and ask them to deal with it. So I did. That evening my wife and I were drifting off to sleep, our son next to us in his cot, when we both noticed a light in our hallway. We looked towards our bedroom door into the hallway – just as a tall pillar of white/gold light drifted down the hallway past our bedroom. 'What the ...!' said the wife. Ahh, I thought. Haven't seen him for many years. Our boy has slept soundly since – well, apart from the teething of course! My perspective was that this *apa* had responded to my call for assistance, and was gliding through our house blazing away whatever had been visiting our boy.

When one considers the concept of psychosis, the definitions of such 'symptoms' as hallucinations, delusions and so on, then by all means what I experience could well fit within that perspective. To see, hear, feel and interact with 'external stimuli' that most people are oblivious to, to hold beliefs in such, to hold them as one's own truth, then absolutely I can see why I was diagnosed with psychosis. The issue with that diagnosis however is that it is one I do not accept for myself. It is not one that fits my experience. It is not congruent with my own life experiences and how my culture construes such experiences.

My perspective is that what I experience is to do with my *whakapapa*. My mother especially experiences what I do in similar – and different – ways. As do many members of my *whanau* and *tipuna*. Such experiences can be handed down from generation to generation just as much as eye colour or other physical characteristics. Genetic disposition – *Whakapapa*. Po-tay-toe – Po-tar-toe. What I experience is to do with what those before me experienced, with what I'm born into rather than any personal presentation, prognosis or diagnosis I may be bestowed with.

I will give the mental health system and my diagnosis of psychosis its proverbial pound of flesh here. I will acknowledge that *if* I don't adequately mitigate what I experience, *if* I don't maintain my spiritual wellness, it has the potential to create physical and mental unwellness within me. I am not by default 'unwell' because I hear, see or feel supposed non-apparent stimuli. Rather, the non-apparent stimuli I hear, see and feel *can* effectively drive me into unwellness if not managed appropriately. Chicken, egg. Egg, chicken.

So how is it managed?

First and foremost I manage it through accepting and understanding it, through seeing it as normal and natural a part of who I am, as my hair colour. Through understanding there *are* some *rules, Tikanga* (codes of conduct), around how you process such experiences – so too a consciousness of the cost to yourself (and others) if you fall foul of them. I also don't manage it alone. I have much assistance – from the living (wife, *whanau*, friends, *Tohunga* and other mentors), from the passed (grandmother, sister, *tipuna* and others) and from beyond (*Apa, Atua* (God/s), and others). In many ways my wellness is not my sole doing – but a collective effort.

It is managed through specific *karakia*, through adherence to the *Tikanga* surrounding it, through other methods and mediums such as the *taonga* (blessed objects) I wear or carry on my person. Much as the more 'Western' approach may be to utilize specific medications, specific therapies and interventions to addresses specific issues – so too does our Māori culture have such. Specific *rongoa* (natural medicines) can be used, specific *karakia*, specific protocols and processes, rituals and methods are utilized to address specific issues one may experience. My management of the experience utilizes these methods to maintain my wellness – my own safety – within the experience.

How did I become unwell to the point of being diagnosed as psychotic?

At 18 years old I attended Waikato University. I had left the support, safety and oversight of my *whanau*, particularly my mother. I left a small village within a small town and moved to the much larger population base of Hamilton. With that came exposure to a far greater number of people – and to the myriad of attachments, issues and *wairua* (spirit) of such a large population. Effectively I was thrust into sensory overload and was simply ill-equipped and unable to deal with the enormous increase in voices, in visions, in what I saw and felt all around me and from those around me.

I went long periods with little sleep. I was unable to sleep. The voices, visions and visitors simply started flooding into my dreams. In a desperate attempt to find some solace within the storm I accepted an offer of marijuana. I slept soundly for the first time in ages. When I woke I experienced something different. I experienced silence. But the voices and visions returned by late morning. They returned much stronger. I tried more marijuana this time. Again I slept and awoke to silence, until after breakfast. It all returned in ever increasing waves. Eventually it didn't matter how much I smoked or what I did – nothing shut it out, nothing quietened it down.

My perspective (and one shared by *Tohunga* I have spoken with) is that the marijuana usage had catapulted me into a sensory level I was not ready for. I was too ashamed to tell my parents what I had done, so I tried to just survive through it. I couldn't. I needed help. Help came – in some way – by a visit to Accident and Emergency and a talk to a Duty Registrar. This resulted in my committal to Tokanui Psychiatric Hospital. It resulted in a diagnosis of Drug Induced Psychosis. Tokanui is a place I choose not to talk about much, other than to say it was not a place of healing for me. Too much pain. Too many memories I'd rather not have.

How did my healing and wellness come?

My healing started when I was discharged to the safety of my *whanau*. My healing came with the assistance of a number of *Tohunga*, male and female. One couple in particular. The woman taught me methods of centring myself, meditation, of finding and if need be forming a calm eye in the spiritual storms around me. Her husband cleansed me and covered me with *karakia* and *rongoa*, removing the physical pollutants of anti-psychotic medications, of alcohol and drugs, and also the spiritual pollutants I was experiencing.

They worked together first to shut me down, to shut off what I was seeing, hearing and feeling. Then they gradually reopened those elements and walked me through them. The hearing. The sight. The feeling. They explained each element. Taught me ways of coping with each, the meaning of each and how to consciously alter the levels in which each *sense* was received. Whenever those senses would overload me they'd shut them down and start again.

It was a gradual process of becoming increasingly aware of the different elements and interactions of the experience. Of learning to actively control those elements myself, until I was able to see, hear and feel constantly while still maintaining balance and wellness. I have enjoyed solid, sustained wellness for many years now. I have not utilized mental health systems or medications for just as long. Yet I continue to see, hear and feel constantly. I see, hear and feel at levels beyond anything experienced before. Well beyond even those that pushed me into unwellness and Tokanui.

The physical world, as perhaps many people see/understand it, and the spiritual world – to me – are constantly interwoven, intermingled. Blended. One. I can still recognize the difference, still make that separation – but the veil that separates is as thin or as thick as it is chosen to be.

How is this in any way possible?

I first need to explain some key contributors to the experience: *Wairua* and *Mauri*.

Wairua: Often this is used to mean 'spirit' or 'spirituality' (*Wairuatanga*). It is a *kupu* (word) that has many layers of meaning to it. One such meaning may be found within the *kupu* itself – and again I acknowledge this is but one, for there are many: *Wai* = unique, special, unprecedented. For instance, we also use *Wa*i to refer to a name. '*Ko wai koe?*' 'Who are you?' *Rua* = abyss, container. *Wai-rua* in a sense could be 'That which is *unique, special* that is contained *within*'.

What is it that is unique within us, unlike any other person living, dead or yet to live? There is really nothing physical that would fit such a condition. There is something spiritual that would – *you*. Your spirit. The essence of who you truly are. That constant inalienable undeniable inner-self. Spirit.

Mauri – Often translated as 'life force', or 'life essence' of sorts. Through breaking down the *kupu* you may gain an understanding of its possible meaning. *Ma* = To be connected to, bound, linked, joined to. *Uri* = Descendents. All things seen and unseen.

The important component there is the *seen and unseen*. The awareness of the physical/seen world and the unseen (to most people) spiritual world. From one perspective *Ma-uri* could mean 'Connection to all living (and non-living) things both seen and unseen.' How do *Wairua* and *Mauri* relate to each other? Mauri is the *connection between* the Wairua and *all things seen and unseen. Mauri* is – in some regards – the way in which our Wairua relates and interacts with *all things seen and unseen*. That connection is also a bit of a two-way street. A two-way line of communication.

An analogy

Think of a tree. Within the branches of that tree is a spider sitting in the middle of its web. The strands of the web spread out and connect with the twigs and branches it is secured to. Along comes a fly. It lands on one of the twigs or brushes one of the strands. The vibrations of its landing are transferred to the strand/s of the web, down the strands to the spider in the middle. The spider receives those vibrations and knows that a fly is about. The strands of the web are like *Mauri*, and the spider, *Wairua*. The spider doesn't have to see the fly. The fly doesn't have to touch the spider. The awareness of the fly's existence exists without visual confirmation, without direct physical contact. *Mauri* is a bit like the strands, like a radar pulsing outwards, pinging any contacts in the vicinity. It's the *Mauri* that receives (and transmits) information regarding *the seen and unseen. Mauri* is your connection. The super-highway of communication and information between *Wairua* and all things seen and unseen.

How does this relate to the experience from a cultural and personal perspective?

Connection.

For whatever reason people are attuned to different things. Attuned to colours and forms like an artist, sounds and beats like a musician, tastes and textures like a chef. Their internal processing is informed by their extraordinary hearing, touch, taste, sight and smell – senses that are attuned at a level beyond most. Some learn to attune and fine-tune those senses – some are born with a little head start. To me the hearing, seeing and feeling experience is like that. It's no more abnormal or special than a great set of ears, or eyes, nose, mouth or hands. All it is is information being delivered to my own internal processes. How is it delivered? *Mauri*. What is it delivered to? *Wairua*.

Implications for understanding

What does all of this mean – at least for me? What relevance, what *purpose*, do these experiences have? Part of understanding of them – I'd say the largest part – extends beyond the base questions of 'What' and 'How', of 'what' the content and context of the experience is, of 'how' such experiences, the mediums of the experience may occur. Rather the larger question – the larger key – to one's understanding, acceptance and ultimately peace with the experience lies within the more potent question of 'Why'. Why do I hear what I do? Why do I see what I do? Why do I feel what I do? Why me? Why now? Why why why? It is the Why that can be the true driver of wellness or unwellness; the Why that turns and burns you at 2am. It's the Why that also brings the understanding, brings the acceptance, brings the peace and ultimately the wellness.

So . . . why?

The answer to that is as individual as the individual. These are just my thoughts as to the Why in regard to my own experiences: Healing.

Some say these experiences are gifts. Personally I don't see them as a gift per se. The popularized perception around the term 'gift' to me seems pretentious. Almost as if the Experiencer is in some way better than, more than, more 'enlightened', more 'connected' than others who perhaps don't experience such. To me these experiences have no intrinsic added value to them. No more so that having acne-free skin or shiny hair or anything else. To me there is nothing special about them that warrants any added kudos. Gifts are only 'gifts' if they are given away, if they benefit other people. Sure, you may feel a sense of pleasure giving a present to someone, seeing the joy and thanks they show you for what you have given. But the feeling itself comes from the knowledge you have given something to someone else. The *good* of it comes from the *giving* of it. Any gift component of the experience rests there – the personal feeling of doing something for someone, of making some kind of a difference. Apart from that, the gift of it all is for the benefit of the receiver.

How does this present itself within my daily life and mahi (work)?

I've worked within the mental health sector for 14 years now. Currently I work as a Māori Mental Health Researcher and Community Liaison Worker for Capital and Coast District Health Board. Part of my *mahi* is within Te Whare Marie – Specialist Māori Mental Health Services. I work alongside our Cultural Therapist, talking with *Tangata Whaiora* ('People seeking wellness' – consumers) who may be experiencing some cultural issues. I speak with them regarding voices, visions, events in their lives and in their *whanau* history that they haven't shared with me. That prior knowledge, that connection with them in regards to their own experiences, certainly aids the process of assisting in whatever cultural interventions may be required to facilitate that person's wellness.

Outside of work I – and my wife – am often called upon by friends and *whanau* for various *mahi*. Be it providing some understanding regarding experiences they may be having, be it cleansing/blessing of houses and bringing some awareness as to what issues may be within that *whanau* house/environment, providing *karakia* to facilitate healing and recovery from some ailment (be it physical or spiritual in nature). That is the role. The function. The reason of it all. At least for me and what I experience.

It is through understanding and accepting that role and reason that my wellness has solidified. Through doing so, the nagging 'Why' no longer exists. It is through understanding and accepting the role that strength is also provided during those times I may see, hear, feel and know things I'd perhaps prefer not to. Not everything I experience is sweetness and delight. Some of it is quite traumatic, quite dark and painful. However the understanding that even those negative experiences can bring positive benefit for someone else certainly keeps you focused. It is through viewing the experience within a Māori cultural context, the validity and value of it within that cultural context, that I find much comfort with and acceptance of the experience.

Implications for practice

The essence of this *korero* (discussion) is a brief glimpse into how I make sense of my *supposed* psychosis. To me how I make sense of 'psychosis' isn't important – as I made sense of and solace with it many years ago. It's how do *you* make sense of it that is the crunch. Are my experiences psychosis? Are they hallucinatory? Are they delusional and/or grandiose? What do your life, your learning and your culture provide by way of an answer?

Within our Māori culture these experiences are nothing new. Generations have been born seeing, hearing, feeling and knowing. People who experience what I do may within our culture be termed *Matakite*. *Mata* = Face. *Kite* = To see, all-seeing. *Mata-kite* = The all-seeing face. Others, depending on what role they play and how they are called to utilize such experiences may be termed *Tohunga*. *Tohu* = Sign, indication, symbol, symptom, advise, instruct. *Nga* = plural, all, many. *Tohu-nga* = someone who can 'read the signs', who is in their 'knowing place'. The intervener on behalf of someone. The Healer. *Matakite* and *Tohunga* have always been within our culture, so these things are not anomalous for Māori. The anomaly happens when non-Māori (dare I say non-*wairua*) perspective is applied to it. Such is the risk of viewing a person's experiences from one set of perspectives, from one set of cultural or clinical concepts and contextual norms. The end result from that perspective can only be that it is perceived as abnormal.

So what am I saying?

What I'm certainly *not* saying is that every person who shows up on your service doorstep experiencing these things is having a purely spiritual experience. What I most definitely *am* saying is that not everyone who does is having a purely psychotic one. The trick is in the differentiation – then providing more appropriate intervention options. But first – even if it's momentary – ask yourself, 'Is there more to this person's presentation than meets the eye and does it need someone else's eyes?' Be more open to other possibilities, no matter how irrational or illogical they may seem to you. Does your service have the ability to provide – or access – cultural assessments? What cultural choices of treatment/intervention/support does your service provide or have access to?

To use a rugby metaphor, it matters not whether it's a clinical or cultural hand that touches the ball over the try-line. It's the score on the board at the end of the game that matters. Ultimately, the person's wellness is the goal. Which path you and they take to get there isn't so important.

'Nau te rourou, naku te rourou, ka ora ai te Iwi'

('By your foodbasket, by my foodbasket, the People will be well (fed)')

All of us have our special treats and treasures to bring to the table. All of us – be we clinician, be we service-user, be we a supportive *whanau* member or friend – come from a collective context. We are a collective construct of our own cultures, our own journeys, our own learning. It is only through combining them that a true feast of wellness can be laid before those we serve.

Clinical and cultural collaboration. That's the key we should seek.

Heoi ano, kua oti enei korero mo tenei wa
(And so, this discussion is finished for now)
Nga mihi aroha ki a koutou e nga mana, e nga reo, e nga maramatanga – e oku Rangatira katoa
(Loving greetings to you [all], the many authorities, many languages, and many different understandings – to you all my Chiefs)
Nga mihi ki a koutou – Ma Te Atua, ma nga Tipuna e awhi e tiaki
(Greetings to you – May God and the ancestors cherish and look after you)
Tena koutou, tena koutou – Mauriora tatou katoa.
(That is you [acknowledgement of your very existence], that is you – Wellness/Good health/Life to us all.)

Recommended online resources

www.mentalhealth.org.nz/file/downloads/doc/file_142.doc
www.tewhaioranga.co.nz/Health-professionals/Understanding-culture/Māori-health-models
www.tewhaioranga.co.nz/Health-professionals/Rongoā-medicine

Chapter 6

Exploring culture, subjectivity and psychosis

Ingo Lambrecht and Melissa Taitimu

Introduction

This chapter aims to examine the context in which subjectivity, culture and psychosis intersect within scientific literature and research. The various ways in which psychosis is experienced and understood across time and geography is arguably a litmus test for the cultural, social and political climate. This chapter also aims to recognize some of the complexities of researching subjectivity cross-culturally.

Contextualizing subjectivity

It is important to recognize the cultural history into which the notion of 'subjectivity' was born. Currently, subjectivity in relation to psychosis can be viewed as a counter-narrative to the objectifying medical model of schizophrenia. Subjectivity and psychosis in modern Western discourse could be construed as being the result of three major streams of thought. The first is the European hermeneutical and phenomenological philosophy that affords primacy to the meaning generated by the subject, exemplified by Jaspers' writings on psychosis, where psychosis is defined as a condition that seizes the individual as a whole, regardless of hereditary factors or brain lesions (Jaspers 1963). This tradition has also entered the fields of sociology and anthropology through qualitative research designs, which explore psychosis in terms of social and cultural relations (Biehl *et al.* 2007).

The second main tradition that addresses subjectivity is psychoanalysis and its various offshoots in which the subjectivity of Freud's '*Ich*' or 'I' got lost in translation, becoming the objectified 'ego' in English language and thought. Nonetheless, the self has a strong position in modern psychoanalytic thought on psychosis (Alanen 2001; Hinshelwood 2004; Martindale 2007; Williams 2001). Benedetti (1995) succinctly linked current psychoanalytic thought with society and culture when he stated the following:

> It is in the psychotic's suffering that the most serious problems of the human mind are encountered. Tackling them means illuminating the human being

with signification and sense, gaining a better understanding of the human being in general, not only of the psychotic person.

(Benedetti 1995)

The third tradition has more of a political background, emerging from the consumer movement, in which users of mental health services have fought against feelings of disempowerment by the objectifying process of language, psychiatric diagnosis and treatment (Anthony 1993; Deegan 1992; O'Hagan 1999). The personal stories of people with psychosis provide a counterweight to the medical model of schizophrenia. The recovery literature, especially in relation to psychosis, gained traction in its focus on an active sense of self and personal agency in the individual pathway to wellness and recovery (Lampshire 2005; Tooth *et al.* 2006). Therefore, in terms of these three major traditions of thought, 'subjectivity' is not a new concept in relation to psychosis; it has a rich conceptual history and cannot be separated from political and cultural contexts, for even some very personal recovery stories echo archetypal journeys (Lambrecht & Lampshire 2009).

Whilst subjectivity is considered to be an important divergence from the current dominance of the medical model, it is equally important that a critical understanding of subjectivity as a concept is retained. Within this chapter subjectivity is recognized as just one of many ways of viewing experience that, like all concepts, has arisen within a particular historical and cultural context. So subjectivity itself is formed and created by history (Foucault 1977; Rorty 2007). In postmodernism, subjectivity no longer holds a privileged position (Lyotard 1984).

Therefore, in this chapter the subjectivity of a person experiencing psychosis is neither rarefied (untouchable truth because it is personal) nor denied (sidelined in the medical model). Rather, equal weight is given to other factors, such as socio-economic factors and cultural practices. The next section will refer to research that demonstrates the relationship between the political, social, cultural and historical context and the content of psychotic experiences. To provide some specific examples, Māori ways of understanding psychosis as well as the psychotic experiences amongst South African shamans are presented.

Culture and content of psychosis

At the beginning of the last century, when 'schizophrenia' had barely been proposed as a diagnosis, psychosis was closely associated with culture. Both Freud (1913/1983) and Jung (1964) thought deeply about psychosis. Freud, in *Totem and Taboo*, considered social structures and the repressive aspects of culture to be forms of protecting groups and individuals from the chaos of violence and madness in the 'return of the repressed' (Freud 1913/1983). For Jung, the imagery or content of psychosis is related to the collective unconscious, which opens psychosis up to myths, symbols and culture (Jung 1964). The mythical figure of the 'wounded healer', namely a healer being transformed by his or her own madness, is very common amongst shamans in traditional societies. This will be elucidated more closely in the next section of this chapter.

In the 1970s, Laing (1972) proposed that psychosis is not so much a form of madness as a healthy response to a mad society. Goffman (1961) and Szasz (1974) emphasized the political relation between psychosis and society, indicating that asylums, labelling, stigmas and social structures may drive us mad. Taken beyond the individual level, it is important to consider how institutional psychiatric cultures affect people with psychosis (Hinshelwood 2004). Indeed, many consumers have commented on the effect psychiatric treatment has had upon the content and meaning of their experience (Read 2004), creating a feedback cycle where the experience and effects of treatments become part of the symptomatology that justifies further treatment. Research conducted in the UK (Hutchinson *et al.* 1996: 780) suggested that an increased incidence of psychosis for second-generation Afro-Caribbeans may be an adaptive response to being a minority.

Overall, evidence suggests that psychosis is permeated and modified by culture. Some research has indicated that the content of delusions that could be labelled clinically as 'paranoid' has been related to the context of colonisation for indigenous populations both in New Zealand (Beaglehole & Beaglehole 1946; Taitimu 2007) and Africa (Sadowsky 2004). Furthermore, Lenz (1964) found the content of delusions to reflect technological progress throughout the 1900s. Delusions regarding electrical current surfaced first, then robots, followed by radio waves. Therefore, an account of psychosis and culture will need to take account of the subtle interplay between content and context (Corin 2007). In this manner, the cultural grounding of the subjective experience of schizophrenia could be considered a paradigmatic case of understanding fundamental human processes of self, social engagement and cultural orientation (Jenkins 2004). Psychosis within cultural relations becomes not so much about psychosis itself but in fact reveals, highlights and presents the processes of culture, society and subjectivity itself.

Culture and the understanding of psychosis

The relationship between culture, subjectivity and psychosis has been investigated in a number of ways with most research falling into one of three research traditions – cross-cultural, transcultural or indigenous – each of which adopts a different position towards the subjective experience of psychosis. The following discussion will outline the tendency for research to silence, objectify or empower subjective accounts of psychosis within the cultures investigated.

Cross-cultural research tends to investigate the *prevalence* of psychotic symptoms within cultural groups with little to no attention afforded to the subjective meaning of their experiences for participants. The WHO International Pilot Study of Schizophrenia is an example of cross-cultural research (World Health Organisation 1973; 1975; 1979). The WHO studies were established in

1967 and have included nearly 30 research sites across 19 countries. Significant commonalities were found in symptomatology across all sites. However, the form and content of symptoms was the major focal point with personal meaning being largely ignored or pathologized. For example, subjective accounts of psychosis recorded within the Agra region were referred to as 'misconceptions and superstitious beliefs about mental illness' that drove the individual to 'faith-healers' (World Health Organisation 1979: 104). Just over 20 years later, further research conducted within India indicated that researchers perpetuated a theme of 'silencing' and pathologizing indigenous constructions when they described spiritual/traditional constructions as 'resistant' and 'persistent' (Das *et al.* 2001; Taitimu & Read 2006).

Despite this tendency to silence indigenous perspectives, understanding more about subjective accounts of psychosis and how these explanations relate to cultural context may explain the finding of better outcomes for those who experience psychosis within non-Western/developing countries compared with Western countries (Castillo 2003). Castillo (2003) proposed that better outcomes may be related to the spiritual constructs these cultures hold regarding psychosis. These constructs tended to externalize the origin of the illness which, he proposed, may lead to increased integration and less stigma within families and societies. Read and Harre (2001) report a similar effect on stigma when comparing cultural and psychosocial explanations with biomedical explanations of psychosis. This finding is consistent with the explanations provided by Māori participants in recent research in New Zealand, where a cultural support worker commented:

> There are a couple of guys from over here [residential mental health setting housing mostly young males diagnosed with a psychotic disorder] who are *matakite* [literally translated, seer of faces, a common term for gifted]. I've been talking to them and helping them understand it . . . it doesn't freak them out now. One guy we had here, he is out in the community with his *whanau* [family] now.
>
> (Taitimu 2007: 152)

Transcultural studies, on the other hand, aim to relate the form and content of psychotic experiences to cultural context and history. The popularized term 'culture-bound syndromes' arose from transcultural research (Mezzich *et al.* 1999). Culture-bound syndromes have since been listed within the appendix of the DSM-IV-TR (Mezzich *et al.* 1999). However, some have argued that the tools for understanding psychosis in one culture cannot be transposed to another without elements being lost in translation, akin to a square peg being pushed into a round hole. Within the DSM-IVR and wider transcultural literature, culture-bound syndromes are often referred to in terms of form and content alone with little attention afforded to subjective explanations; when explanations *are* acknowledged, they appear to be objectified as interesting alternative explanations for psychosis as opposed to being centralized as legitimate and valid explanations derived from long-standing, complex knowledge systems. Fanon (1963) referred to the process of indigenous knowledges being 'whitened' so that information could be digested by Western psychology as 'lactification'. Overall, transcultural research is often conducted by members of Western academia and aims to *look upon* predominantly non-Western groups or individuals and *describe* the meaning they place on their experience to the West in a form that is often unrecognizable to the original custodians (Jahnke & Taiapa 1999). Bishop (1998: 200) compared this form of research to the colonization process within New Zealand when he said that 'many misconstrued Māori cultural practices and meanings are now part of our everyday myths of New Zealand, believed by Māori and non-Māori alike.'

By contrast, indigenous psychology has developed a tradition whereby research is commonly conducted from *within* a cultural group by one or more members of the group for the benefit of the group itself. This form of research seeks to centralize indigenous ways of knowing and recognize this knowledge as legitimate in its own right without having to ascribe to another body of knowledge for validation. Subjective explanations are empowered through a collaborative meaning-making process where researchers and participants share at least some common cultural values, explanations and experiences. Often, indigenous researchers and participants experience difficulty in explaining the complexity and depth of their cultural explanations of experiences. For example, the difficulty in defining Māori spirituality within research is evident in the following comment: 'To ask my father what *mātauranga* Māori [Māori knowledge systems] is would be like asking a fish what water is. It remains invisible to them' (Royal 1998). Indeed, some participants within recent research conducted in New Zealand regarding Māori ways of understanding psychotic experiences (Taitimu 2007) expressed concern that the *wairua* [spirituality] of the conversations and the complexity of the meanings shared during the research interviews would be lost when put in a written format.

Taitimu (2007) aimed to research Māori constructions of the symptoms of schizophrenia and how these constructions compared with Western psychiatric constructions. The theoretical assumptions for Taitimu's research were that: the investigation is conducted from within the cultural context; the process of construction is influenced by personal, social, cultural and historical factors; researchers and participants are subject rather than object; individuals have agency (self determination or *Tinorangatiratanga*) in their construction of experiences; change can occur on an individual, social and political level through indigenous research that supports individuals to voice and/or reconstruct their experiences.

Overall, Taitimu's (2007) research indicated that Māori hold multiple explanatory models for extra-ordinary experiences with the predominant explanation being spiritual. Other explanations included psychosocial constructions (trauma and drug abuse), historical trauma (effects of colonisation) and biomedical constructions (chemical brain imbalances). These findings are consistent with the growing body of international literature which has found that individuals and cultural groups hold multiple explanatory models for experiences labelled psychotic (Angermeyer & Klusmann 1988; Das *et al.* 2001; Geekie & Read 2009; Grof & Grof 1990; Joel *et al.* 2003; Lapsley *et al.* 2002; Sanders 2006). Further, participants in Taitimu's (2007) research suggested that spiritual constructions of psychotic symptoms may lead to more positive outcomes by contextualizing the experience and providing the individual with an expectation of recovery. Alternatively, participants proposed that psychiatric constructions may affect outcomes negatively by internalizing the problem and being associated with a more chronic course.

Cultural or indigenous phenomenonology of psychosis as spirit possession would not merely be a good example of a curious or interesting transcultural explanation, but also may stand as a complex and central way of understanding in its own right and lead towards effective means of healing what we might call psychosis in other settings (Castillo 2003). To illustrate this point, we will consider an example of this complexity from indigenous research on shamanic trance states in South Africa (Lambrecht 1998). We will argue that specific possession trance states in relation to psychosis cannot simply be subsumed within Western psychiatric discourse.

From a Western psychiatric standpoint, it is understandably difficult to distinguish between two forms of spirit possession in South Africa, namely the *amafufunyana* and the *ukuthwasa*. From a Western psychiatric perspective both categories would be considered to include psychotic symptoms (Zabow 2007), dominated by auditory hallucinations and social withdrawal, i.e. positive and negative symptoms of schizophrenia (Niehaus *et al.* 2004).

The South African shaman or *sangoma* would differentiate between these two states most concisely. For example, in South Africa, the shamanic Zulu and Xhosa traditions differentiate clearly between *amafufunyana*, which is considered a spirit possession illness requiring healing, and the *ukuthwasa*, which is an initiation illness (a sign that someone has a gift and requires training). One *sangoma* in Lambrecht's research stated that when

> you get like that, you don't know that you get very sick. Where other people get put away in Sterkfontein [mental inpatient unit], these people are not sick, they just need to go to school. [. . .] They said I was crazy, some of the people told me I knocked people out.
>
> (Lambrecht 1998: 362)

'School' here refers to the lengthy shamanic training programme. In this example, a cultural shamanic understanding of psychosis is similar to the afore-mentioned mythical 'wounded healer'. This is different to the Western psychiatric interpretation of psychosis. Currently, both *amafufunyana* and *ukuthwasa* are considered to be culture-specific disorders (Krüger *et al.* 2007) or 'culture-bound syndromes' (Mezzich *et al.* 1999) by psychiatric discourse. While a shamanic initiation illness may be considered to have dissociative features, it cannot be reduced solely to a dissociative trance disorder or a culture-specific disorder, for *sangomas* do not consider the shamanic crisis to be merely defined by functional impairment.

> All too frequently broad brush statements appear in literature that use explanations of spirit experiences, magic or witchcraft, to account for psychiatric symptoms, and vice versa. Before comparing symptoms of schizophrenia, it is necessary to question rather than assume what it is for the person to think, feel and interact with humans, spirits, God or other beings.
>
> (Barrett 2004: 107)

Implications for understanding

Subjective explanations of psychosis can provide an insight into historical, cultural and political practices and events. All individuals with psychosis engage in a meaning-making process that is influenced by wider cultural and political constructs of psychosis. Further to this, cultural and subjective explanations of psychosis are organic and always changing in an adaptive manner.

Implications for practice

Clinical practices and practitioners require flexibility and active inclusion of various cultural and subjective explanations and practices. For example, many cultures have structured and effective cultural shamanic healing processes. Further to this, individuals with psychosis may seek traditional cultural healing together with psychiatric interventions. Indeed, some research indicates that consumers want to access Western psychiatric interventions when needed in conjunction with traditional cultural practices (Taitimu 2007; Allen 2002; Lambrecht 1998). It is expected that supporting consumers to integrate various healing options as well as develop their own subjective meanings, derived from both Western psychiatry and their own cultural background, may result in more positive outcomes. However, it is acknowledged that such combinations are not always simple and require significant paradigm shifts in educational and clinical practices.

References

Alanen, Y. O. (2001) *Schizophrenie*. Klett-Cotta: Cotta'sche Buchhandlung.

Allen, M. (2002) *Identity and resistance in Okinawa*. New York: Rowman & Littlefield Publishers.

Angermeyer, M. C. and Klusmann, D. (1988) 'The causes of functional psychoses as seen by patients and their relatives', *European Archives of Psychiatry and Neurological Sciences*, 238: 47–54.

Anthony, W. A. (1993) 'Recovery from mental illness: The guiding vision of the mental health service system in the 1990s, *Psychosocial Rehabilitation Journal, 16*: 11–23.

Barrett, R. J. (2004) 'Kurt Schneider in Borneo: Do First Rank Symptoms Apply to the Iban?' In J. H. Jenkins and R. J. Barrett (eds) *Schizophrenia, Culture, and Subjectivity: The Edge of Experience*. Cambridge: Cambridge University Press (pp. 87–109).

Beaglehole, E. and Beaglehole, P. (1946) *Some Modern Māoris*. Auckland: Oxford University Press.

Benedetti, G. (1995) *Introductory Lecture* at the Tenth International Symposium for the Psychotherapy of Schizophrenia, Stockholm, Sweden.

Biehl, J., Good, B. and Kleinman, A. (2007) 'Introduction: Rethinking Subjectivity'. In J. Biehl, B. Good and A. Kleinman (eds) *Subjectivity: Ethnographic Investigations*. Berkeley: University of California Press (pp. 1–23).

Bishop, R. (1998) 'Freeing ourselves from neo-colonial domination in research: A Māori approach to creating knowledge', *Qualitative Studies in Education*, *11*: 199–219.

Castillo, R. (2003) 'Trance, Functional Psychosis and Culture', *Psychiatry*, *66*: 21.

Corin, E. (2007) 'The "Other" of Culture in Psychosis: The ex-centricity of the subject'. In J. Biehl, B. Good and A. Kleinman (eds) *Subjectivity: Ethnographic Investigations*. Berkeley: University of California Press (273–314).

Das, S., Saravanan, B., Karunakaran, K. P., Manoranjitham, S., Ezhilarasu, P. and Jakob, K. S. (2001) 'Effects of a structured educational intervention on explanatory models', *Journal of Psychiatry*, *188*: 286–287.

Deegan, P. E. (2001) 'The independent living movement and people with psychiatric disabilities: Taking back control over our own lives', *Psychosocial Rehabilitation Journal*, *15*: 3–19.

Fanon, F. (1963) *The Wretched Earth*. New York: Grove Press.

Foucault, M. (1977) *Discipline and Punish*. London: Penguin Books.

Freud, S. (1913/1983) *Totem and Taboo*. London: Ark Paperbacks.

Geekie, J. and Read, J. (2009) *Making Sense of Madness: Contesting the Meaning of Schizophrenia*. Hove, England: Routledge.

Goffman, E. (1961) *Asylums: Essays on the Social Situation of Mental Patients and Other Inmates*. New York: First Anchor Books Editions.

Grof, C. and Grof, S. (1990) *The Stormy Search for the Self: A Guide to Personal Growth through Transformational Crisis*. New York: Jeremy P Tarcher.

Hinshelwood, R. D. (2004) *Suffering Insanity: Psychoanalytic Essays on Psychosis*. London: Routledge.

Hutchinson, G., Takei, N., Fahy, T. A., Bhugra, D., Gilvarry, C., Moran, P. . . . Murray, R. M. (1996) 'Morbid risk of schizophrenia in first-degree relatives of white and African Caribbean patients with psychosis', *British Journal of Psychiatry*, *169*: 776–780.

Jahnke, H. T. and Taiapa, J. (1999) 'Maori and Research'. In C. Davidson and M. Tolich (eds) *An Introduction to Social Science Research in New Zealand*. Auckland: Addison Wesley Longman.

Jaspers, K. (1963) *General Psychopathology*, trans. J. Hoenig and M. W. Hamilton. Manchester: Manchester University Press.

Jenkins, J. H. (2004) 'Schizophrenia as a Paradigm Case for Understanding Fundamental Human Processes'. In J. H. Jenkins and R. J. Barrett (eds) *Schizophrenia, Culture, and Subjectivity: The Edge of Experience*. Cambridge: Cambridge University Press (pp. 29–61).

Joel, D., Sathyaseelan, M., Jayakaran, R., Vijayakumar, C., Muthurathnam, S. and Jakob, K. S. (2003). 'Explanatory models of psychosis among community health workers in South India', *Acta Psychiatra Scandanavia*, *108*: 66–69.

Jung, C. G. (1964) *Man and his Symbols*. New York: Anchor Books.

Krüger, C., Sokudela, B. F., Motlana, L. M., Mataboga, C. K. and Dikobe, A. M. (2007) 'Dissociation: A preliminary contextual model', *South African Journal of Psychiatry*, *13*: 13–21.

Laing, R. D. (1972) 'Transcendental Experience'. In J. White (ed.) *The Highest State of Consciousness*. New York: Anchor Books (pp. 104–113).

Lambrecht, I. (1998) *A Psychological Study of Shamanic Trance States in South African Shamanism*. In fulfilment of the degree in Philosophy of Arts in Psychology. Johannesburg: University of the Witwatersrand.

Lambrecht, I. and Lampshire, D. (2009) Presentation at the International Symposium for the Psychotherapy of Schizophrenia: *Screaming in Whispers: A Dialogue Between an Expert Voice Hearer and a Psychologist/Shaman*. Copenhagen, Denmark.

Lampshire, D. (2005) *From Psychosis to Personhood: The Dollhouse Effect*. Paper presented at the 3rd annual Making Sense of Psychosis Conference. Auckland, New Zealand.

Lapsley, H., Nikora, L. W. and Black, R. (2002) *Kia Mauri Tau! Narratives of Recovery from Disabling Mental Health Problems*. Wellington: Mental Health Commission.

Lenz, H. (1964) *Vergleichende Psychiatrie: Eine Studie über die Beziehung von Kultur, Sociologie und Psychopathologie*. Vienna: Wilhelm Maudrich.

Lyotard, J. (1984) *The Postmodern Condition: A Report on Knowledge*. Minneapolis: University of Minnesota Press.

Martindale, B. (2007) 'Psychodynamic contributions to early intervention in psychosis', *Advances in Psychiatric Treatment*, *13*: 34–42.

Mezzich, J. E., Kirmayer, L. J., Kleinman, A., Fabrega, H. Jr, Parron, D. L., Good, B. J. . . . Manson, S. M. (1999) 'The place of culture in the DSM-IV', *Journal of Nervous and Mental Disease*, *187*: 457–464.

Niehaus, D. J. H., Oosthuizen, P., Lochner, C., Emsley, R., Jordaan, E., Mbanga, N. . . . Stein, D. (2004) 'A culture-bound syndrome "amafufunyana" and a culture-specific event "ukutwasa": Differentiated by a family history of schizophrenia and other psychiatric disorders', *Psychopathology*, *37*: 59–63.

O'Hagan, M. (1999) *Realizing Recovery: Six Challenges to the Mental Health Sector*. Realizing Recovery Conference. Wellington: Mental Health Commission.

Read, J. (2004) 'The invention of schizophrenia'. In J. Read, L. Mosher and R. Bentall (eds) *Models of Madness: Psychological, Social and Biological Approaches to Schizophrenia*. Hove, East Sussex: Brunner-Routledge.

Read, J. and Harre, N. (2001) 'The role of biological and genetic causal beliefs in the stigmatisation of "mental patients" ', *Journal of Mental Health*, *10*: 223–235.

Rorty, A. O. (2007) 'The vanishing subject: The many faces of subjectivity'. In J. Biehl, B. Good and A. Kleinman (eds) *Subjectivity: Ethnographic Investigations*. Berkeley: University of California Press (pp. 34–51).

Royal, C. (1998) *Te Ao Marama – A research paradigm*. Paper presented at the Te Oru Rangahau, Māori research and development conference, Massey University, New Zealand.

Sadowsky, J. (2004) 'Symptoms of Colonialism: Content and Context of Delusions in Southwest Nigeria, 1945–1960'. In J. H. Jenkins and R. J. Barrett (eds) *Schizophrenia, Culture, and Subjectivity: The Edge of Experience*. Cambridge: Cambridge University Press (pp. 238–252).

Sanders, D. L. (2006) *Illness Representations of Mental Illness in New Zealand*. Unpublished MSc, University of Auckland, New Zealand.

Szasz, T. (1974) *The Myth of Mental Illness: Foundations of a Theory of Personal Conduct.* New York: Harper & Row.

Taitimu, M (2007) *Nga whakawhitinga: Māori ways of understanding extra-ordinary experiences and schizophrenia.* Unpublished doctoral thesis, University of Auckland, New Zealand.

Taitimu, M. and Read, J. (2006) 'Explanatory models of schizophrenia', *British Journal of Psychiatry, 189*: 284.

Tooth, B., Kalyanansundaram, V. and Glover, H. (2006) *Recovery from Schizophrenia: A Consumer Perspective.* Adelaide: Health and Human Services Research and Development Grants Program.

Williams, P. (2001) *A Language of Psychosis.* London: Routledge.

World Health Organization (1973) *Report of the International Pilot Study Of Schizophrenia.* Geneva: WHO.

World Health Organization (1975) *Schizophrenia: A Multinational Study. A Summary of the Initial Evaluation Phase of the International Pilot Study of Schizophrenia (IPSS).* Geneva: WHO.

World Health Organization (1979) *Schizophrenia: An International Follow-up Study.* London: Wiley.

Zabow, T. (2007) 'Traditional healers and mental health in South Africa', *International Psychiatry, 4*: 81–83.

Part III

Spirituality

Following on from the preceding two chapters, which looked at the role of culture in the subjective experience of psychosis, we now move on to consider another often overlooked, yet clearly important, aspect of the experience of psychosis: spirituality. As both the following chapters illustrate, spiritual concerns are often of paramount importance to the individual who experiences psychosis and these concerns can, as Patte Randal's story so beautifully illustrates, provide an adaptive framework for understanding the experiences.

As with previous personal accounts, Patte's story shows us that the experience of psychosis can often be traced to earlier life experiences (in her case, boundary violations). Also, in keeping with the previous accounts, Patte's story illustrates that through the building of a personally meaningful understanding of the experience and with validation through a group of like-minded people, learning helpful ways to manage – even value – the experience becomes possible.

David Lukoff's chapter reminds us that the relationship between psychosis and spirituality has a long history with spiritual concerns commonly being pathologized, despite research showing that spirituality is often associated with better, not worse, outcomes in a wide range of health matters. Again, both these chapters address an issue (in this case, spirituality) which mental health services have struggled to deal with, despite the fact that subjective accounts of psychosis show us that these are often important concerns for the individual which can be associated with positive outcomes.

Chapter 7

Subjective experience of spirituality and psychosis

Patte Randal

My spiritual heritage

My maternal grandparents were Zionist Jews who migrated from Lithuania, via Germany, to Palestine, where my mother was born in 1926. When my mother was nine, her mother died. My mother came to believe that if there was a God, 'He didn't care' about her, and subsequently described herself as an atheist. My father, born in 1911 and left motherless at the age of seven, was a British policeman stationed in Palestine before the war. He married his young Jewish bride and took her to Britain. Although agnostic, a remnant of his Protestant upbringing was his bedtime ritual of saying, 'Good night, God bless.'

My mother tried to assimilate her family into British culture by sending us to Sunday school. One day I was found standing on the window sill saying, 'Please God make me die. I want to go to Jesus.' I was five years old. There was no more Sunday school after that. My mother told us that the English version of the Bible was mistranslated and misleading. Our Jewish identity was acknowledged through the implicit message that we were different and special – 'the chosen ones' – but this was not reflected in any rituals or practices.

Formative experiences

My parents valued education above all else, and I came to think of myself primarily as a scientist. I remember feeling elated when I learned about the Periodic Table, and glimpsed the order that lay behind the emotional chaos of life. Family life was mixed and intense: repeated asthma attacks; playing with my five siblings; noticing with silent shock my school friend sitting on her father's lap – how come my father never held me like that?; absorbing the confusing, unbidden secret attention from my mother's 37-year-old brother stroking my 11-year-old nipples and kissing me with his tongue, whispering, 'I love you, I love you'; my mother saying, 'that couldn't have happened or if it did, it's because he's an artist', and dismissing my attempts to tell her of my confusion.

By the time I was 23, I had been married, completed the first part of my medical training and started work on my doctorate in psychology. I had had a baby and when he was seven months old I had been deserted by my husband. I was in therapy with the clinician who ran the student health service, seeing him irregularly. I had no understanding about what to expect in therapy. We had a lot of physical contact; sometimes he would hold me close. This was not sexual touching but it was confusing. I felt I loved him, and wanted to know he loved me. He said he loved me 'in ways'.

My research was in traditional acupuncture. I was reading many stimulating books about the Chinese philosophy of health, *Chi* energy, and related topics; meeting new people; trying to manage as a single mother. So much had changed so suddenly in my life.

Spiritual emergency?

Shortly after my husband left, I was high. High high high. Life was tremendous. It was as if I was in love, but with no object of my passion. I needed very little sleep. Colours were unusually bright. Many insights occurred to me; I felt so clear about things, so knowing, with many solutions to great problems. I wrote in my diary '*mind=energy=matter*'. The energy, my own energy, seemed to be Reich's orgone energy or Chinese 'Chi' energy. I was rushing round, talking to lots of people, feeling ripples of energy flowing through me. I became very thin, losing 8 lbs over ten days. It was as if my body was being converted into mind energy. The clarity of my thinking disturbed me, but I just felt so good, so real, so alive, so in touch with myself. I was delighted with everything and everybody. My therapist said I was 'enchanting'. I felt that I would be like this forever. The whole world seemed to have changed.

> *This is the beginning of the revolution; there will be a cascade effect; soon everyone will feel like this. All we have to do is trust each other, and not be frightened to show our true selves.*

I was amazed by how insightful the lady who ran the crèche sounded. I didn't realize it was my interpretation that had changed. I remember looking down over the university from a hill thinking that I was the mother of the world. I saw myself as out of reach of any man, and suddenly felt acutely terrified that I would be alone for the rest of my life.

My therapist was concerned about the down that would inevitably come. He said he wanted me to learn to feel sad as well as elated. He wanted to make sure he was around when I crashed. I couldn't believe his prediction. Again I felt confused. Did he want me? I could easily interpret his behaviour as very loving and close. He talked about 'real life' and 'boundaries', but his office wasn't anything to do with real life. What was he talking about? I needed him to explain to me why he wouldn't let me love him or make love with me. We went over this repeatedly during the ensuing months.

Psychosis?

When my son was 14 months old, my father died in front of me, gasping for his last breath after a nine-month struggle with lung cancer. The whole world seemed grey, bleak, pointless. My therapist seemed unable to contain my sense of meaninglessness. I wanted to dissolve into him, but he didn't have time. The chaos of life continued and yet I persisted with my reading, writing, and research.

In the maelstrom of emotional confusion, denial and avoidance of my repeatedly broken heart, I had a puff of marijuana, and . . . . time stopped. I could hear the same sound over and over, and let out a terrified, choking scream. Hell . . . This was hell . . . I was no longer in my body. I found myself trapped forever in this hell-like state of utter terror as if I had been totally obliterated yet was conscious of my non-existence. Paradoxically, this state alternated with an experience of utter ecstasy; acquiescence into the arms of everlasting trusting love. These two polar extremes went on interminably, culminating in a state of eternal orgasmic bliss.

The sequence of events continued to unfold like a roller coaster ride. Within weeks of my father's death, a baby died in our university crèche. After a string of brief sexual encounters, I began to fall in love with my doctoral supervisor, who appeared to reciprocate and then went away on a trip. I became elated by the sense of being able to become my true self. I was writing everything down – all the gems of thought. I felt I was on the verge of something important in my development. I wasn't sure what, but it was exciting and frightening at the same time. There was a sense of urgency to it all.

> *I must follow my inner voice; do anything I feel I must do. Something big is really happening – something much bigger than me – something that many other people also feel. Am I in the vanguard, somehow setting the pace? I am to disperse my knowledge; tell others about the meanings that are being revealed to me; we should all allow ourselves to be open to change.*

My awareness seemed to be growing; ideas on philosophy, life and the puzzles of the universe. I stayed up talking all night with a friend, writing down all I had discovered. What I wrote seemed immensely profound, as if I'd cracked some vast riddle. The pattern of existence had emerged before my eyes. It involved macrocosms and microcosms; spirals; the double helix; behaviour being written into the genes. My experiences seemed to exemplify a process which was necessary to all humankind.

> *Everyone has to experience self-discovery before we can progress as a species.*

I felt so alive; each minute seemed so important. I phoned my therapist to tell him that I had written a very important work, equivalent to the I Ching.

That night I had a strong sense of my destiny. *This is my last supper.* I went to bed, but I didn't sleep. Instead I slipped back into that same state I had experienced weeks previously when I had inhaled the marijuana. *The paradox, the fear, the orgasm. I'm truly trapped. This surely is hell!!!!* The same sounds as I recalled from before. Time had truly stopped. The heat. The sense of being obliterated. Again I screamed, as I'd screamed before. The reality of non existence. The terror. It was as if that first hell merged into this one. My writing lay on the floor for the entire world to see.

> *What if it contains a fatal error that will mislead humanity? What if the baby's death is linked with me? Should I stay, or should I move on from this world?*

In the morning there was a postcard from my supervisor. I read it as a sign that everything would be all right.

> *I must burn my manuscript. I mustn't look at what I've written. Don't think. Don't look back. Don't stop. Ashes to ashes. Dust to dust. All the written truth must be destroyed. The only truth is inner truth. I must not speak. I must just allow myself to Be. The world must reach this state without a dogma.*

Covered in ash, I went to have a bath, my mind devoid of words. I slipped down into the water, sensing that I was to drown. My head was filled with an immense pressure. It seemed to go on forever. My death needed to happen for the sake of humankind; the whole of humanity was with me. Suddenly, I could feel myself breathing. I could hear myself crying! In dying, I had been reborn! I opened my eyes. I was alive! I sensed that everyone needed to be reborn in this way. I sensed I had a mission ahead, that anything was possible. I awaited instructions.

The phone rang. It was a friend telling me that he had found his little adopted baby dead in her cot that morning! A second baby dead within one week! It confirmed my belief that everything had changed and that I had some kind of mission to carry out. I told my friend, 'Everything will be all right in the end.'

I desperately needed to see my therapist, and hitchhiked to the University. I walked across the car park, towards the steps between the physics and biology buildings. Below me were 13 deep concrete steps. I felt a sweeping sense of elation. This new life was an adventure, full of possibilities. *I'm travelling on the edge of time.* When I reached the top step it became apparent to me that gravity no longer operated in this new reality, and I could simply step down to the bottom of the flight – a mere 15 feet or so. Without running, I launched myself off – *awesome!* I landed at the bottom, falling onto my knees. To my surprise, I felt as if I'd broken every bone in my body. Down on road level a group of people stopped to look at my flight in amazement. They stood motionless, waiting to see what had happened.

Two men asked if I was hurt. 'Yes. I think I might have broken every bone in my body. Please can you help me?' They were taken aback, afraid to touch me. *I have to convince them that they can heal me.* I was certain my legs were shattered. As I spoke to them they seemed to grow taller and taller, until they looked like glowing, beautiful giants. They asked me if I was wasting their time and I said, 'If you really believe that, then it is so!' I jumped up. *A miracle! I'm healed!* These men looked like beautiful gods, heroes. I hugged them both, and exclaimed, 'We're all the same. We're equal and the same.' The men looked askance at me and said, 'she's crazy,' but I had already run away, my arms outstretched to embrace this wonderful new world of equal, loving, all-powerful God-like people.

I felt so happy. *This is the Truth – The Way Things Are Meant to Be.* Rather than being so different, as I had been told in my growing up years, I knew now that we were all the same – and all God-like. I ran along the road embracing people, shouting, 'Brothers, sisters, we're all the same!' Somebody said, 'But I don't know you!' I said, 'That doesn't matter. We're all the same.' I rushed to my therapist's office, throwing open the door. He was talking with a student. 'What are you doing here?' I asked, 'You're the same as him. What can he give you that you can't give him?' My therapist said something like, 'Yes, we might be the same, but I've got work to do,' and indicated the door.

Eventually he admitted me to the university sickbay, and gave me chlorpromazine, which I took for several days. I began to feel so dreadful that I hid all the subsequent doses in a handkerchief and a week later presented a handful to him as proof that I had recovered and was back to my normal self. He did not insist that I take further medication, and stayed in relationship with me for a number of years, allowing me to contact him whenever I needed him. Despite suffering from jaundice for several months as a side effect of the chlorpromazine, I recovered quickly, and completed my DPhil.

A sense of pathway

I did not reflect on the detail of what I had experienced, but realized that it had something to do with my uncle's behaviour towards me. I was left with a new sense that life had some mystical meaning and purpose, although I didn't quite know how or what. I had what I called 'a sense of pathway'. I felt I was here for a reason. I had also discovered the concept and experience of 'synchronicity' or meaningful coincidence. Despite now being a trained scientist, it began to seem to me as if the universe was not a chance or haphazard phenomenon, but had some meaningful design of which I was a part. I certainly did not see myself as having been mad or mentally ill. I was not ashamed of what had happened, or stigmatized by it, and I readily talked to people about it. Although aspects of the experience had been utterly terrifying, there were ways in which I found it fascinating and compelling. My family and friends were very shaken by it all, but quickly put this aside as I rapidly resumed my life course. After completing my doctorate I went on to finish my medical degree, and undertook General Practice. Eventually, I remarried and had two more children. I went to live with my second husband in his country of origin and there, at age 33, began my training in psychiatry.

Over the ensuing 19 years, I went on to have many experiences similar to those in my early twenties, which I came to recognize as being episodes of 'psychosis'.

I began to take regular antipsychotic medication which eventually resulted in a very rare form of tardive dystonia leaving me unable to speak without great effort.

After my third such episode, and for reasons that I have explained elsewhere (Randal 1999; Randal *et al.* 2008), I lost my place in the psychiatry training scheme, and was told that my 'ideas and theoretical frameworks did not fit with the way psychiatry was to be practiced.' For a brief time I believed that I had been entrapped by 'the devil'. Although I continued to practice medicine, and subsequently was accepted back into psychiatry, at the time I felt as if my pathway had been blocked by an insurmountable brick wall. Perhaps life had no meaning after all, except to be born, have children, and die. One day I considered the possibility of suicide; my children were asleep in the car and apart from them and my husband, I could see no reason to carry on.

'Knock and the door will be opened. Seek and you will find'

I remember looking up into the sky and saying out loud, 'God, if you're up there, and I don't for a minute believe you are, I need to know right now!' Prior to this moment, even though I had the 'sense of pathway', I had never considered the possibility of the existence of a personal, loving God who might want to help me.

There followed a sequence of synchronous events beginning with being prayed for by an acquaintance who suggested I read the Gospel of John – a completely novel idea for me, especially in view of my mother's disdain for the New Testament. When I read it I was surprised by how it reminded me somehow of my own journey of meaning-making, and felt intrigued to realize that this represented 'the truth'. When I was later with a patient who was in great distress, I prayed for her (this was a most unusual thing for me to do, but as I had experienced such surprising comfort when I had been prayed for, I spontaneously offered her the same intervention). Leaving in my car after this unusual encounter, I turned on the radio and heard the words of a then popular song 'We all need a little divine intervention'. I thought back to my recent heartfelt cry to the God who I did not believe in.

I began to read the Bible and to attend a small local Church, where we learnt songs about 'Spiritual Warfare', a new concept to me. One song had the words 'It is written in Ephesians chapter 6 verses 10–12: Be strong, put on God's armour; we're not fighting human enemies, we're fighting a war in the spirit.' I related this to my many experiences of hell, the obliterative forces that I felt had almost destroyed me, and my brief encounter with 'the devil'. One evening soon after this I came across this scripture in two different contexts. The next day, I was in my car at traffic lights, praying, when a man cycled up, asked if I read the Bible, and handed me a small piece of paper on which was written:

> The Full Armour of God: Ephesians: 6 v.10–18: The girdle of TRUTH; The breastplate of RIGHTEOUSNESS; The shoes of PEACE; the shield of

FAITH; the helmet of SALVATION; The SWORD OF THE SPIRIT – THE WORD OF GOD; PRAYER. Please keep this in your Bible. DO NOT LEAVE HOME WITHOUT IT.

My hair stood on end. I thought, 'Does God really exist after all? And does He (or She) send letters?'

Since that time I have read the whole Bible many times, and have become integrated into a faith community of like-minded people who worship and pray together. It was humbling to realize, initially to my shame and to my mother's consternation, that I had come upon the so-called 'Christian God'. Only gradually did I discover that I had connected with my ancestral Jewish heritage in finding 'Yeshua' (Jesus), the historical person I now believe to be the Messiah foretold in the Hebrew Scriptures. I experienced relief to realize that in His death, the 'suffering servant' of Isaiah took upon *Himself* the world's pain, grief and destructiveness; it was not *my* role to do that!

I slowly discovered the love and forgiveness of the incarnate living God who my mother had told me either did not care about her or more probably did not exist. I began to reframe my psychotic experiences as 'spiritual emergencies' (Randal & Argyle 2005) culminating in the emergence of a Christ-centred spirituality that now makes sense to me. I was able to stop all medication and to maintain my equilibrium despite further recent experiences of abandonment, betrayal and rejection.

I now understand the story of my own spiritual development in the context of the Biblical meta-narrative that traces the history of the Jewish people to the birth of Jesus as the fulcrum of history, and beyond to the heritage of the New Testament writers. Their accounts of their own experiences bring hope that we might all be instrumental in bringing 'the now and the not yet' of the Kingdom of Heaven to be manifest on earth.

I hope and believe that my small contribution to psychiatry lies in the construction of the 'Re-covery Model' (Randal *et al.* 2009), which comes partly out of my own journey of recovery. Oddly (in view of the visions I experienced at 24) this model includes a spiral or helical representation of bio-socio-psycho-spiritual and cultural development. It provides a new, more hope-inspiring context for understanding mental health crises and extreme states as providing opportunities for victorious cycles of meaning-making and spiritual development, rather than the vicious cycles of stigma and hopelessness so often encountered by those people who have endured experiences such as mine.

Implications for understanding

Personal reflections

I now understand that my parents and my uncle were emotionally compromised by the loss of their mothers in early childhood. Although my parents did the best they could, I probably developed an insecure ambivalent attachment style, tending to idealize others, without a steady capacity to integrate the 'good' and the 'bad', or to name or regulate my intense emotions. I became spiritually and emotionally vulnerable to my uncle's inappropriate sexualized involvement with me. My boundaries were severely damaged by both his intrusive advances, and my mother's denial of my reality and lack of capacity to acknowledge or contain my pain. This, in turn, left me vulnerable to sexualizing other relationships with men, such as with my therapist and my supervisor. I was re-traumatized as a result of confusing boundary violations.

My tendency to form insecure ambivalent attachments left me unable to sustain nourishing marital relationships when my needs for validation, holding and recognition were not met. I was unable to manage my inevitable disappointment. Similar dynamics created the pattern of betrayal I experienced within the psychiatry training.

The lack of a foundation of spiritual identity or existential holding left me vulnerable to ontological insecurity and the terror of obliteration when faced with extreme circumstances (such as the death of my father, breakdown of my marriage and rejection from psychiatry). No attention was paid at any stage in my journey by any of my caregivers, therapists, psychiatrists or colleagues to addressing my spiritual history or my need to explore my cultural and spiritual heritage. I was forced by my circumstances to make the almost impossible transition from the worldview I was brought up in, where meaning was found solely in intellectual and educational achievement, and vulnerability was to be avoided at all cost, to one where I am loved unconditionally by a Divine Father with my many vulnerabilities and failings. Once I discovered the trustworthiness of a loving Divine Father, I gradually learned to acknowledge my own vulnerability and to grieve my many losses. I slowly developed a resilient sense of my own worth, value, purpose, meaning and vocation.

General reflections

Traumatic early developmental experiences in the context of insecure parental attachment and invalidation create a predisposition to emotional and relational dysregulation. The 'transference' of these parental attachment patterns onto the imagining of God may result in ontological insecurity and experiences of obliteration terror. The concept of 'spiritual emergency' appears to be useful as a way of framing experiences which would otherwise be deemed 'psychotic'. This explanatory model is potentially less stigmatizing, bringing hope of restoration and healing with the emergence of a spiritual understanding. The development of a more hopeful narrative which makes sense of suffering brings with it the possibility of making a meaningful contribution and may aid in the reduction of the need for medication.

Implications for practice

My story highlights the importance of exploring spiritual heritage, spiritual development and indicators of spiritual vulnerability. Making sense of the meaning of extreme experiences in the context of early attachment patterns, trauma and boundary violations may aid with understanding ontological insecurity and obliteration experiences. Reframing these extreme states as 'Spiritual emergencies' and helping to find the emerging narrative of spiritual meaning-making may bring sufficient reduction in anxiety/terror to create the pathway for reducing antipsychotic medication. Believing in the possibility that specific imagery experienced during these states is meaningful and may be prophetic of positive future initiatives may aid with validating personal narratives and creating spiritual resilience.

References

Randal, P. (1999) 'Loving relationship is at the root of recovery'. In J. Leibrich (ed.) *A Gift of Stories. Discovering How To Deal With Mental Illness* (pp. 137–144). Dunedin: University of Otago Press/Mental Health Commission.

Randal, P. and Agyle, N. (2005) 'Spiritual emergency – A useful explanatory model? A literature review and discussion paper', *Spirituality Special Interest Group Publications Archive*. Retrieved from: www.rcpsych.ac.uk/pdf/DrPRandal-DrArgyleEmergency.pdf

Randal, P., Geekie, J., Lambrecht, I. and Taitimu, M. (2008) 'Dissociation, psychosis, and spirituality: Whose voices are we hearing?' In A. Moskowitz, I. Schafer and M. Dorahy (eds) *Psychosis, Trauma and Dissociation: Emerging Perspectives on Severe Psychopathology*. Chichester: Wiley-Blackwell.

Randal, P., Stewart, M.W., Proverbs, D., Lampshire, D., Symes, J. and Hamer, H. (2009) 'The Re-covery Model – An integrative developmental stress-vulnerability-strengths approach to mental health', *Psychosis, 1*: 122–133.

Chapter 8

Spirituality and psychosis

David Lukoff

Cross-cultural and historical perspectives

Psychotic and spiritual experiences have been associated since the earliest recorded history. Hallucinatory and visionary experiences of Biblical prophets and saints have played an essential role in religion for thousands of years. Socrates, who had a personal Daemonic voice that guided him, declared, 'Our greatest blessings come to us by way of madness, provided the madness is given us by divine gift' (Dodds 1951). Based on a cross-cultural survey, the anthropologist Prince (1992) concluded that:

> Highly similar mental and behavioural states may be designated psychiatric disorders in some cultural settings and religious experiences in others ... Within cultures that invest these unusual states with meaning and provide the individual experiencing them with institutional support, at least a proportion of these individuals may be contained and channelled into socially valuable roles.
>
> (Prince 1992: 289)

In a study of visions among Hispanic clinic patients, Lata (2005: 27) found that 'psychotic phenomena could occur in connection with spiritual experiences. Visions of loved ones who have died occur constantly, as well as visions of saints, angels, Jesus, and Mary.' Other anthropological accounts show that babbling confused words, displaying curious eating habits, singing continuously, dancing wildly, and being 'tormented by spirits' are common elements in shamanic initiatory crises. In shamanic cultures, such crises are interpreted as an indication of an individual's destiny to become a shaman, rather than a sign of mental illness (Halifax 1979). In Asian cultures, problems associated with spiritual practices, such as disorientation and hallucinations, that in the West could be labelled as psychotic, are recognized phenomena distinguished from psychopathology.

Contemporary perspectives

In recent years, religious institutions and the mental health field – especially in the West – have tended to take a dichotomous view of spirituality and psychosis.

When spirituality and psychosis overlap, the experience has usually been viewed as pathological. The mental health professions have a long history of ignoring and pathologizing religion and spirituality in all forms (Lukoff and Turner 1992). For instance, Freud described religion as an obsessional neurosis (Freud 1989). Albert Ellis asserted, 'The less religious [patients] are, the more emotionally healthy they will tend to be' (Ellis 1980: 637).

However, it seems that mainstream mental health is undergoing a change in perspective. Partly this can be traced to the consensus of research findings such as by Koenig *et al.* (2001) that religion is overwhelmingly associated with positive health including mental health. Their chapter on 'Schizophrenia and Other Psychoses,' summarized research showing that persons with mental disorders utilize their spiritual resources to improve functioning, reduce isolation, and facilitate healing.

Transpersonal psychologists maintain that some episodes of psychosis are part of a natural developmental process with both spiritual and psychological components. They point out similarities between psychotic symptoms and spiritual experiences (Lukoff 1988; Perry 1998) and argue that psychotic experiences are better understood as crises related to the person's efforts to break out of the standard ego-bounded identity: 'Trials of the soul on its spiritual journey' (House 2001: 124–125). Stanislav and Christina Grof (1989: 254) coined the term 'spiritual emergency' to describe this and similar episodes that 'take the form of nonordinary states of consciousness and involve intense emotions, visions and other sensory changes, and unusual thoughts, as well as various physical manifestations.'

Beginning in the 1960s, interest in Asian spiritual practices such as meditation, yoga, and tai chi, as well as experimentation with psychedelic drugs, have been documented to trigger psychotic experiences (Lukoff 2007). Surveys show a significant increase in participation in spiritual practices such as meditation, yoga, *qi gong* sweat lodges, drumming circles, and other practices which can induce intense spiritual experiences (Pew Forum on Religion and Public Life 2008). The majority of these experiences are not problematic and do not disrupt functioning, nor necessitate mental health treatment. However, with increased utilization of spiritual practices and participation in groups that induce intense spiritual experiences, it can be expected that the incidence of spiritual-practice-induced and spiritually themed psychotic episodes will increase. As Caplan comments:

> The contemporary spiritual scene is like a candy store where any casual spiritual 'tourist' can sample the 'goodies' that promise a variety of mystical highs. When novices who don't have the proper education or guidance begin to naively and carelessly engage mystical experiences, they are playing with fire.
>
> (Caplan 1999: 74)

Implications for understanding the relationship between spirituality and psychosis

Both psychosis and intense spiritual experiences such as mystical experiences involve escaping the limiting boundaries of the self, which leads to immense elation and freedom as the outlines of the confining selfhood melt down (Boisen 1962; Buckley 1981; James 1958). The need to transcend the limiting boundaries of the self has been postulated to be a basic neurobiological need of all living things (Newberg *et al.* 2001). However, during psychotic episodes, if 'the sense of embodied self is transcended before it has been firmly established . . . disintegration and further fragmentation are the likely results' (Mills 2001: 214).

Research confirms the overlap between psychotic and spiritual experiences. Peters *et al.* (1999) assessed the incidence of delusions among members of New Religious Movements (NRMs), such as Moonies, nonreligious people, Christians, and patients hospitalized for psychotic disorders. They found that those in the NRM group could not be distinguished from the inpatients by the presence of delusions, but the patient group had a significantly higher level of distress. In another study, religious experience and psychopathology were compared across three groups in the US, matched for age and gender: 30 psychotic patients at a psychiatric hospital, 30 religious contemplatives, and a comparison group of individuals. Contemplatives were nationally recognized Buddhist meditation teachers, Hindu centre directors, and Christian monks and nuns. Psychotic inpatients and religious contemplatives had similar scores on measures of mysticism, and both groups scored significantly higher than the comparison group. The patients were distinguished only by having significantly lower levels of adjustment than the other two groups (Stifler *et al.* 1993).

Detailed case studies have shown that psychotic symptoms occur in the context of spiritual experiences (Lukoff 1991; Lukoff and Everest 1985). Greenberg *et al.* (1992) described four young men who explored Jewish mysticism and became psychotic. Their hallucinations, grandiose and paranoid delusions, and social withdrawal were indistinguishable from those of many mystics.

Several survey studies have shown that more than half the normal population has some experience with voices (Posey & Losch 1983), and approximately 10 per cent of the general population has the experience of hearing a comforting or advising voice that is not perceived as being one's own thoughts (Barret & Etheridge 1992). Voices and visions frequently occur in people during bereavement, life threatening situations, and stressful traumatic situations such as sensory deprivation, sleep deprivation, illness, and solitary confinement (Forrer 1960). Inner voices have played a significant role in the lives of many noted individuals including Carl Jung, Elisabeth Kubler-Ross, Martin Luther King, Jr., and Winston Churchill (Liester 1996). Hearing inner voices is often experienced as helpful by people who are experiencing a spiritual awakening (Heery 1989). These accounts and empirical studies comparing individuals who are both religious and deluded call into question diagnostic criteria for delusions that emphasize the content (i.e. bizarreness or falsity) of beliefs to classify them as pathological (Brett 2002). Pathological and spiritual experiences cannot be distinguished by form and content, but need to be assessed in the light of the values and beliefs of the individual and the social context.

Implications for practice: persons in acute psychotic episodes

Spiritually oriented psychotherapy can help individuals probe the personal meaning of their symptoms, see the universal dimensions of their experiences and shape a psychotic episode into a coherent narrative that leads to a new, life-affirming personal belief system. There is already a body of clinical literature, particularly detailed case studies (Cortright 1997; Lukoff & Everest 1985; Lukoff 1988, 1991), that illustrates effective approaches for working with spiritual crises. Clarke (2008) describes how cognitive therapy can be used to normalize psychotic experience by emphasizing to the patient the overlap with spiritual experiences.

Exploration of the many spiritual and mythic symbols encountered in psychosis can be an important part of the recovery process. In a study of 30 successful recovery narratives, Jacobson (2001) found a recurrent theme that emphasized 'what happened' as a spiritual or philosophical crisis during which the self is destroyed and then recreated in the light of a newly realized truth. Many found a community of practising Buddhists, the Bible, or philosophy helped them to recreate a new sense of an enlightened self with enhanced wisdom and compassion.

Through psychotherapy, individuals may be able to salvage personally valid spiritual dimensions of their psychotic experience. People recovering from psychotic disorders have rich opportunities for spiritual growth, along with challenges to its expression and development. Unfortunately, many beliefs that people develop around an episode of psychosis are dysfunctional and emphasize pathological qualities.

Some residential treatment approaches have addressed spiritual dimensions of psychosis. Perry (1974), who founded Diabysis, a Jungian-oriented group treatment home for people experiencing a first psychotic episode, found themes including the destruction of the world, a cosmic fight between good and evil, the appearance of a messiah that the client identifies with, and a sense of rebirth of the world into a more loving place. Perry encouraged clients to express and explore the symbolic aspects of their psychotic experiences. Therapy, conducted thrice weekly, consisted of listening to clients and helping them to interpret the powerful and spiritual symbols within their hallucinations and delusions. Medications were rarely used. Perry reported that severely psychotic clients became coherent within two to six days *without* medication. The outcomes appeared better for those who had had fewer than three previous psychotic episodes. Diabysis closed down in 1980 due to budget cutbacks in the mental health system.

A similar program, Soteria House, located in San Jose, California, provided more empirical support for this model (Mosher & Menn 1978, 1979). Soteria House ran from 1971 to 1983, roomed six clients, with three to four staff on premises at one time. The staff was trained to view psychotic experiences as a developmental stage that can lead to growth, which often contains a spiritual component of mystical experiences and beliefs. Medication was typically not prescribed unless a client showed no improvement after six weeks (only 10 per cent of clients used medication at Soteria), since it was believed to stunt the possible growth-enhancing process of the psychotic episode (Mosher & Menn 1979).

Outcomes from Soteria were compared to a 'traditional' program, a community mental health centre inpatient service consisting of daily pharmacotherapy, psychotherapy, occupational therapy, and group therapy (Mosher, Menn & Mathews 1975). Clients' length of stay was longer at Soteria than in the comparison program (mean of 166 days versus 28 days) (Mosher & Menn 1978). But most patients recovered in six to eight weeks without medication (Mosher et al. 2004). A recent meta-analysis of data from two carefully controlled studies of Soteria programs found better two-year outcomes for Soteria patients in the domains of psychopathology, work, and social functioning compared with similar clients treated in a psychiatric hospital (Bola & Mosher 2003).

Lukoff developed a holistic program for patients with diagnoses of schizophrenia that addressed the spiritual side of their lives. He contrasted the effectiveness of a 12-week holistic health program with a social skills training group, randomly assigning inpatients at a state mental hospital to either treatment (Lukoff et al. 1986). The holistic program consisted of 20 minutes each of daily yoga and meditation. Clients also attended a weekly 'Growth and Schizophrenia' session examining the positive, especially the spiritual dimensions of their hallucinations and delusions. Overall, the study provided some support to the idea that spiritual interventions can be used in persons with schizophrenia without causing harm, and with possible benefits.

Implications for practice: spirituality in recovery from psychosis

Many mental health systems around the world are undergoing a quiet revolution as former patients and other advocates are working with mental health providers and government agencies to incorporate spirituality into mental health care.

A diagnosis of a serious mental problem does not affect the deepest drives of humanity – to live with purpose and become active participants in the community. Understanding one's problems in religious or spiritual terms is an extremely powerful alternative to a biological or psychological framework.

'Serious mental illness' – even when viewed through the most optimistic recovery framework – is usually perceived as a gloomy diagnosis. If the experience is framed in spiritual terms, on the other hand, the end result of all the pain and hard work may be envisioned as spiritual development – a worthy if difficult goal (Blanch 2007: 259).

Many studies show that spirituality often plays an important role in recovery. Several studies document that patients with psychotic disorders use religion to cope with their illness (Chu & Klein 1985) and that the intensity of religious beliefs is not associated with psychopathology (Pfeifer & Waelty 1995). In fact, religious practices (such as worship and prayer) appear to protect against severity of psychiatric symptoms and hospitalization, and enhance life satisfaction and speed recovery in mental disorders (Koenig *et al.* 2001). Kirov *et al.* (1998) found that 61.2 per cent of patients with acute psychotic symptoms reported they used religion to cope with their illness and to assist recovery.

Studies have found that the religious beliefs, practices and commitments of psychiatric patients are similar to or stronger than the general population and that they turn to religious resources during such crises (Fitchett *et al.* 1997). In Lindgren and Coursey's (1995) interviews with people in psychosocial rehabilitation programs, 80 per cent said spirituality/religion had been helpful to them. In a study of psychiatric inpatients, Fitchett *et al.* (1997) found that 88 per cent reported three or more current religious needs, but patients had lower spiritual well-being scores and were less likely to have talked with their clergy than higher-scoring patients. They concluded that religion is important for the psychiatric patients, but they may need assistance to find resources to address their religious needs.

However, some patients have been found to hold dysfunctional beliefs about their disorder. One study of psychiatric inpatients found that 23 per cent believed that sin-related factors, such as sinful thoughts or acts, were related to the development of their illness (Sheehan & Kroll 1990). This is clearly a guilt-inducing belief for which there is no evidence, and one that the vast majority of religious professionals would challenge.

Fallot (1998, 2001) analysed the key religious and spiritual themes in recovery narratives drawn from spiritual discussion groups, trauma recovery groups and other clinical groups for people diagnosed with severe mental problems. He found that although organized religion had been experienced as stigmatizing and rejecting on some occasions, on the whole a personal, spiritual experience of a relationship with God was helpful in building hope, a sense of divine support and love, the courage to change and to accept what can't be changed, connection with faith communities, as well as supporting practices such as prayer, meditation, religious ritual, religious reading, and listening to religious music. The authors found three key themes. First, spirituality played a positive role in coping with stressful situations, using prayer and religious role models, as well as avoiding drug use and negative activities. Second, church attendance and a belief in a higher power provided social and emotional support. Third, spirituality enhanced the sense of being whole.

Many people experience recovery from a psychotic disorder as part of their spiritual journey. Many years after her psychotic episode and two-year hospitalization, Sally Clay went back to review her case records, and found herself described as having 'decompensated with grandiose delusions with spiritual preoccupations' (Clay 1987: 90). She complains that 'Not a single aspect of my spiritual experience at the [Yale Medical School affiliated] Institute of Living was recognized as legitimate; neither the spiritual difficulties nor the healing that occurred at the end' (ibid.). Clay is not denying that she had a psychotic disorder at the time, but makes the case that, in addition to the disabling effects she experienced as part of her illness, there was also a profound spiritual component which was ignored. Nevertheless she has persevered in her belief that:

> For me, becoming 'mentally ill' was always a spiritual crisis, and finding a spiritual model of recovery was a question of life or death. Finally I could admit openly that my experiences were, and always had been, a spiritual journey – not sick, shameful, or evil.
>
> (Clay 1994: 3)

Personal stories of recovery and spirituality are easily accessed on websites (e.g. sallyclay.net), and organizational resources (e.g. realization.org; spirituale-mergence.net, spiritualrecoveries.blogspot.com).

Pat Deegan, who is both a consumer and a psychologist, also makes the point that psychosis can be a genuine route to spirituality:

> Distress, even the distress associated with psychosis, can be hallowed ground upon which one can meet God and receive spiritual teaching . . . Those of us who are diagnosed can have authentic encounters with God [which] encourage the healing process that is recovery.
>
> (Deegan 2004)

Consumer advocate Jay Mahler expresses it this way:

> My being aware that I'm on a spiritual journey empowers me to deal with the big, human 'spiritual' questions, like: Why is this happening to me? Will I ever be the same again? Is there a place for me in this world? Can my experience of life be made liveable? If I can't be cured can I be recovering . . . even somewhat? Has my God abandoned me . . . That's my spiritual journey, that wondering. That's my search.
>
> (Weisburd 1996: 2)

Jerome Stack, a Catholic Chaplain at Metropolitan State Hospital in Norwalk, California, for 25 years, observed that many people with psychotic disorders do have genuine religious experiences:

> Many patients over the years have spoken to me of their religious experience and I have found their stories to be quite genuine, quite believable. Their

experience of the divine, the spiritual, is healthy and life giving. Of course, discernment is important, but it is important not to presume that certain kinds of religious experience or behavior are simply 'part of the illness'.

(Stack 1997: 24)

Some clinicians have expressed the concern that having patients discuss their delusional experiences could exacerbate their symptoms by reinforcing them. Lukoff's holistic program (described earlier) was conducted at a state psychiatric hospital and participants actively explored their psychotic symptoms without detrimental effects. Their symptom ratings improved as much as the group that did not discuss their psychotic experiences.

'Spiritual issues groups' for persons with psychotic and other serious mental problems are another area of innovation appearing in the scientific literature (Phillips *et al.* 2002). These programs have ranged from time-limited sessions of a psycho-educational format (Lindgren & Coursey 1995) to longer-term psychodynamic interventions (O'Rourke 1997). Unlike some of the transpersonal therapies, these groups clearly demarcate the boundaries by not including religious or spiritual practices in the treatment session itself (Kehoe 1998). These programs have focused on helping patients to understand the religious identity and experiences of those with psychotic disorders and how it affects their lives (Genia 1990). There is a balance of exploring both religious resources and spiritual struggles in these groups. Questions such as 'Is it OK to be angry with God' and 'If God loves, then why is there suffering' are explored to normalize such concerns and assuage guilt (Kehoe 1998). They are a place for clients to discuss and heal from spiritual struggles, such as feeling abandoned by God or ostracized by their religious community. They also provide opportunities for clients to discuss positive religious experiences which may enhance self-esteem and a sense of self-worth. Finally, these groups differentiate religious delusions from helpful religious coping strategies.

Spiritual support involves the degree to which a person experiences a connection to a higher power (i.e. God or other transcendent force) that is actively supporting, protecting, guiding, teaching, helping, and healing. Some researchers have suggested that the subjective experience of spiritual support may form the core of the spirituality–health connection (Mackenzie *et al.* 2000). Persons with psychotic disorders utilize spiritual support to improve functioning, reduce isolation, and facilitate well-being.

Spiritual support can include:

• Educating clients about recovery as a spiritual journey with a potentially positive outcome.
• Encouraging clients' involvement with a spiritual path or religious community consistent with their experiences and values.
• Encouraging clients to seek support and guidance from credible and appropriate religious or spiritual leaders.

- Encouraging clients to engage in religious and spiritual practices consistent with their beliefs. At times, this might include engaging in a practice together with the client such as meditation, silence, prayer, or singing.
- Modelling one's own spirituality (when appropriate), including a sense of spiritual purpose and meaning, along with hope and faith in something transcendent.

Spirituality is an important coping mechanism because individuals seek meaning when experiencing severe illnesses. Therefore, promoting religious and spiritual beliefs and practices is appropriate with patients who are open to accepting that approach.

References

Barret, T. R. and Etheridge, J. B. (1992) 'Verbal hallucinations in normals, I: People who hear voices', *Applied Cognitive Psychology*, 6: 379–387.

Blanch, A. (2007) 'Integrating religion and spirituality in mental health: The promise and the challenge', *Psychiatric Rehabilitation Journal*, 30: 251–260.

Boisen, A. T. (1962) *The Exploration of the Inner World*. New York: Harper and Row.

Bola, J. R. and Mosher, L. R. (2003) 'Treatment of acute psychosis without neuroleptics: Two-year outcomes from the Soteria project', *Journal of Nervous and Mental Disease*, 191: 219–229.

Brett, C. (2002) 'Psychotic and mystical states of being: Connections and distinctions', *Philosophy, Psychiatry & Psychology*, 9: 321.

Buckley, P. (1981) 'Mystical experience and schizophrenia', *Schizophrenia Bulletin*, 7: 516–521.

Caplan, M. (1999) *Halfway Up the Mountain: The Error of Premature Claims to Enlightenmen*. Prescott, AZ: Hohm Press.

Chu, C. C. and Klein, H. E. (1985) 'Psychosocial and environmental variables in outcome of black schizophrenics', *Journal of the National Medical Association*, 77: 793–796.

Clarke, I. (2008) *Cognitive Behavior Therapy for Acute Inpatient Mental Health Units: Working with Clients, Staff and the Milieu*. NY: Routledge.

Clay, S. (1987) 'Stigma and spirituality', *Journal of Contemplative Psychotherapy*, 4: 87–94.

Clay, S. (1994) 'The Wounded Prophet'. In *Recovery: The New Force in Mental Health*. Columbus, OH: Ohio Department of Mental Health.

Cortright, B. (1997) *Psychotherapy and Spirit: Theory and Practice in Transperonal Psychotherapy*. Albany, NY: SUNY Press.

Deegan, P. (2004) Spiritual Lessons in Recovery. Retrieved from: www.patdeegan.com/blog/archives/000011.php.

Dodds, E. (1951) *The Greeks and the Irrational*. Berkeley, CA: Univeristy of California Press.

Ellis, A. (1980) 'Psychotherapy and atheistic values: A response to A. E. Bergin's Psychotherapy and Religious Issues', *Journal of Consulting and Clinical Psychology*, 48: 635–639.

Fallot, R. (1998) 'Spiritual and religious dimensions of mental illness recovery narratives'. In R. Fallot (ed.) *Spirituality and Religion in Recovery From Mental Illness*. Washington, DC: New Directions for Mental Health Services.

Fallot, R. (2001) 'Spirituality and religion in psychiatric rehabilitation and recovery from mental illness', *International Review of Psychiatry*, *13*: 110–116.

Fitchett, G., Burton, L. A. and Sivan, A. B. (1997) 'The religious needs and resources of psychiatric patients', *Journal of Nervous and Mental Disorder*, *185*: 320–326.

Forrer, G. R. (1960) 'Benign auditory and visual hallucination', *Archives of General Psychiatry*, *3*: 119–122.

Freud, S. (1989) *The Future of an Illusion*. New York: W. W. Norton & Company.

Genia, V. (1990) 'Interreligious encounter group: A psychospiritual experience for faith development', *Counseling and Values*, *35*: 39–51.

Greenberg, D., Witzum, E. and Buchbinder, J. (1992) 'Mysticism and psychosis: The fate of Ben Zoma', *British Journal of Medical Psychology*, *65*: 223–235.

Grof, S. and Grof, C. (eds) (1989) *Spiritual Emergency: When Personal Transformation Becomes a Crisis*. Los Angeles, CA: Tarcher.

Halifax, J. (1979) *Shamanic Voices*. New York: Dutton.

Heery, M. (1989) 'Inner voice experiences: An exploratory study of thirty cases', *Journal of Transpersonal Psychology*, *21*: 73–82.

House, R. (2001) 'Spiritual experience: Healthy psychoticism?' In I. Clarke (ed.) *Psychosis and Spirituality: Exploring the New Frontier*. London: Whurr Publishers.

Jacobson, N. (2001) 'Experiencing recovery: A dimensional analysis of recovery narratives', *Psychiaric Rehabilitation Journal*, *24*: 248–256.

James, W. (1958) *The Varieties of Religious Experience*. New York: New American Library of World Literature.

Kehoe, N. C. (1998) 'Religious-issues group therapy', *New Directions for Mental Health Services*, *80*: 40–55.

Kirov, G., Kemp, R., Kirov, K. and David, A. S. (1998) 'Religious faith after psychotic illness', *Psychopathology*, *31*: 234–245.

Koenig, H., Mccullough, M. and Larson, D. (eds) (2001) *Handbook of Religion and Health*. New York: Oxford University Press.

Lata, J. (2005) 'Visual hallucinations in Hispanic clinic patients: A need to assess for cultural beliefs'. PhD thesis, Carlos Albizu University, Miami, Florida.

Liester, M. (1996) 'Inner Voices: Distinguishing Transcendent and Pathological Characteristics', *Journal of Transpersonal Psychology*, *28*: 1–31.

Lindgren, K. N. and Coursey, R. D. (1995) 'Spirituality and serious mental illness: A two-part study', *Psychosocial Rehabilitation Journal*, *18*: 93–111.

Lukoff, D. (1988) 'Transpersonal therapy with a manic-depressive artist', *Journal of Transpersonal Psychology*, *20*: 10–20.

Lukoff, D. (1991) 'Divine madness: Shamanistic initiatory crisis and psychosis', *Shaman's Drum*, *22*: 24–29.

Lukoff, D. (2007) 'Visionary spiritual experiences', *Southern Medical Journal*, *100*: 635–641.

Lukoff, D. and Everest, H. C. (1985) 'The myths in mental illness', *Journal of Transpersonal Psychology*, *17*: 123–153.

Lukoff, D., Wallace, C. J., Liberman, R. P. and Burke, K. (1986) 'A holistic health program for chronic schizophrenic patients', *Schizophrenia Bulletin*, *12*: 274–282.

Lukoff, D., Lu, F. and Turner, R. (1992) 'Toward a more culturally sensitive DSM-IV: Psychoreligious and Psychospiritual Problems', *Journal of Nervous and Mental Disease*, *180*: 673–682.

Mackenzie, E. R., Rajagopal, D. E., Meibohm, M. and Lavizzo-Mourey, R. (2000) 'Spiritual support and psychological well-being: Older adults' perceptions of the religion and health con', *Alternative Therapies in Health and Medicine*, *6*: 37–45.

Mills, N. (2001) 'The experience of fragmentation in psychosis: Can mindfulness help?' In I. Clarke (ed.) *Psychosis and Spirituality: Exploring the New Frontier*. London: Whurr Publishers.

Mosher, L. and Menn, A. (1978) 'Community residential treatment for schizophrenia: Two-year follow-up', *Hospital and Community Psychiatry*, *29*: 715–723.

Mosher, L. and Menn, A. (1979) 'Soteria: An altenative to hospitalization'. In H. R. Lamb (ed.) *Alternatives to acute hosptialization* (pp. 73–84). San Francisco, CA: Jossey-Bass.

Mosher, L., Menn, A., and Mathews, S. (1975) 'Soteria: Evaluation of a home-based treatment for schizophrenia', *American Journal of Orthopsychiatry*, *45*: 455–467.

Mosher, L., Hendrix, V. and Fort, D. (2004) *Soteria: Through Madness To Deliverance*. Philadelphia: Xlibris Corporation.

Newberg, A., D'aquili, E. and Rause, R. (2001) *Why God Won't Go Away: Brain Science and the Biology of Belief*. New York: Ballantine Books.

O'Rourke, C. (1997) 'Listening for the sacred: Addressing spiritual issues in the group treatment of adults with mental illness', *Smith College Studies in Social Work*, *67*: 177–196.

Perry, J. W. (1974) *The Far Side of Madness*. Englewood Cliffs, NJ: Prentice-Hall, Inc.

Perry, J. (1998) *Trials of the Visionary Mind: Spiritual Emergency and the Renewal Process*. Albany, NY: State University of New York Press.

Peters, E. R., Joseph, S. and Garety, P. A. (1999) 'The assessment of delusions in normal and psychotic populations', *Schizophrenia Bulletin*, *25*: 553–576.

Pew Forum On Religion And Public Life (2008) *US Religious Landscape Survey*. Washington, DC: Pew Research Center.

Pfeifer, S. and Waelty, U. (1995) 'Psychopathology and religious commitment – a controlled study', *Psychopathology*, *28*: 70–77.

Phillips, R. E., III, Lakin, R. and Pargament, K. I. (2002) 'Development and implementation of a spiritual issues group for those with serious mental illness', *Community Mental Health Journal*, *38*: 487–496.

Posey, T. B. and Losch, M. E. (1983) 'Auditory hallucinations of hearing voices in 375 normal subjects', *Imagination, Cognition and Personality*, *3*: 99–113.

Prince, R. H. (1992) 'Religious experience and psychopathology: Cross-cultural perspectives'. In J. F. Schumacher (ed.) *Religion and Mental Health*. New York: Oxford University Press.

Rosen, G. (1968) *Madness in Society*. New York: Harper & Row.

Sheehan, W. & Kroll, J. (1990) 'Psychiatric patients' belief in general health factors and sin as causes of illness', *American Journal of Psychiatry*, *147*: 112–113.

Stack, J. (1997) 'Organized religion is but one of the many paths toward spiritual growth', *The Journal*, *8*: 23–26.

Stifler, K., Greer, J., Sneck, W. and Dovenmuehle, R. (1993) 'An empirical investigation of the discriminability of reported mystical experiences among religious contemplatives, psychotic inpatients, and normal adults', *Journal for the Scientific Study of Religion*, *32*: 366–372.

Weisburd, D. (1996) 'Spirituality: Publisher's note', *The Journal*, *8*: 2–3.

Part IV

Existential/sense of self issues

Whatever name we may choose to give them, the kind of experiences associated with the term 'psychosis' can, as the following two chapters demonstrate, be closely associated with what we might refer to as 'existential issues': one's sense of self and sense of being in the world, issues that have commonly been the domain of philosophers. In Arnhild Lauveng's account of her personal experience, we find a valiant effort to articulate aspects of experience that lie largely on the boundaries of what our language can easily express (and, that she does so in a language that is not her mother-tongue makes her account all the more remarkable).

In her account we hear how her loss of her sense of self was at the core of her experience, underpinning other aspects of the experience (such as hearing voices), and contributed to her struggle in carrying out everyday activities (echoing Larry Davidson's chapter earlier). Again, Arnhild points out how her experience, while unusual, is understandable if we take into account her life experiences (in particular the loss of her father and how she was treated by peers at school). Jim Geekie's chapter details his research into the subjective experience of clients of a first episode psychosis service and we find that the existential concerns expressed by Arnhild are shared by participants in his research.

Both chapters point, once again, to aspects of the experience of psychosis which are easily overlooked if subjective experience is not properly attended to. Again, we find that sense of self and the need to develop personally meaningful narratives, which are validated by others, permeate the subjective experience of psychosis.

Chapter 9

When you have lost yourself, there's really not very much left

Arnhild Lauveng

In my everyday life, I occupy a number of different roles with different behaviour. I'm a professional clinical psychologist, I'm a lecturer, a friend, a private person. These different roles have different demands, and I use slightly different traits and items from my personality in each of them. I can say and do different kinds of things as a lecturer than as a private person, and vice versa. And besides the different roles, other things can also affect my behaviour. Sometimes I'm tired, or have received good news; I can be in a good or bad mood, comforting, hurt, angry or unreasonable. But even if my feelings and my behaviour can change depending on circumstances, mood and roles, I'm always myself. I can sometimes wonder what on earth I was thinking about when I did something especially stupid, but I'm never in doubt that it was me that took that decision. I can question some of my choices, or doubt my skills, but I never doubt being alive. I always know that I'm alive, and that I am myself.

But it has not always been this way. When I was seventeen years old I got the diagnosis of schizophrenia. For about ten years I went in and out of psychiatric wards. I had hallucinations. I hurt myself when the voices told me to. I was thought disordered and delusional. It was all very confusing, scary and painful, but most frightening of all was the persisting feeling that I had lost my self. I didn't know who I was any more. I often thought that I was a zombie, one of the living dead, or just a person in a book or in someone's imagination. Or, even more commonly, I had no explanations at all; I was just confused and scared, feeling that I was no longer a person, not able to recognize my self or to feel that I was an independent individual who could make my own choices or control my own actions. It was really the most frightening experience I've ever had, because normally, when you get in trouble, you can trust that your head, or your experience, or your personality will find some way to help you. Maybe you can do it yourself, or you can ask someone else for help, or support. But what can you do when the problem is that you have lost your self? Then you're *really* lost.

In this chapter I will look at some existential issues or 'sense of self' in psychosis, how it can be experienced – from the 'inside' – and how this experience can make sense when you take into account the patient's subjective story of life. Finally, I will consider implications for understanding and treatment derived from this experience.

The feeling of losing my self

It started gradually. It was like fog appearing on a sunny day. First the silhouettes of items far away became less distinct, then the world slowly got smaller. Things far away disappeared, and even the things near me seemed more and more cloudy and unreal. It was like driving in a foggy landscape. I couldn't see the road in front of me, I didn't know where I was, and I became scared of losing my way.

And so the fog got thicker, so thick that it got inside me, so eventually it was not only other people, but also myself who became grey and foggy and unreal. I couldn't recognize my surroundings. I could, of course, see them – I was not blind – and some parts of me knew that they were exactly as they had always been. But at the same time, they didn't appear the same. I could not name any specific differences, but I just didn't recognize them as familiar. And, even more importantly, I couldn't recognize myself anymore. I would not have been able to describe the changes at that time, but I did know that something was really different. I had changed, and I didn't know myself any more.

And that was probably the main problem: I couldn't recognize myself. And when I no longer knew who I was, how could I know or recognize anything else? I didn't feel alive, like a unique, integrated person. Even now, it's really hard to describe this feeling, because the feeling of self is so integrated and automatic that we hardly ever think about it, and this makes it difficult to describe the differences that appear when this feeling disappears. I started to think about myself as 'she'. 'She went to school'. 'She was sad'. And I wondered who 'she' was. Was 'she' 'me'? But, no, that could not be true, because the sentences I heard in my head told me that 'she' was sad, and wanted to kill herself, but I was not sad, as far as I could tell. But, really, I couldn't know, because I didn't exist any more. And, if I was 'she', who then was the 'I' wondering if 'I' was 'she'? Was that another 'I'?

Of course I didn't tell anybody. It happened so slowly there was really nothing to tell. And even when I noticed that things had gone far out of control, and I really needed some help, I still didn't tell anybody; simply because I didn't know what to say. What could I say? That I didn't exist any more? That would have sounded very strange. But I tried anyway. I went to the school nurse and said that there was really nothing seriously wrong with me, but I felt that everything was a little bit 'difficult'. I was asked some questions, first by her, and then by a school psychologist. They asked me if I was afraid of being alone, or going by bus, or going shopping, but I was not. Then they asked me if I was eating properly, and at that time, I was. They asked about suicidal thoughts, and I really didn't know what to answer, because I knew that 'she wanted to kill herself', but I didn't know if she was me, so I just said that I didn't know for sure. I tried to tell the psychologist that I didn't feel that I had control over my self anymore, that something had changed. He responded by drawing circles of id, ego and superego, and at that moment I realized that I would never be able to explain to him what was really going on. So I said I was ok, and cancelled all further appointments. I didn't want to do that, because I knew that I was in need of help, but I didn't know what else to do. I had no words for what was happening to me. And, most of all, it was too difficult for 'me' to tell what 'I' felt; when the problem was that 'I', in fact, didn't feel that I was a person any more.

Or, at least, that was my experience, at that time. In retrospect, I can see that in fact 'I' was there all the time. I have read research claiming that people with psychosis can 'lose their identity'. I totally agree that identity problems are central to understanding psychosis, but my personal experience, supported both from my own story and from my work with patients suffering from psychosis, is that it is not identity itself that is lost, but the person's *experience* of his or her identity. I felt that 'I' didn't exist any more. Now I can see that my identity was in fact rather stable, even if I couldn't see or feel that at the time. I had my interest in animals and my tendency to think and speak in metaphors. I had my personality, my strengths and weaknesses, my humour and my stubbornness. I was myself all the time; even if I could not recognize myself for a while.

Consequences of losing the sense of identity

The feeling of being alive, of being a unique person, able to control your own actions or to have at least some control over your thoughts and feelings is, of course, a crucial aspect of life. And when this most basic experience is changed, very much in life will change as a consequence of this.

Some of the first changes I noticed were that my perceptions started to change and that I could no longer rely on my senses. A normal shadow could suddenly become threatening and dangerous, subjects and people I knew I ought to know could seem strange and unfamiliar. Sometimes the buildings I passed would grow and become huge, leaving me like a scared little mouse, just waiting to be crushed by giants. When I didn't have a stable experience of myself as a constant identity, separated from my surroundings, and stable despite emotional changes, my comprehension and perception of the world around me could not be constant either, but were infected by my feelings and thoughts.

Later on, I started to hear voices. In the beginning, it was just my perception of sounds that changed, just like my perception of vision had changed. Sounds that used to be loud and distinct and important, like the sound of my friends' voices, or the teacher's lectures, became low and blurry. And sounds that used to be ignored, like the sound of my steps, got loud and scary and took away the focus from the things I was supposed to concentrate on, like a conversation. This was really disturbing and frightening enough, but after a while I also started to hear the sound of someone talking. At first it was just the sound of voices, mumbling without words, but then The Captain appeared. One evening, writing my diary, I noticed a sentence that ended in a completely different way from what I'd planned. So I continued to write, and asked 'who wrote that?', and 'he' answered (using my hand to write the answer), 'It was me. I'm The Captain.'

And he really was a captain. He would decide anything. He told me that I was not allowed to sleep more than three hours a night, not allowed to eat more than five times a week. He was never satisfied with my homework; even if I got a top grade he told me that it was not good enough – even if the teacher hadn't noticed, he had. I was not good enough. Never. Then, he started to hit me. And this is a bit strange, because I say 'he hit me'. Today, as a psychologist, I of course know that he was a representation of my own feelings and memories. Even at that time I could see that it was my arm that hit me. But when I didn't exist, how could I claim the right to be the only owner of the hand, I, who didn't even know if I was a living person? I could not. So he used my arm and hit me, and at that time, I did not understand anything. I was very confused. And of course very, very scared. The Captain and the other voices constantly screamed in my head and said I was a bad person; I was always hungry and tired, because The Captain wouldn't let me sleep or eat enough, and he said he would kill me if I did not obey. Even at that time I knew he would use my body to kill me, my arms would get the rope or my legs would jump out of the window. I knew that others would call it a suicide, but I had lost control and was afraid that the parts of me that still wanted to live would not be able to stop 'him' if he really tried to kill me. It was really frightening, for there is no place on earth you can hide from yourself and when 'I' was no longer there to stop my destructive impulses, anything could happen. I knew I could kill myself, even if I didn't want to die, and there was nothing 'I' could do to stop it. Because 'I' was no longer there. I was lost.

And when 'I' was lost, I also lost the relationship to others. I had never had many friends, but at least I had some. Now I had difficulties keeping those relationships alive. Sometimes I just couldn't understand what my friends were talking about, or, even if I did understand, it didn't seem important to me. I often got confused, forgetting which person had told me what, or who people really were. Now, of course, it is strange to realize that it took me so long to understand this. But when I consider the fact that I did not have a stable and secure experience of my identity at that time, the situation makes sense. If I don't know myself, how can I possibly know others?

Implications for understanding

But how can we understand all this? Why did it happen?

When I was three years old, my father got cancer. Two years later, when I was five, he died. Those years, between three and five, children usually use to do some – often rather noisy – work on their identity. But it is not so easy to do this if you are waiting for your father to die. It's too scary. I couldn't scream or get angry or have tantrums in a safe manner, because I could never know if daddy would be there in the morning. Maybe he would be dead. And maybe that would be my fault. Because, that's another thing about being four or five years old: the world is magic and you are the centre of the universe. If you do the right things, counting all your steps or saying some magic words or something, things will work out just fine. But, if you have naughty thoughts or make mistakes, something terrible can happen. Of course I didn't want my father to die, so I did my very best to prevent it. But I failed. And he died.

And this is really a rather difficult situation. The 'choices' I had, unconsciously, of course – I was five years old! – were both equally painful. I could 'choose' to admit that the world is totally unfair and unpredictable, you can do your very best and be as kind as possible, but terrible things can still happen, totally out of your control. Or I could 'choose' to admit that I failed. I hadn't done enough to save my dad; it was my fault that he died. The first option is of course the healthier one, but despite that I 'chose' the latter one. That made me a terrible person, not deserving to live, but it also made the world more predictable; if I did better next time, no more disasters would happen. It was a lie, and it was a terrible explanation to live with, but it was better than the alternative – at least for a while. I was bad, very bad, but the world was, in a way, still safe. And for a five-year-old kid, just losing her big, strong daddy, that was the most important thing of all, at that time.

One year later, when I was six, I started school. The other children thought I was strange, and, in fact, I was, because I was grieving. They started to avoid me, and after a while, to bully me. They said I was stupid, ugly, bad, a terrible person. They hit me, and, even worse, they did not see me. When I said 'Good morning' or asked about homework or something, they just didn't answer. If some of them stood talking, and I went over, no one noticed me, and no one made a space for me. The only people speaking to me at school were the teachers.

Of course, only communicating with the teachers, always being preoccupied with being a clever student, is not a good way to make friends. I got more and more annoying, always knowing the answers to any questions, never doing anything wrong, and the more annoying I got, the more my schoolmates bullied me and so on. And there were no grown ups there to stop the destructive games.

Think of the situation: no one says hello, or answers your greetings, not for the whole day. Nor the next day. In first grade, second, third, all the way. Every day. In fact, I don't think it's so strange that I eventually started to wonder if I really existed. The strange part is really that I could survive for so many years, before I started to wonder. And The Captain? He just said all the things my classmates used to say, and the teachers used to show me: 'You're worth nothing in yourself. Only when you work can we like you and accept you.' And more than that, he also repeated my one fear as a preschooler: how could daddy just die and leave me? I must have done something terrible; it might be my fault that he died.

So then The Captain, and the feeling of not being a person, does not seem so strange any more. And the same for the other symptoms: perceptual disorders, hallucinations, delusions, lack of interest in activities and persons, and thought disorders. In fact, it all becomes rather understandable. I could not feel sure of my own identity because I had been disturbed in the work of building that identity and because I had experiences that taught me that I was a terrible person, not worth enough to be alive. Most of the time I wondered if I was still alive, and even when I thought I might be alive, I was scared, because I never felt that I deserved to live;

I was too evil. And when I no longer had a secure and safe identity, very many other functions were disturbed too.

My story will always be just that, my own personal story, and could never be generalized to be used as a model to understand other people's stories, or as an example of 'what to do' to get people well. That is not the point. My purpose in telling this story is in fact rather the opposite: not to suggest that professionals 'do the same' or 'look for the same', but rather that they look for the unique. The great tragedy in treating psychosis today is, in my opinion, the fact that many professionals still think they are supposed to treat psychoses. We are not supposed to do that. Our responsibility should always be to treat individuals. To search for their unique stories, their unique personalities, and their unique strengths and needs. And, in cooperation with these findings, use whatever approach and treatment necessary for this special person to understand and manage his or her special life and living condition. And these approaches of course also have to take into account not only the individual's personal story and personality, but also his or her relatives, network and living conditions, as well as practical matters and the social and cultural context in general.

This will make treatment a bit more complicated. We can no longer do 'as usual', because 'as usual' will be to have that healthy curiosity that forces us to do something new every time, and this will always be more complicated. But also more satisfying. Because it will more often help people to find their self again. If we accept the view held by many scientists today (Møller 2005; Blankenburg 2001; Parnas & Handest 2003; Sass & Parnas 2003) that lack of, or damage to, the person's own feeling of identity is a core problem in the severe psychoses, the natural treatment will be to strengthen the person's experience of themselves as a unique person. And to do that, treatment 'as usual' or 'general treatment for psychoses' is not enough. In my opinion, 'best practice' treatment for psychoses should always involve inventing a 'new', specially adjusted treatment for each individual patient. If we want people to find something so unique and special as their own self, we have to search for the unique history of their life, and to treat them as the special persons they in fact are. And, maybe, after a while, they will be able to experience this by themselves.

Implications for practice

It takes time to get sick, and it will take time to get well. To have that time and to have the opportunity of being in a stable and long-lasting relationship will always be of the utmost importance. We know from developmental psychology some of the things that are important for children to build a healthy personality. Shared attention is important, as are mirroring, the forming of stable relationships over time, the caregiver's ability to adapt to the child's needs and wishes, and giving the child time and space to explore his or her special talents, needs, strengths and weak points. No child grows up and builds their identity in six months or one year – it takes a long time. And when the development of a safe identity has gone wrong, it will naturally take some time to get it right. In this process, it is essential not to be alone. Identities are built in relationships with others, and the attitudes of other people are crucial for this development. Benedetti (1964) states that psychotherapy for psychoses involves a certain attitude, not a certain technique, and so the important thing is not only *what* you do, but *how* you do it. To listen to what people say, even if it may seem confused, to look for the feelings, history and meaning behind the symptoms, and to respond to those feelings will often support people's sense of identity. Telling a person that he or she acts strangely because he or she is 'schizophrenic' will not support the development of a secure sense of identity.

When I was sick, I often saw big, scary wolves. Some of the nurses and therapist told me that these were not real, and that I was only confused because I was sick. Their statements confused me even more. I felt alone, and scared, and the wolves, which were really manifestations of my feelings of impotence and anxiety, would become even stronger as a result of my growing anxiety. Other nurses and therapist said that they could not see my wolves, but that *if* they had seen wolves they would have been scared, and they wondered how I felt now.

If we consider these different responses in terms of shared attention, secure relationships and adapting to someone's needs, it is easy to see that in the first approach above none of these core factors for developmental psychology are met. In the latter approach, most of these needs are met. When the nurses talked with me about my experiences, instead of just telling me that this was not 'true', they shared their attention to the topic of most importance for me. They confirmed my experience, but, at the same time, informed me that their experience was somewhat different. They explored my emotions, offering suggestions for what I might feel, and through their interest and support created a secure setting for exploring feelings. Their support and interest showed that they cared and that my well-being was important to them, and – most of all – that I was not alone any more. When my father died and my mother became occupied with her own grief, or at school, when no one tried to stop the bullying, or asked me how I felt, I was all alone. And the fact that no one seemed to care underlined the feeling that I really was a terrible person, not allowed to live, or maybe not a real, living person at all. Telling me that I was a 'chronic schizophrenic' and using forced treatment, isolation cells or behaviour therapy did not change that feeling. Giving me time, creating safe, kind and long-lasting relationships did. In the cooperation with people who treated me as a unique human being, worthy of being alive and worthy of good experiences, I learned to find and accept myself. I can have bad and nice traits. I can be kind or difficult, happy, scared, angry or loving. But through all emotional and behavioural changes I am myself. Always. And I'm never ever in doubt of that any more.

References

Benedetti, G. (1964) *Klinische Psychoterapie*. Bern: Verlag Hans Huber.
Blankenburg, W. (2001) 'First steps toward a psychopathology of common sense', *Philosophy, Psychiatry & Psychology*, 8: 303–315.

Møller, P. (2005) 'Schizofreni og selvet – eksistensielle perspektiver på forståelse og utredning', *Tidsskrift for den norske lægeforening*, *125*: 1022–1025.

Parnas, J. and Handest, P. (2003) 'Phenomenology of anomalous self-experience in early schizophrenia', *Comprehensive Psychiatry*, *44*: 121–134.

Sass, L. A. and Parnas, J. (2003) 'Schizophrenia, consciousness, and the self', *Schizophrenia Bulletin*, *29*: 427–444.

Chapter 10

The uncertainty of being

Existential aspects of the experience of psychosis

Jim Geekie

> I think that's sort of shaken my belief system and my direction in life, you know, my purpose in life. Sort of like my belief system, my self, my personality, you know.
>
> (Paul, research participant)

We see, in the above quote by Paul – a client of a first episode psychosis service reflecting on aspects of the impact of his experience of psychosis – an expression of important existential concerns, relating to how and what he believes, his sense of purpose and his very sense of self. I propose that existential concerns such as these, and others which will be explored in this chapter, lie at the heart of human experience, although, generally speaking, these concerns are part of the tacitly held, rarely noticed and even more rarely questioned taken-for-granted notions that each of us operates with in our day-to-day lives. Under certain circumstances, these 'taken-for-granteds' may be called into question, and this may shake the foundation of the framework we use for navigating the world. It is my contention that the experience of psychosis is one such set of circumstances where aspects of our fundamental ways of being-in-the-world may be called into question. In this chapter, I want to show that when we attend more closely to the subjective experience of psychosis, important aspects of the experience, such as those expressed by Paul above, which I refer to here as 'existential concerns', are apparent. The bulk of this chapter will be dedicated to discussing findings from my own research into the subjective experience of psychosis, focusing in some detail on three such existential concerns: Authoring, Ontological Insecurity and Epistemological Uncertainty. After outlining what I mean by these terms, I will briefly consider implications for practice and research which emerge from consideration of these notions.

There is a growing body of research into subjective aspects of psychosis which shows that the concerns of the individual who experiences psychosis may not always be congruent with an exclusive focus on the so-called 'positive symptoms' (such as hallucinations, delusions and thought disorder) which tend to be the primary concerns of researchers and clinicians working in this area. For example, Wagner and King (2005: 142) asked hospitalized psychotic clients in Brazil about their needs and found that 'existential needs were the most important and pressing theme for people with psychotic disorders.' However, they go on to report that participants expressed considerable discontent about the clinical service they received, feeling that these concerns were rarely addressed adequately.

Wagner and King's findings point to a discrepancy between what the individual who experiences psychosis identifies as important and the tendency of clinicians (and researchers) to focus on those aspects of the experience that are identified as part of diagnostic criteria for various putative conditions, such as schizophrenia. Paying greater attention to the subjective experience of psychosis can help to counteract this unfortunate state of affairs where potentially very important aspects of the experience can be overlooked by clinicians and researchers who, if they rely excessively on diagnostic criteria to guide their investigations, may find themselves neglecting other significant facets of the experience. This is a classic example of Korzybski's (1933) notion of 'mistaking the map for the territory' where over-reliance on the 'map' (in this case diagnostic criteria) may blind us to important features of the 'territory' (here, the subjective experience of psychosis). While it may be impossible for us ever to escape the need to rely on a 'map' to guide our explorations, I believe that the maps we choose to use in investigations into human experience must be subject to constant revision and improvement, and we should forever be alert to the risk of allowing our reliance on maps to obscure from view important features of the territory we hope to explore. Focusing on subjective experience is a useful way of 'recalibrating' our maps to ensure that they remain faithful and useful tools to assist us in navigating the at times murky waters of human experience and behaviour.

Parnas and Sass (2001) provide us with an example of how sensitive consideration of subjective experience might help us to refine our understanding of diagnostic categories such as 'schizophrenia'. They posit that anomalies of 'self-experience' are central to the development of 'schizophrenia' and propose that 'disorders of the Self represent the experiential core clinical phenomenon of schizophrenia' (ibid.: 101). By using clinical material to support their argument, Parnas and Sass make a persuasive case that self-experience lies at the heart of the condition referred to as 'schizophrenia', yet this is largely absent from the criteria most often used in reaching this diagnosis. Lysaker and Lysaker (2008) discuss the importance of sense of self in historical conceptualizations of schizophrenia in the work of Jaspers, Kraepelin, Bleuler and others. In addition, they develop a helpful framework for considering the various ways in which sense of self has been conceptualized in terms of its relationship to psychotic experience, from theoretical perspectives including psychodynamic, existential and dialogical.

Research into the process of recovery from psychotic experience has also identified a central role for the experience of self. Andresen *et al.* (2003) reviewed published personal accounts of recovery from schizophrenia and found that self-experience was a key feature of the experience, and re-establishment of a sense of identity and finding meaning in life were crucial components of recovery. Similarly, Davidson and Strauss (1992) interviewed 66 people with experience of psychosis and report that taking stock of self and developing a more active sense of self were central to the process of recovery. Consistent with these findings, Dilks *et al.* (2010) conducted a qualitative study based on recordings and first-person accounts of psychosis and concluded that 'negotiating selfhood' was one of the main themes to emerge from their analysis.

Research findings such as the above point consistently to the importance of the experience of self in the development of and recovery from the experience of psychosis. I will now move on to discuss my own research in this area. This research was conducted in a public mental health service in Auckland, New Zealand with clients of a first episode psychosis service. With clients' consent, recordings were made of psychotherapy sessions which were later analyzed, using a grounded theory framework, by the author (who was also the psychotherapist). Fifteen clients participated in this research (11 male, 4 female), and in total 62 psychotherapy sessions were recorded and analyzed. Findings from this research have been published elsewhere (Geekie 2004; Geekie & Read 2009), where more details on methodological considerations can be found. Here, the focus will be on specific findings relating to the experience of self as expressed by research participants. Three constructs (Authoring, Ontological Insecurity and Epistemological Uncertainty), each of them central to existential aspects of the experience of self, will now be discussed in some detail. These constructs emerged from the author's in-depth analysis of the subjective experience of psychosis as expressed by clients in therapy sessions. Quotes from research participants (whose names and other identifying characteristics have been changed to protect anonymity) will be used to support and illustrate the arguments being made. It is my hope that these three constructs go some way towards identifying important aspects of the experience of psychosis and, as such, may be helpful in guiding research and clinical endeavours in this field.

Authoring

Making sense of the experience of psychosis was a major concern for participants in this research. An important consideration here was that participants emphasized the importance of telling their *own* story, which made *personal* sense to them, rather than simply accepting a 'ready-made' explanation of what their experience should mean to them. For example, Sara, who had been briefly hospitalized following concerns about her disorganized behaviour and persecutory beliefs, expressed her need for a personal understanding of her experience thus: 'Um, just because, I mean, because I want to find out why it has happened and why it has happened to me.'

Another participant, Paul, was quite explicit in his rejection of standardized impersonal explanations for his experience. After reading a generally well-regarded (by clinicians and clients alike) 'What is psychosis?' information pamphlet provided by the clinical team, he politely reflected: 'Well, yes, that's very interesting. But I need to make my own sense of it.'

Borrowing from Shotter (1981), I refer to this need to be an active agent in making sense of one's experience as 'authoring'. Shotter (1981) argues that being author of one's own experience should be thought of as a moral right and a requirement for a sense of autonomy. The importance of being author of one's own understanding of experience is also stressed by Roe and Davidson (2005) who, drawing on recovery research, conclude that authoring (or re-authoring) one's story is central to recovering from psychosis and developing a more integrated sense of self.

It is important to recognize that authoring is not a purely internal psychological process, but that it takes place in social contexts (including, but not limited to, the clinical setting) and that the responses of others to the individual's efforts to author his or her experience are also important. Feeling that significant others were available to listen respectfully to their individual story was valued highly by participants in my research. Michael, who experienced a range of confusing and debilitating psychotic phenomena, including menacing visual hallucinations, here identifies feeling understood as beneficial:

> Like, when I was talking to my friend one time, I just started talking to him about it [psychosis], and I was in a bad mood to start off, and all of a sudden I felt like I was . . . I felt really healthy right, and my head was working perfectly and . . . like, as it should be working, like. But the only difference was I could explain myself and he understood it all.

Conversely, feeling either silenced or invalidated in efforts to author one's own story was experienced by participants as damaging. Sara complained that she felt silenced at home, where family members quashed her attempts to discuss her experience, a process that she saw as undermining her capacity to author her experience: 'We spoke about it a couple of times, but he [husband] says don't think about it and try to get better as soon as possible.'

Feeling that other people were dismissive of one's attempts at authoring was commonly experienced as invalidating. This was the case for Margaret, a woman in her thirties who had heard voices which she felt were of spiritual significance. She felt friends, including members of her spiritual group, dismissed this out of hand without adequate consideration. This was particularly painful for her, as she felt her mother had experienced something similar, many years before: 'Well, I feel like I've been written off as a bloody nutcase, like my mother was written off too.'

Others struggled with the idea that their experience could be explained as 'psychosis'. This, they felt, invalidated their authorship, by denying them the right to determine the meaning of their own experience. This was a major issue for Isa, a young articulate Polynesian man: 'I feel down when I think other people are judging me or categorising me. I feel good when I feel validated.'

In short, then, we might conclude that for those who experience psychosis making sense of the experience and having the opportunity to share this sense with others is an important requirement in coming to terms with the experience

Implications for understanding

In terms of how we understand the experience of psychosis, research such as that outlined in the present chapter demonstrates the importance of ensuring that our theoretical models of psychosis (or, to return to Korzybski's analogy, our 'maps') do not neglect subjective aspects of the experience. This is critical for both our theoretical understandings and our clinical approaches to psychosis. For example, the research discussed above makes a strong case for viewing the experience of self as having a major role to play in the experience of psychosis, yet this is not reflected in diagnostic criteria nor in the bulk of mainstream literature on psychosis and schizophrenia where the emphasis tends to be on the 'positive' symptoms.

If we hope to enhance our understandings of the experience of psychosis then attending more closely to subjective aspects of the experience may be an imperative. As in much of the research discussed in this chapter, we may find that this points us in the direction of some of the underlying processes implicated in the experience. Such underlying processes may be more fundamental than the more obvious manifestations of psychosis, such as hearing voices or delusional beliefs. We may find that philosophical and existential considerations relating to the experience of self, to the nature of being and of knowing, have an important role to play in the emergence of psychosis. Clearly, such an understanding would have important implications for how we go about offering support to those who may be troubled by such experiences.

Implications for practice

The research outlined in the present chapter also has implications for clinical practice. Clinical approaches to psychosis are dominated by efforts to control positive symptoms. Yet research suggests that these may not be the primary concern for clients. It seems that a comprehensive clinical approach would need to extend beyond this focus to include consideration of other important aspects of the experience for clients. Research consistently finds that the search for meaning is of vital importance to many of those who experience psychosis, and that being author of this meaning is critical for many. Clinical services, if they are to be truly responsive to the needs and wishes of clients, need to take this into consideration and look at ways in which clients can be offered opportunities to explore what their experiences mean to them. This may prove challenging for services, particularly if the risks of invalidating the clients' efforts at authoring are to be taken seriously. Clinicians need to recognize that a didactic approach, where clients are 'told' what their experience means, may have just such an effect. Here, Margaret expresses the consequences of having her efforts at authoring invalidated: 'I feel almost like unheard and unaccepted. Not good enough to have those experiences. That makes me feel inferior, you know.'

Instead of such direct challenges, it may be more helpful to develop a supportive relationship where meaning can be discussed and negotiated within a context which recognizes that there are multiple ways of making sense of psychosis and that for the client a sense of agency in this process is important (possibly even more important than the particular sense that happens to be made).

It may also be helpful for services to recognize that clients may experience what I've referred to in this chapter as 'ontological insecurity' and 'epistemological uncertainty' associated with the experience of psychosis and that these experiences may precede and/or follow the so-called positive symptoms of psychosis. First, it would be helpful for clinicians to enquire about this, to ascertain if clients are feeling insecure in their sense of self, or uncertain about whether or not they can trust their ways of knowing about the world. Clinicians may be able to support clients in re-learning how to trust their own ways of knowing about and being in the world (for example, through looking at ways clients can reliably check out their own perceptions, or ways that clients can recognize when perceptions may be suspect). This may be a gradual process where the client tests out his or her perceptions, perhaps with the support of a friend or family member, as faith in the self is gradually reacquired. Mark, a participant in my research who had found he had considerable self-doubt following his experience of psychosis, developed just such a graduated process, which assisted him in coming once again to feel more secure in his sense of self and in his ability to make sense of the world in a way he could trust:

> Well, as life goes by one day at a time and you do the normal things that you should do, it's coming back just by maybe a little repetition of maybe the same thing. Or simply that nothing has actually gone wrong while I have been trying to get myself back on track. And so if I can trust – OK that went all right – so I can try doing the next thing. OK that went fine. That means I can trust myself in those two avenues. The next one and the next one, just like steps.

References

Andresen, R., Oades, L. and Caputi, P. (2003) 'The experience of recovery from schizophrenia: Towards an empirically validated stage model', *Australian & New Zealand Journal of Psychiatry*, *37*: 586–594.

Davidson, L. and Strauss, J. S. (1992) 'Sense of self in recovery from severe mental illness', *British Journal of Medical Psychology*, *65*: 131–145.

Dilks, S., Tasker, F. and Wren, B. (2010) 'Managing the impact of psychosis: A grounded theory exploration of recovery processes in psychosis', *British Journal of Clinical Psychology*, *49*: 87–107.

Geekie, J. (2004) 'Listening to what we hear: Clients' understandings of psychotic experiences'. In J. Read, L. Mosher and R. Bentall (eds), *Models of Madness: Psychological, Social and Biological Approaches to Schizophrenia* (pp. 147–161). Hove, East Sussex: Brunner-Routledge.

Geekie, J. and Read, J (2009) *Making Sense of Madness: Contesting the Meaning of Schizophrenia*. London: Routledge.

Jaspers, K. (1963) *General Psychopathology*. Manchester: Manchester University Press.

Korzybski, A. (1933) *Science and Sanity: An Introduction to Non-Aristotelian Systems and General Semantics*. Lancaster, PA: International Non-Aristotelian Library Publishing Co.

Laing, R. D. (1960) *The Divided Self: A Study of Sanity and Madness*. London: Tavistock.

Lysaker, P. and Lysaker, J. (2008) 'Schizophrenia and alterations in self-experience: A comparison of 6 perspectives', *Schizophrenia Bulletin, 36*: 331–340.

Parnas, J. and Sass, L. A. (2001) 'Self, solipsism, and schizophrenic delusions', *Philosophy, Psychiatry, Psychology, 8*: 101–120.

Roe, D. and Davison, L. (2005) 'Self and narrative in schizophrenia: Time to author a new story', *Journal of Medical Humanities, 31*: 89–94.

Shotter, J. (1981) 'Vico, moral worlds, accountability and personhood'. In P. Hellas & A. Lock (eds), *Indigenous Psychologies: The Anthropology of the Self* (pp. 266–284). London: Academic Press.

Wagner, L. C. and King, M. (2005) 'Existential needs of people with psychotic disorders in Porto Alegre, Brazil', *British Journal of Psychiatry, 186*: 141–145.

Part V

At risk mental state

The study of 'at risk' mental state is a fairly recent area of interest in the study of psychosis, and one that is not without its critics, who fear that introducing this concept may lead to widespread, and unhelpful, medicating of a vulnerable group. As the two following chapters indicate, identification of an 'at risk' group need not lead to immediate medicating, but may open the door for other forms of support, such as psychological therapies.

Rory Byrne shares with us his story of experiencing such an 'at risk' mental state, the difficulties he had in accessing help and the kind of support which he ultimately found helpful. While he identifies his own reticence at expressing his concerns to health professionals, his account points to the importance of the context in determining if, how and to what extent individuals are likely to feel comfortable enough to share their concerns. He identifies a 'normalizing', rather than pathologizing, approach as being of importance here. Presumably such an approach is more likely to provide validation of the individual's concerns and so make expression of these concerns feel less threatening.

Kate Hardy's findings from her research into the subjective experience of the 'at risk' mental state are consistent with Rory's position, suggesting that a 'normalizing' approach which validates the individual's concerns is most conducive to engaging with services. Her research also demonstrates that, despite previous claims to the contrary, those who experience 'at risk' mental states hold multiple explanatory models for this experience and they can, if given the opportunity, articulate subjective aspects of this experience.

Chapter 11

At risk of developing psychosis

A personal account

Rory Byrne

Introduction

I am a researcher in the area of early detection and intervention for psychosis, and I have personal experience of psychosis-like psychological problems. I was considered at risk of developing psychosis around ten years ago, and received Cognitive Behavioural Therapy (CBT) as part of a psychology research trial in the UK (Morrison *et al.* 2004). In this chapter I describe some of the factors I think were most important in the development of my psychological problems, and in my recovery. It is hard to summarize such complex and personal issues in this short space so I will only be focusing on key elements and events. The four parts below are brief summaries of: negative life experiences; becoming overwhelmed by my psychological problems; my experiences of receiving professional help and recovery; and suggestions for improvements in understanding and treating unusual psychological experiences or psychosis.

Negative life experiences

Difficult life experiences

Difficult life experiences have had a negative impact on my emotional and psychological well-being for a long time, leading to serious depression and stress before the worst of my problems developed. I was adopted as a child and I grew up with identity and attachment problems, and with a sense of being different to others. When I was 13, I moved with my family from one country to another. The loss of childhood friends and surroundings and the strangeness of being in a new country were all unsettling changes. A number of other significant disruptions occurred over the next few years, making life more difficult, such as moving from a relatively comfortable neighbourhood where I lived near my friends and school to a more deprived area a few miles away.

Traumatic experiences

From around the age of 18, a number of violent attacks contributed to my psychological problems. For example, I was stabbed during a mugging; a year later I was threatened with a knife during what was probably the most traumatic experience I've had. Knowing the attacker's history and personality, I believed him when he held a very sharp knife to my throat and threatened to kill me. Perhaps the most damaging effect of that assault was that afterwards I felt I had to change and become 'hard' to protect myself. Adopting a 'hard' persona was really only a superficial change and over time I actually became more and more insecure.

A few years later, when I was 22, I was violently assaulted in three different attacks within a short space of time. I was knocked unconscious outside a local pub during an unprovoked attack; a few weeks later I was robbed and assaulted at gunpoint when using a local ATM. Those incidents were particularly unsettling because of their proximity to my own home. During the third incident, I was assaulted by a number of youths while working in a city centre nightclub. They were recognized as members of a notorious local gang and after they had been ejected a car drove past the front of the club and a number of gunshots were fired at the front door. No one was hurt, but I was anxious as I left to go home that night as I assumed the shooting was related to my assault. I increasingly felt that I was being targeted or persecuted, though I had no real idea of why or how, and without knowing how or why it would happen, I came to think that I might be killed in the near future.

Drugs

From the end of my teenage years I began to smoke cannabis quite regularly. I also used other recreational drugs from time to time. Taking LSD in particular had some serious effects, inducing very unusual psychological states and vivid visual hallucinations. Smoking cannabis came to have a negative effect over time, especially by increasing my tendency to be introspective and to live 'in a world of my own'. When my psychological problems later got much worse, my use of strong cannabis led to feeling increasingly strange and nervous in social situations and distanced or dislocated from others and the world around me. Many associations have been made between the use of illicit drugs and the development of psychosis or psychosis-like experiences, and I'm sure that in my own case drug use contributed significantly, especially smoking 'skunk' cannabis.

Becoming overwhelmed by psychological problems

Stress

In 1998, when I was 23, a range of different life events led to the build up of quite serious emotional and psychological stress. In July of that year my Dad had a serious stroke and was left badly affected afterwards. It was a shock to see him so seriously ill and more than once close to death. At times, I also felt that my Dad's stroke had been something more than a natural misfortune. The night before he had the stroke, I was coming home from a situation where I thought I'd done something wrong, when I saw a neon-lit cross on the top of a church. At the time it seemed like some kind of 'sign', signifying something ominous, and when my Dad fell ill the next day, he was at mass. It seemed that the 'sign' I'd seen had been real and that my Dad's stroke was somehow related to me and my actions.

Around the same time, going to work became very stressful. I worked in a busy call centre which I found more and more claustrophobic and I was finding it increasingly difficult to interact with customers and colleagues because of how stressed I often felt. For a number of reasons I'd also started to think I was disliked or personally rejected by friends and colleagues, and that had a particularly negative effect on my general mood and self-esteem, along with sometimes making me feel paranoid.

Later in the year I started a psychology course at college, hoping to go to university the following year. Working and studying at the same time was difficult, and studying psychology may in itself have been unhelpful as it seemed that the more I learned the more uncertain I felt about my own psychological well-being. I'd worried before then about having a serious mental health problem because of how unhappy I'd been and it seemed that things were continually getting worse. Learning about mental health problems, especially conditions such as schizophrenia, was particularly unsettling for me, perhaps because such conditions were most often described in terms of 'illness' and 'disease', which in turn implies a permanent and sometimes horrific deterioration of one's brain or mind. I think that for me, it would have been more helpful to have been taught more about evidence-based psychosocial approaches to mental health problems than about theoretical medical models.

Losing control

During 1999 my life became more difficult and the most distressing of my psychological problems emerged. I never really talked about my problems with anyone and that meant I was always 'bottling up' my emotions and feeling increasingly stressed, depressed and unsettled as the year went on. The kinds of unusual psychological experiences I'd had before then became more frequent and I became more conscious of unusual coincidences and seeing or hearing things that seemed to relate to me.

On one occasion, I was feeling very angry after a stressful incident at work, when a heavy thunderstorm grew and broke outside. As with anything like this, it's hard to adequately describe why or how, but the thunder seemed to be some kind of echo of my own mood. It felt as though whatever 'higher power' I believed in was somehow aware of me, responding to my stress and anger, and indicating to those around me that I was special or important.

Feeling strange

During that summer my emotional and psychological problems became over-whelming and I felt stressed almost all the time. I remember in particular the day I handed in my final piece of coursework for college; it had been a difficult time, I hadn't slept much for a few days and I'd been drinking a lot of coffee. On my way home in the early evening I felt strange, as if I was dreaming, but 'on edge' and unable to relax. That feeling remained over the next few days and I started to think that something was really wrong with me. I felt nervous and unsure of myself when I was talking to people and I was especially disturbed by the way that eye contact with others became very difficult. I was worried because until then I'd attributed any problems like this to my misuse of cannabis, but by then I hadn't smoked for about a month and was still feeling unsettled and strange.

Social anxiety

I came to feel increasingly uncomfortable and nervous in social situations and especially at work. I worked in an open-plan office and I often felt very exposed and self-conscious, as if other people were looking at me. I spent most of my time at work talking on the phone and, because our calls were randomly monitored, I also worried about being listened to by supervisors as I'd been finding it more and more difficult to speak to customers. Before long I began to feel as though I was being looked at or watched by others wherever I was and especially in busy public places. Over the next couple of months my self-consciousness turned to serious social anxiety and panic. I couldn't ever really relax, my heart always seemed to be racing and sometimes I felt like I couldn't breathe. There were times when I felt so nervous in public situations that I had to mentally talk myself through the process of walking.

Social breakdown

The serious problems I experienced with social relationships and social situations were the most difficult aspects of the condition I came to be in. I felt increasingly uncomfortable and unable to spend time with others, even in calm and safe situations. I was always very self-conscious about feeling strange and seeming strange. It felt as though I spent most of my time just trying to maintain a 'normal' appearance, trying to seem calm when I was nervous, and trying to seem happy when I was seriously depressed. The anxiety I experienced also led to difficulties with my concentration and memory so at times it was very hard to maintain even short conversations. I also sometimes felt that people around me could hear what I was thinking, which was very worrying. After a while my anxiety was almost constant and at times nightmarish, as though the world around me was intruding into my consciousness. I often felt like I couldn't think straight and that I was losing control of my thoughts or forgetting how to think and act. It felt as if I was falling apart, or as if an abyss had opened inside me and I was falling into it. I felt more and more insecure about myself and who I was, and the more difficult I found it to be in social situations the more I kept to myself, spending more and more time on my own.

Professional help and recovery

Seeking help

I'd wanted to talk to someone for a long time, but I was always reluctant to burden friends or family with my psychological problems, and I worried that if I did they'd think I was crazy and then dislike or even reject me. I knew that I really needed help though so I went to my GP and told her I felt very depressed and anxious, and worried that something was wrong with me. I was unsure of how to explain my difficulties and I didn't tell her about the more unusual psychological experiences or beliefs I'd had. The GP didn't seem to offer much time or attention to what I was saying, which was disappointing, though I understand GPs have only a limited time to see each patient and may only have a limited understanding of psychological problems. I was given a prescription for anti-anxiety medication, but I didn't like it as it didn't seem to reduce my anxiety and it made me feel numb. Being given the medication also made me think the anxiety I experienced was a physical disorder and for me that wasn't helpful as I worried that it meant the problem would be permanent.

Counselling

After some time I went back to my GP to ask if I could be referred to a therapist as I was still feeling anxious and confused. My GP referred me to a counsellor who worked at the same practice and I remember the appointment as being helpful, as I got the chance to disclose more fully how anxious and strange I felt. I didn't disclose everything because I still worried that however I tried to explain myself, the counsellor would think I was strange or 'mad'. I don't know if the session was helpful overall though as I had talked about a wide range of issues without any clear structure or feedback from the counsellor herself, so I may have felt more confused afterwards, and I also thought she had seemed a little unsure of how to respond to the issues I was discussing. Although perhaps I should have tried again, I didn't arrange any further appointments.

Psychiatry

I realized that I needed to speak to someone trained to deal with more serious psychological problems, so I returned to my GP again to ask if I could be referred to a psychologist or a psychiatrist to talk through my concerns more fully. There was a long waiting list to see a psychologist, so it wasn't really possible to see one. I told my GP that I felt my need to speak to someone was becoming urgent, so I was referred to see a psychiatrist within a few weeks.

The psychiatrist's evaluation was fairly brief and I only really remember the psychiatrist asking me about my depression and anxiety in a kind of 'box ticking' way. I know that this can be a helpful way to identify psychological problems quickly, though I think it could also at times be an inappropriate way to treat people seeking help for serious psychological distress. I don't think I felt particularly comfortable discussing my problems with the psychiatrist and I was still worried about being told there was something seriously wrong with me, so again I essentially concealed the most 'crazy' of my unusual thoughts and experiences. I can't remember exactly what the outcome of that appointment was, but I wasn't offered any further appointments and I didn't meet the psychiatrist again.

University counselling

I had seen a sign for a counselling service after I'd started at university and in February 2000 I went to ask for an appointment. The counsellor I met was friendly and easy to talk to. I remember feeling more calm when I was talking to her than I had for quite a while. I was able to disclose things I hadn't talked about with anyone until then and being able to unburden myself was a huge relief and a very important part of the process of recovering from my difficulties. Our sessions came to an end after a few months and I felt that the counsellor had really helped to reduce the depression and stress I'd felt. However, even though I'd been comfortable discussing a lot with the counsellor, I still hadn't disclosed the most 'mad' thoughts or beliefs I'd had. With those concerns still unresolved I went back to the counselling service later in the year and asked to speak to someone again. After a couple of sessions I explained more fully what I was worried about, especially my fear that I was going mad. Fortunately, the counsellor was aware of a local psychology research trial that was looking at those more unusual issues and referred me to them.

The EDIE trial

The research trial, known as the EDIE project (Early Detection and Intervention Evaluation), was aiming to identify people like myself who were having difficulty with unusual psychological experiences, and to assess the use of Cognitive Behavioural Therapy (CBT) to prevent our experiences becoming full episodes of psychosis. I first met with an assistant from the trial at the university counselling service as I was already comfortable attending appointments there. We worked through a set of questionnaires to assess the types of difficulties I was having, which also gave me an opportunity to explain the life stresses and experiences I thought had contributed to them. The assistant responded in a very calm and understanding way when I disclosed my concerns and that helped me to worry less about discussing those things from then on.

Cognitive Behavioural Therapy (CBT)

Following the assessment I was included in the research trial and then randomly allocated to the group of participants who would receive CBT. When I met the therapist I told him what I was most worried about and we worked out a problem list to address my difficulties in a practical way. As with the assistant I'd met, the therapist was understanding and easy to talk to, and he didn't use any words like 'mental illness' or 'psychosis', which for me was helpful.

After talking things through, we didn't actually spend much time discussing the more unusual thoughts and beliefs I'd had, as those didn't cause me that much distress compared with the anxiety I'd felt, especially social anxiety. We discussed the negative thought processes and behaviours that were maintaining my anxiety and worked out how to improve the way I coped with it by learning not to worry or panic when I felt anxious, and to think about the things I was worried about more practically. It was very helpful to learn that the kind of psychological problems I'd experienced were understandable, even normal considering how difficult some of my life experiences had been. This 'normalization' of my difficulties was one of the most helpful elements of therapy as it very quickly reduced my fear of being 'mad', which had been the most disturbing of my worries. After six or seven therapy sessions, I felt we'd covered the issues I'd been most worried about and so we drew therapy to a close, though we agreed that I should get back in touch if things changed or I felt I needed help again. I don't remember any particularly negative aspects of the CBT, though in hindsight I don't think what I learned has been as effective for dealing with my depression as it was for my anxiety and unusual psychological experiences. I also know that for some people CBT won't be as effective as it was for me, or may be more difficult to engage with.

Recovery

I had recovered from the worst of my difficulties before my involvement with the research trial ended. My social and general anxiety had been effectively reduced so that I could cope with social situations and stress much better, and these were the most important improvements for me. Although unusual thoughts or beliefs continued from time to time they didn't cause me serious concern or distress because I'd learned to think about them in a more realistic way and no longer worried that they meant I was 'mad'. Therapy gave me a new way of understanding my psychological difficulties, and helped me to improve my ability to cope with them. The coping skills I gained were also helpful for dealing with difficult life circumstances and events that continued after I had finished therapy.

Although I'd withdrawn a lot socially, my family and friends always kept in touch and as I recovered from the worst of my difficulties it got easier and more enjoyable to spend time with others. I also felt much more 'grounded' and optimistic after therapy because I'd seen that by thinking and acting in more positive, practical ways I could address and overcome the most serious of problems. I've also learned to value the resilience I developed from getting through some very difficult times. I managed to stay at university through the worst of my difficulties and to graduate with a good degree even though there were times when I thought I wouldn't.

Beyond recovery

After graduation I went back to full-time work. I had been in contact occasionally with the EDIE researchers after the trial ended, and was invited to participate in a number of focus groups with other service users. This then led to further involvement with the research team, and later to my employment as a user-researcher. I've now worked as a researcher for the past three years and I'm currently working through my second year of a PhD study looking at subjective experiences of unusual psychological difficulties and psychosis, along with exploring service users' priorities and preferences for treatment of those problems. I've been very fortunate in my role, having had excellent supervision and personal support, great colleagues, and some brilliant opportunities. I hope to continue working in this field for some time, either as a researcher or, if possible, as a therapist or clinical psychologist. I think it could be very helpful for clients with difficult psychological experiences to meet with a mental health professional who has not only had some of the same kinds of difficulties but who has also recovered from them. This could be normalizing for clients and could reflect an example of recovery that can only be given from a first-hand perspective. As Pitt et al. (2007) suggests, 'Service users need more access to other people's stories of recovery. This can be inspiring and a great source of hope'.

Implications for understanding

Although I'd had unusual psychological experiences and beliefs for quite a few years, they only became particularly worrying after serious anxiety had developed and led to the fear that I was really 'going mad'. I think one of the most important steps mental health professionals need to take is to *normalize* psychotic-like experiences and psychosis itself as much as possible, in the first instance through evidence-based education of professionals themselves. The establishment of a primarily normalizing rather than pathologizing paradigm for academic and clinical conduct could reduce the service-based stigma currently experienced by those with such difficulties. In the long term this should also reduce the stigma and fear still associated with psychosis at the societal level and could contribute to a reduction in the general incidence of psychosis by reducing delays in getting help for those with emerging psychosis-like experiences and enabling access to effective treatments (e.g. CBT) that may prevent the onset of full psychosis.

Implications for practice

The normalizing and practical needs-based approach of CBT was particularly effective for me and quickly improved the way I coped with anxiety and unusual beliefs. For some clients, though, it may be important to be offered longer-term support, as the kinds of personal and psychological problems that can underlie psychotic phenomena will often remain even after the psychotic or unusual psychological experiences have been addressed or resolved. For example, addressing continued problems with anxiety, depression, low self-esteem, drug or alcohol abuse, or financial or housing problems may be as important for improving service users' recovery and quality of life as addressing psychotic experiences themselves. In many cases the staff who could offer such support would not need to have expensive specialist or clinical training. Finally, I'd highlight and recommend for greater attention some of the non-specific benefits of therapeutic interventions that may be most highly valued by service users themselves: simply having someone to talk to about private issues in confidence, being listened to and feeling understood and accepted as a person, and being helped to regain a sense of hope for the future.

References

Morrison, A. P., French, P., Walford, L., Lewis, S. W., Kilcommons, A., Green, J. *et al.* (2004) 'Cognitive therapy for the prevention of psychosis in people at ultra high risk: Randomised controlled trial', *British Journal of Psychiatry*, *185*: 291–297.

Pitt, L., Kilbride, M., Nothard, S., Welford, M. and Morrison, A. P. (2007) 'Researching recovery from psychosis – a user-led project', *Psychiatric Bulletin*, *31*: 55–60.

Chapter 12

At risk of developing psychosis

The research perspective

Kate Hardy

Introduction: the origins of defining the at risk mental state

Identification of individuals at risk of developing psychosis is a recent expansion of the early intervention in psychosis paradigm. Early intervention targets individuals in the critical period following the onset of their first episode of psychosis with the aim of improving outcomes (Birchwood 2000). Early detection aims to identify people who may be at risk of developing psychosis and endeavours to provide treatment options to prevent or delay the onset and impact of psychosis. These individuals are identified through specific assessments focusing on both state and trait factors. State factors include the presence of attenuated psychotic symptoms or brief limited intermittent psychotic symptoms (known as BLIPS) while trait factors include having a diagnosis of a schizotypal personality disorder, or a first degree relative with a diagnosis of a psychotic disorder, plus a recent deterioration in functioning.

Generally, it is more common for individuals to present to early detection teams with attenuated psychotic symptoms. Attenuated symptoms are characterized by occurring less frequently and with less intensity than symptoms defined as psychotic. For example, someone experiencing a fully psychotic paranoid delusion might be *convinced* that there were cameras in their home recording their every movement and may change their behaviour accordingly (stay away from certain rooms, speak in a whisper or take other measures to ensure their safety) while someone in the at risk period might *question* that there were cameras in the home but would be less convinced of this, would be able to provide reasons why this might not be true (e.g. no evidence of recording equipment) and, importantly, would not change their behaviour. Attenuated symptoms are conceptualized as symptoms that have not yet reached a psychotic level (Yung & McGorry 1996a) and are best thought of as lying along a continuum of experiences such as that described by Bentall (1993: 234): 'Madness and sanity are but points on a continuum along which we are all inclined to move during difficult moments in our lives.'

The period during which psychosis-like phenomena develop is termed the prodomal period. However, since the prodrome is a term that can only be accurately applied retrospectively (i.e. once the individual has made a transition to psychosis) these individuals are referred to as being 'at risk' (Yung & McGorry 1996a). To apply the term 'prodrome' to people who are experiencing attenuated symptoms implies an inevitability of making a transition to psychosis which is only true of a minority of those assessed as being at risk (French & Morrison 2004). Although rates of transition to psychosis vary between studies (Yung *et al.* 2006), it is generally agreed that the risk of developing an axis 1 psychotic disorder over the following 12 months is greatly increased in those assessed as being at risk.

Subjectivity and the at risk mental state

Research in this field has typically focused on the identification of those at risk, prospective studies to explore risk and protective factors, and possible treatment options to prevent or delay the transition to psychosis including cognitive therapy (Morrison *et al.* 2004), low-dose antipsychotics (McGlashan *et al.* 2003) or a combination of the two (McGorry *et al.* 2002). Although there has been much published in recent years on these topics there is relatively little literature on the *subjective experience* of those identified as being at risk of developing psychosis.

The principles that drive the publication of subjective accounts of psychosis and psychotic experiences apply as strongly to the at risk population as to any other. Narratives should be actively sought in line with recent advances in the field of psychosis away from the predominant medical model towards a holistic model that incorporates individual explanations. This is in line with recommendations that the acknowledgement and consideration of subjective narratives is an essential part of treatment, research and service development. For example, the British Psychological Society (2000: 58) recommended that 'service users should be acknowledged as experts on their own experiences' and that 'services must respect each individual's understanding of their own experiences.' Other authors have called for increased value to be placed upon the subjective experience of the service user, with May (2004: 246) arguing that it is more beneficial to 'see each individual's mental health as a unique and evolving story' and Ridgway (2001) stating that there is more than one view of psychosis and that adopting an illness model is not the only way to recovery.

In 2005 the International Early Psychosis Association emphasized the need for more research into the subjective experience of being at risk of developing psychosis and stated that 'priority should be given to research on representative early psychosis populations to obtain a deeper understanding of the processes associated with the onset of psychosis' (IEPA writing group 2005: 121). One way to gain a deeper understanding of these processes is to directly ask those identified as being at risk to describe those experiences as they occur and to utilize this information to inform providers at a variety of levels including treatment and service development. This is not to say that the subjective narrative of those at risk is the only way to conceptualize these experiences or is in some way superior to other sources of information about this period but rather that gaining perspectives and information from multiple sources on these experiences can add to the overall breadth of knowledge thus benefitting service users, clinicians and researchers alike. As Geekie (2004: 150) argues in relation to the subjective experiences of people diagnosed with schizophrenia, 'it is a legitimate form of knowledge and, as such, has an important contribution to make'; the same is equally true of the subjective accounts of individuals at risk of developing psychosis.

Accessing the subjective experience of the at risk period retrospectively

Most of the research in this area has been retrospective studies of the at risk period in which individuals who have experienced their first episode of psychosis are asked to reflect back on the months and years preceding the onset of psychosis and to recall changes that occurred over this time. Yung and McGorry (1996b) conducted a retrospective qualitative study of the changes experienced prior to the onset of psychosis with 21 first episode psychosis participants. They argued that in taking this qualitative approach to explore the subjective experience of the period preceding a transition to psychosis they were able to access 'rich descriptions of prodromal phenomena' (ibid.: 598) instead of focusing only on behavioural features. As will be seen, behavioural changes are a core feature of the period before the onset of psychosis but Yung and McGorry asserted the importance of other factors such as subjective experiences. In accessing the subjective experience retrospectively they were able to further develop assessment tools to identify the at risk population with a specific focus on phenomena experienced by the individual including attenuated psychotic symptoms such as changes in thinking ('It was just like my head went blank') and perception ('Everything was heightened, sounds, the birds. It was really acute') (ibid.: 593).

Other retrospective explorations of this period have sought to explore the factors that impact upon delays in help seeking. Møller and Husby (2000) concluded that prior to the onset of psychosis the participants had experienced difficulties in interpreting and talking about their experiences resulting in a delay in seeking help. They also identified what they termed two 'core dimensions' of the pre-psychotic phase: 'disturbance of perception of self' with one participant reporting that 'I totally lost myself. Had to remind me about who I was' (ibid.: 222) and 'extreme preoccupation by and withdrawal to overvalued ideas' represented by the quote 'The new ideas about supernatural mental phenomena gradually took over my life and way of thinking' (ibid.). These core dimensions capture the insidious nature of the onset and progress of these experiences which the authors argue 'reflect pervasive and enduring changes' (ibid.). Møller and Husby also note that participants recognized behavioural changes over this period including termination of school or work, changes in interests and alteration in social interaction (either passivity or active avoidance). Typically these behavioural changes are observed and reported by the individual prior to the experience of attenuated psychotic symptoms and this is consistent with the reports of family members interviewed retrospectively about their child's prodromal period (Corcoran *et al.* 2007).

One of the striking elements of research into the subjective experience of being at risk is the high level of awareness reported by participants, at least retrospectively, of changes in their thinking and behaviour. When Boydell *et al.* (2006: 57–58) explored delays to help-seeking during the period before the onset of psychosis they found that the participants were highly aware of their experiences and made choices as to how to manage these experiences including ignoring ('I was hearing a lot of voices, you know? For like ten months, I just ignored it'), hiding ('I didn't want to worry them [parents] so I told them I was normal') and eventually disclosing their difficulties ('It got to the point where I couldn't take it any more . . . The shadows would turn into something . . . they'd turn into cartoons . . . it was freaky. . . . I said I gotta tell someone . . . I told my mother'). This discomfort in disclosing their difficulties resulted in delayed help-seeking and consequently delays in accessing treatment. A possible explanation for this delay in disclosure could be that although individuals were aware of their experiences, and they recognized the need for treatment, they avoided services for fear of stigma (Judge *et al.* 2008). When discussing the clinical implications of their work Judge *et al.* (2008) stated that the participants in their study had all demonstrated a need to understand and make sense of their experiences, they concluded that the development of this personal narrative is important in helping the individual to understand their symptoms in the context of their own personal experience and that this in turn can aid engagement in a population that is notoriously difficult to reach.

Accessing the subjective experience during the at risk period

From the retrospective research described it is possible to make certain assumptions about the subjective experience of someone at risk of developing psychosis. These assumptions would suggest that this is a difficult and distressing period, that the individual experiences changes in their behaviour and mood which are observable to family members (Corcoran *et al.* 2003; Møller & Husby 2000; Yung & McGorry 1996a), recognizes specific changes in themselves (Judge *et al.* 2008) and may choose to hide or ignore these (Boydell *et al.* 2006). However, these findings are based entirely on the observations of family members or on the retrospective accounts of the service user. A more accurate line of inquiry into the subjective experience is to directly ask the service user about these experiences while they are in the at risk period.

While working in an Early Detection Service in the UK, I interviewed ten individuals who were assessed as being at risk of developing psychosis. The results of this study have been presented elsewhere (Hardy *et al.* 2009) so I will provide only a brief summary here. We aimed to explore how these individuals understood and made sense of their experiences. At that time no other research had been published that explored the subjective experiences of individuals at risk of developing psychosis, possibly due to the belief that individuals in this period would not be able to reflect on their experiences. For example, Corcoran *et al.* (2003: 317) stated that they chose to interview parents of those identified as being at risk, rather than the individuals themselves, based on the belief that 'symptomatic individuals may have difficulty in describing their experience when "prodromal" given possible limitations in insight, sensory misperceptions, suspiciousness, emerging negative symptoms and cognitive impairment.'

All participants in our study had entered the service through the attenuated symptoms (symptoms that have not reached a psychotic level) route and were at one of three stages of an early detection service: assessment for entry into the study, treatment or follow-up monitoring. The mean age of the participants was 21.8 years (ranging from 16 to 30) with six females and four males.

It was noticeable that the participants did not necessarily focus on the symptoms that had brought them into the service. Unpublished data from this research suggested that when the participants did speak about their symptoms they took a holistic approach to explaining the origin of these and drew upon multiple explanatory frameworks including traumatic early experiences ('I think like some of the triggers is coz I've always been in kids homes. . . . it's very scary . . . I'm just wondering if it's something to do with that, I just get nervous when there's more than three people, two or three people, I start thinking they're planning to do something to me'); drug use ('taking the drugs didn't help and what have you, it's fifty fifty init, it's meself as well as I don't know what . . . just how I am'); and the start of 'madness' ('no, it was the beginning of craziness, I still think I was going mad').

A central narrative emerged that described their progress or lack of progress in their lives. This theme was termed 'journey' and reflected their experience of moving forwards, a sense of regression in their lives and at times of stasis. One participant summed up this experience with the statement 'it's like a big long road' while another likened it to 'climbing a ladder and you get to the top and you can't get no higher, yet you still want to go up more.' Additionally, the participants appeared to be very aware of what was required in order to continue on this journey. This 'perception of needs' (as the topic was termed) included what the participant felt they required from family, friends and the service and was a catalyst for initial help-seeking.

All participants were oriented to their own personal future and this was dependent on where they perceived themselves at the time of the interview. This orientation was related to their own hierarchical needs from the need for housing to more complex psychological needs such as the desire of one participant to have a baby once her mental health problems were resolved.

This research contradicted previous beliefs (Corcoran *et al.* 2003) that at risk individuals would not be able to provide subjective accounts of their experiences. In contrast, the participants in this study provided rich and coherent narratives of their mental health problems which included both positive attenuated symptoms, such as voice hearing and suspiciousness, and general mood symptoms, including anxiety and depression. We wanted to call attention to the 'positive contribution this group can make in providing rich and meaningful data that aid our understanding of accessing early detection services' (Hardy *et al.* 2009: 56) and concluded by emphasizing the importance of eliciting and respecting the subjective narrative as a means to access a holistic understanding of the individual's clinical needs and priorities.

More recently this research has been adapted and developed by Byrne and Morrison (2010) as a user-led exploration of the relationships and communication difficulties of the at risk population. This research takes a unique approach to the investigation of the subjective experience of this population as the lead researcher and interviewer, Rory Byrne, identified himself to participants as a previous 'at risk' client. This approach is arguably a validating experience for the participants interviewed and the study found that the participants typically appreciated the interviewer disclosing his role as a former service user. The study concluded that participants had often experienced significantly difficult interpersonal relationships including conflict, abuse and exposure to domestic violence. Additionally, there was a reference to the difficulties in disclosing psychological problems which is consistent with previous research (Møller & Husby 2000). These participants identified this difficulty as being linked to a central concern that these experiences meant that they were 'going mad' with one participant saying: 'I just keep it to myself . . . you feel a bit like, they're gonna think you're going mad.' However, all the participants in this study did at some point decide to disclose their experiences and so a theme emerged relating to their experience of this. This research also examined the subjective experience of interpersonal relationships and communication difficulties for this population including social isolation as a result of bullying ('basically it was bullying at school . . . it's my instinct to run away and be alone instead of being with the group') and difficulty communicating mental health concerns to others ('I've always really wanted help but I had trouble admitting I had problems . . . it was hard to admit to myself, like, it was even harder to admit it to somebody else'). This is crucial since people presenting to services exist within a system larger than their mental health problems and, as such, family support, experience of relationships and past and present experience of disclosing their difficulties should be assessed, respected and integrated into treatments.

Implications for understanding

There are several implications for our understanding of the at risk period. Importantly, this research challenges the previously dominant view that it is not possible to access first-hand accounts of the at risk period in 'real time' (Corcoran *et al.* 2003). The subjective accounts described increase our understanding of this typically difficult and distressing time during which the individual is aware of changes in their perception and thinking and may be actively involved in trying to make sense of these experiences. Another implication for understanding this period is an insight into what factors precipitate and/or delay help-seeking in this population. Increased understanding of this process may aid the development of educative outreach programs and may inform service development to promote easier and earlier access.

At present it would appear that just two studies exist that have explored the subjective experience of the at risk client during this period. Further research should focus on explanatory models developed during this period, exploration of differences across cultures and repeated longitudinal interviews with at risk clients as they move through the early detection service into recovery or, as is possible, into a transition to psychosis. This research can be service-user-led, possibly resulting in greater disclosure and an increased validation of experiences (Byrne & Morrison 2010).

Implications for practice

Exploring the subjective experience of the at risk client has implications for practice at a number of levels. At a service development and delivery level, eliciting subjective experiences can provide an insight into what is important to the service user in terms of accessing and using services. Increased exploration and publication of these narratives would increase access to subjective accounts for consumers new to services and may aid normalization of their experiences and decrease the sense of isolation often reported by consumers during this period.

Clinically, it has been seen that individuals welcome the opportunity to talk about their experiences both during this period and retrospectively and benefit from this experience. Additionally, for clinicians and treatment providers this experience offers the opportunity to gain a different perspective and to challenge the traditionally pessimistic discourse related to the potential onset of psychosis. It encourages a deeper level of understanding for the service provider so that they can better appreciate the different experiences that this population presents with.

Cognitive Behavioural Therapy treatment manuals that exist for working with this population (French & Morrison 2004) highlight the importance of addressing issues placed on the problem list by the service user. This can only be successfully achieved by engaging in a close discourse with the service user and should be a collaborative process resulting in a treatment plan developed through mutual agreement. Any concerns that mental health providers may have had that this population is not able to articulate their needs or recognize the importance of accessing care should hopefully be dispelled by the research presented here.

Conclusions

The field has much to learn from accounts of the subjective experience of these individuals, while consumers who are assessed as being at risk of developing psychosis for the first time should have more access to narratives provided by this population (for example that provided by Rory Byrne in the previous chapter) in order to be exposed to realistically optimistic stories of recovery.

References

Bentall, R. P. (1993) 'Deconstructing the concept of 'schizophrenia', *Journal of Mental Health*, 2: 223–238.

Birchwood, M. (2000) 'The Critical Period for Early Intervention'. In M. Birchwood, D. Fowler and C. Jackson (eds), *Early Intervention in Psychosis: A guide to Concepts, Evidence and Interventions*. Chichester: Wiley.

Boydell, K. M., Gladstone, B. M. and Volpe, T. (2006) 'Understanding the help seeking delay in the prodrome to First Episode Psychosis: A secondary analysis of the perspectives of young people', *Psychiatric Rehabilitation Journal*, 30: 54–60.

British Psychological Society (2000), *Understanding Mental Illness: Recent Advances in Understanding Mental Illness and Psychotic Experiences*. Leicester: British Psychological Society.

Byrne, R. and Morrison, A. P. (2010) 'Young people at risk of psychosis: A user-led exploration of interpersonal relationships and communication of psychological difficulties', *Early Intervention in Psychiatry*, 4: 162–168.

Corcoran, C., Davidson, L., Sills-Shahar, R., Nickou, C., Malaspina, D., Miller, T. and McGlashan, T. (2003) 'A qualitative research study of the evolution of symptoms in individuals indentified as prodromal to psychosis', *Psychiatric Quarterly*, 74: 313–332.

Corcoran, C., Gerson, R., Sills-Shahar, R., Nickou, C., McGlashan, T., Malaspina, D. and Davidson, L. (2007) 'Trajectory to a first episode of psychosis: A qualitative research study with families', *Early Intervention in Psychiatry*, 1: 308–315.

French, P. and Morrison, A. P. (2004) *Early Detection and Cognitive Therapy for People at High Risk of Developing Psychosis: A Treatment Approach*, Chichester: Wiley.

Geekie, J. (2004) 'Listening to the voices we hear: Clients' understandings of psychotic experiences'. In J. Read, L. R. Mosher and R. P. Bentall (eds), *Models of Madness: Psychological, Social and Biological Approaches to Schizophrenia*. Hove, East Sussex: Brunner-Routledge.

Hardy, K. V., Dickson, J. M. and Morrison, A. P. (2009) 'Journey into and through an early detection of psychosis service', *Early Intervention in Psychiatry*, 3: 52–57.

IEPA Writing Group (2005) 'International clinical practice guidelines for early psychosis', *British Journal of Psychiatry*, 187 (*S48*): 120–124.

Judge, A. M., Estroff, S. E., Perkins, D. O. and Penn, D. L. (2008) 'Recognizing and responding to early psychosis: A qualitative analysis of individual narratives', *Psychiatric Services*, 59: 96–99.

McGlashan, T. H., Zipursky, R. B., Perkins, D., Addington, J., Miller, T. J., Woods, S. W. . . . Breier, A. (2003) 'The PRIME North America randomized double-blind clinical trial of olanzapine versus placebo in patients at risk of being prodromally symptomatic for psychosis. I: Study rationale and design', *Schizophrenia Research*, 61: 7–18.

McGorry, P. D., Yung, A. R., Phillips, L. J., Yuen, H. P., Francey, S., Cosgrave, E. M. *et al.* (2002) 'Randomized controlled trial of interventions designed to reduce the risk of progression to first episode psychosis in a clinical sample with subthreshold symptoms', *Archives of General Psychiatry*, 59: 921–928.

May, R. (2004) 'Making sense of psychotic experience and working towards recovery'. In J. F. M. Gleeson and P. D. McGorry (eds), *Psychological Interventions in Early Psychosis*. Chichester: Wiley.

Møller, P. and Husby, R. (2000) 'The initial prodrome in schizophrenia: Searching for naturalistic core dimensions of experience and behaviour', *Schizophrenia Bulletin, 26*: 217–232.

Morrison, A. P., French, P., Walford, L., Lewis, S. W., Kilcommons, A., Green, J. *et al.* (2004) 'Cognitive therapy for the prevention of psychosis in people at ultra high risk', *British Journal of Psychiatry, 185*: 291–297.

Ridgway, P. (2001) 'Restorying psychiatric disability: Learning from first person narratives', *Psychiatric Rehabilitation Journal, 24*: 335–343.

Yung, A. R. and McGorry, P. D (1996a) 'The prodromal phase of first episode psychosis: Past and current conceptualizations', *Schizophrenia Bulletin, 22*: 353–370.

Yung, A. R. and McGorry, P. D. (1996b) 'The initial prodrome in psychosis: Descriptive and qualitative aspects', *Australian and New Zealand Journal of Psychiatry, 30*: 587–599.

Yung, A., Stanford, C., Cosgrave, E., Killackey, E., Phillips, L., Nelson, B. and McGorry, P. D. (2006) 'Testing the ultra high risk (prodromal) criteria for the prediction of psychosis in a clinical sample of young people, *Schizophrenia Research, 84*: 57–66.

Part VI

Trauma

A number of previous chapters have referred to the relationship between trauma and psychosis. The following two chapters focus specifically on this relationship. This can, of course, at times confront the reader with moving accounts of difficult and unpleasant experiences which, in turn, may stimulate the desire to avoid such material. Both the chapters which follow recognize this tendency, though they also demonstrate convincingly that, ultimately, accepting the reality of the existence and impact of traumatic experiences can lead to the development of more sensitive understandings of and more helpful approaches to the kinds of experiences that we refer to as 'psychosis'.

In the first of the two chapters, Wilma Boevink, with support from her collaborator Dirk Corstens, shares what she refers to as her 'intimate story of suffering' (though we should point out that ultimately it is also a story of courage and recovery). We should not be surprised to find that, once again, the issue of sense of identity permeates much of Wilma's story. We see also, as with previous personal accounts, that how Wilma understands her experience has a great impact on how she relates to and manages it.

John Read, in reviewing research in this area, points out that quantitative research has a role to play and need not overlook subjective aspects of experience. He reminds us that mental health services have a history of denying the importance of trauma, which contrasts with the views of both the general public and those who experience psychosis, both of whom hold complex, multi-factorial understandings of psychosis, with trauma and abuse commonly identified as important factors.

A thread running through both chapters is the recognition that there are many ways of attending to experience, both one's own experience and the experience of others, and that recognizing and accepting the existence and impact of traumatic experiences is a challenge which requires both courage and patience.

Chapter 13

My body remembers; I refused

Childhood trauma, dissociation and psychosis

Wilma Boevink and Dirk Corstens

In memory of Sharon Lefèvre

Preferring psychosis

I cannot remember any violent struggles connected to forced sexual contact, to abuse. At least I cannot remember a fight. At most some pushing and pulling on an unwilling child. That child, that's me. Inside, that child continues to brace. By bracing I try to defend my inner self enormously. The worst moment is when my body surrenders. The moment at which my body becomes unresisting. 'OK, go ahead, do what you want.' That is the worst moment: to surrender. From then, my body is doing something other than what I want inside. I turn my head and die a little. Inside I scream 'no, no' and I weep for the bad thing being done to me. Inside, I am overwhelmed by despair. But that should not come out, that may never be expressed, may not be seen. Fear. From that moment on there is a shell, that thing, that body and an 'I'. I do not want to be that body. Take it away from me. Get me out. I'd rather be psychotic.

Making it exist

A story about abuse is an intimate story of suffering. Yet I want to tell my story. I just have to find the right words because after 40 years it is not easy to just tell what happened, to present the facts instead of prolonging the fiction of normality as some sort of 'survival strategy'. It took me 40 years to be able to really go back to how it all started. All these years I did not know what kept me caught by fear, what made me become a chronic psychiatric patient. It is only recently that I started to search for the right words to tell my story. And now I have found a few and used them. Now my story exists and it can be told. Now I can start working on the integration of the words in my head, the sensations of my body and all those long forbidden emotions.

Many stories of one reality

There are many stories about me: a story about a mental health activist, about a social scientist, about a recovery coach. There is also the story of a chronic mental health care patient which is partly written in psychiatric files, reduced to a list of symptoms, psychiatric diagnoses and medications. During my psychiatric career I got reduced to different diagnoses and became detached from my original experiences. My symptoms and the context in which they developed lost their meaningful connection. For a long time I have considered myself as mentally ill, disturbed, psychotic. I had experiences I did not understand, which made me feel powerless. I considered these experiences to be a consequence of brain disease. I felt myself a failure of nature: 'I am a mentally ill person, a patient in psychiatry.' For years and years I believed psychiatry could cure me, that doctors could intervene in the course of 'my illness', taking away the symptoms. I felt powerless and passive. I was not able to see how I had already taught myself to survive. I was blind to my own ways of coping with my psychotic experiences and the ways I maintained some kind of sense of self, despite being admitted to a psychiatric institution for many years. Now, looking back, I can see those strategies. I also see why they didn't work in the long run: they were built on quicksand.

The courage to discover

Survival is not the same as healing. It is merely an attempt to hang on, to keep on breathing. Healing means more than that. Healing for me means finding the courage to start on the road of discovery. It means creating space for the damage, for the madness felt inside. And exploring the many sides of being a victim of abuse. Healing for me now means being able to hear my voices, to listen to the damaged child inside, to make room for my outrage, grief, shame and fear, to accept the battle that is going on inside. It is my battle which I know I have to fight to banish monsters from my past. It is a battle that cannot be fought in solitude. I learned that I need allies, that only in contact with others is healing possible. Now that I have found them, I know how important they are: reliable persons, not afraid to see and accept me and my madness and who have the courage to accompany me on my road of discovery and give me support and hope every time I lose hope myself.

The eye

When my children were still small I had a terrifying experience. It was just one of many psychotic experiences I had at the beginning of my motherhood. These always originated from fear of an emerging war, and the necessity to flee. And in an endless row of fugitives my children would die from famine and I would have to leave them behind.

The most striking experience was when I was alone one day. I was cleaning the house and saw a big eye in my children's toy castle. I saw this eye watching me through the little windows and doors. A tremendous fear took hold and paralyzed me. When my family returned home I tried not to look at the eye any more. Nothing seen, no harm done. Keep up normality. A few days later my husband put the castle in a box. But I still felt the presence of the eye. I avoided the room. In time the walls of the room became alive, pulsating as if a big heart pounded in that room.

Later I was asked: 'What does the eye do?' Then, I dared to look at it. To my astonishment it wasn't an angry or threatening eye. It was a big friendly eye that blinked now and then. It looked like a cow's eye that winked at me encouragingly. What had made me so anxious? I was paralyzed from fear because I knew I saw something that wasn't there. I was frightened by my madness and not by the eye.

The eye was familiar to me. It was a maternal eye, comforting, giving a sense of safety. It was not my biological mother's eye, but it reflected the soul of Diana, my favourite cow on the farm where I grew up. I learned to milk by hand; in the mornings and evenings I sat leaning against her fat, warm belly and heard the gurgling and ruminating noises she was making inside. But she fell ill and it was uncertain if she would get better. My parents told me that they would have to sell her at the market. She would be sure to find a good new home, my mother said. When I heard that, I rushed to the field where Diana was lying. I crawled up against her, weeping, snuggled up against her warm, soft belly. She turned her head and looked at me, blinking with her friendly eyes, comforting me, as if it was I and not her being sent away.

The suggestion that she was going to find a good home by being sold of course was a lie, because the treatment animals received at the cattle market was often rough and abhorrent. It turned out to be a double lie. The next day I returned home to find my mother and grandmother busily cutting up meat. I heard my grandmother ask my mother whether I had been told Diana had been slaughtered. To my face they denied it completely. But I knew it was her who was lying there in pieces. That scene is closely related to the content of my psychoses. The great lumps of bloody meat, the big jug full of blood, the sausage machine. For me, that is so close to life, my life. It's as if it is not my 'mom' but me lying there in bloody pieces. For me, it is total surrender.

Wet dogs

There are periods in my life, lasting days or weeks, when I find myself surrounded by a certain smell. A stench that penetrates everything, even my body. It smells like mouldy humidity, clothes that have not been dried properly or rotting wood. During these periods I get very restless, constantly trying to find the source of the stench. I ask people around me whether they smell it too, but apparently it is for my nose alone. Sometimes the wet smell develops as a cloud of destruction and I am afraid it stems from my body. The penetrating smell convinces me that I produce death, not life.

What smells wet like my olfactory hallucinations I finally identified as wet dogs. Dogs having been in the water and not dried off yet. Just like the dogs of a man I visited every once in a while when I was a child. I was a little afraid of his dogs. I remember that they smelled wet, just like their owner, who liked me a lot.

He always loved seeing me. He was a hunter. He shot animals for fun. He liked me, giving me candy, pulling me onto his lap, touching my little body, especially when he was drunk. For fun. And he liked taking me to the woods in his car, showing me the deer. I do not remember seeing any. I remember that the man was nervous, driving back and forth in his car in a brusque manner. I felt threatened by him, hunted. I tried to avoid him, but as a child you can't direct the course of your life. The man with the wet dogs was the first one who in his way used this body I am in for his sexual needs. He would not be the last.

Werewolves

Recently I had to travel to Freiburg, Germany, to give a lecture on recovery. This town sits in the shadow of the Black Forest. I think I was already heading towards psychosis, or too tired to make the long trip and be on my own in a strange country and city. Or was it the other way around? Did something during the trip trigger my psychosis? I don't know. But I started becoming psychotic. My hotel room was in a noisy street with a lot of traffic, so I slept poorly. There was no host to welcome me. Of course, as a professional, well-paid lecturer, you should be independent. But, I am also an expert by experience, and these experiences are not always in the past – something most people don't realize or want to see. Like me. I feel very vulnerable sometimes and need some support. At that time I was unable to admit this and arrange some supportive contacts during my stay.

I felt very isolated. My fears and confusion came out during my excursion into town the second day. There was a very strange atmosphere: a mist was hanging low over the town. It felt like there was something fundamentally wrong with this world, but I couldn't specify what this was. I saw in the mist the contours of something black hanging over the city. I walked through the streets with a map, trying not only to behave like a tourist, but to feel like one as well. All to allay my fears and hang on to normality. I didn't succeed. I felt more and more, because of the mist and the dark decor, as if I was in a film studio. It didn't seem real, this world. No one else seemed to notice. Perhaps I was the only 'outsider' there? Perhaps I was a spy! Then I saw a war memorial which startled me: a war memorial in Germany? Did they honour the dead soldiers that fought for Hitler in his dirty war? Perhaps I had a spying mission in this neo-fascist town? I noticed that all the city buses had this war memorial as an end station, which felt like a message, a warning to me. Next it occurred to me that I never saw any dogs. How come? I found the explanation in the *mutants* I met. Several men already had the first signs of their transition to werewolves. Their ears grew, their beards became like wolves' fur. They showed their teeth and their fingers and nails grew longer and thinner. Freiburg was inhabited by werewolves, proving it was a fascist bastion. Werewolves fought with and ate dogs. That's why I didn't see any dogs.

Being hunted in a hostile world is a recurring theme in my psychoses. Do I have the genes of a paranoid schizophrenic? In fact, every time, my psychotic adventures are a repetition of what I experienced when I was young. Then too I felt haunted in a hostile world. When I get afraid, when my old fears are triggered, the world becomes threatening and populated with werewolves. This is a sharp representation of how grown-ups, especially men, behaved during my childhood. My father was a community man, very active in our village, popular and respected. But for me, he was angry and aggressive, unreliable, unpredictable and short tempered. Other men during my youth mutated in the same way: they started off being nice and friendly, but at some point showed their true evil faces. What they really wanted was my body, to get sexual fulfilment. I learned to see their 'wolf side', despite the fact that to the outside world they were just good men.

Voices

My head is full of sounds, echoes, animals, music, screaming, crying and voices. For a long time it was just a bunch of noises, being the voice of Evil. It was my punishment. No one knew how bad I was, only the Evil which the noise inside my head represented. It got worse, more threatening, when I had done something wrong. I communicated with that noise. Evil had me in its power. I felt I was at the mercy of something that wanted bad things of me.

Over the years I started to distinguish specific sounds – some nice, others scary. A tree full of birds twittering, a football field of little boys shouting and sometimes cheering, angry voices, heavy breathing, screaming of little children and animals, cows or pigs screaming in pain and panic.

I have a family of heavy breathers inside my head: on the right side there is the always-present father and on the left side sometimes his son appears. The son is unreliable, more impulsive and aggressive, while his father is stable, always hissing: 'I watch you, you cannot escape, I am always watching you.' The son is always sexually aroused; dad is sometimes. It is difficult to have them both at the same time, because they don't breathe simultaneously. If they are both there, I always get dizzy and confused: whom should I serve? Whom should I listen to? Their breathing is destructive and threatening for me, because it makes me feel very dirty, ugly and used, as if they constantly want to remind me that abuse is the only thing I deserve.

I hear another voice as well. At first I thought the breathers were the only inhabitants in my head, but now I am not sure. Father and son are bad guys, but they don't seem evil enough to give me all these messages: 'Whore, kill yourself, you're not worth living, be there for me, I want you, you are nothing, ugly one, you're mine, listen to us or we will get the ones you love.' These messages are so negative that it is very hard to reject and resist them. Sometimes I don't succeed and have to give in and harm myself to make him satisfied and silent for a while. It is very hard and exhausting to deal with these negative and destructive inhabitants and not get upset, desperate or confused. I suppose these negative voices represent people who subjected me to abuse; the abuse made me hate my body. The voices hate me.

There is someone or something else inside me. I often have a heavy stone in my stomach which is the source of my nausea and extreme uneasiness. Sometimes I can hear someone crying inside my body. It is heartbreaking to hear that. I think it is a very little girl. She doesn't have words, but she definitely is very upset.

Quicksand

Hanging on to normality to cover up reality helped me through my childhood. Perhaps that is why I used this splitting between apparent normality and reality in life again. After I broke down at around the age of 20 I was in a psychiatric hospital for three years. During these years I prolonged the splitting: the violence I had been a victim of was never mentioned. My breakdown was said to be the consequence of my psychiatric disorder. I survived by getting away as far as possible from my 'undertow'. Once I restored normality I was discharged and faced with the task of building a new life. I developed a grim determination. I went to university, got a job as a researcher and later developed my career as an experiential expert. Together with others I developed the Towards Recovery, Empowerment and Experiential Expertise (TREE) (Boevink *et al.* in progress) program for users of long-term mental health care to support them in their recovery and their career as experts by experience. We create jobs in psychiatry to work together towards healing-based help for people with severe human distress. And we are developing a research program in this area.

I worked and worked. I learned what love is and became a mother as well. My normality became a wonderful reality. But every now and then I stumble, because of exhaustion, ugly memories, flashbacks, nightmares and psychotic experiences – as if my dissociation from the dark side of my life isn't strong enough. Every now and then my dragon taps me on my shoulder reminding me he is still there and that there will come a moment when I will have to look him in the eye. I don't want to and try to postpone this moment as long as possible. For this I pay a price of drifting every now and then into this endless world of psychosis. I built myself a life, but it is based on quicksand, because I deleted the dark side and tried to live just in the light.

Listening to my body

For as long as I can remember I have considered myself mainly as brains for which unfortunately I need the rest of this body I am in. I never was friends with this shell. I ignored it and refused to listen to it. To suppress whatever difficult sensations or emotions I must have had during the course of my life, I worked very hard, got psychotic, then used psychopharmacological medication, alcohol, drugs and self-harm. Thus I could keep up some kind of normality.

In the past year my body gave up. I got contaminated with the mononucleosis virus and had to stop working and being active in the outside world because of an invalidating exhaustion. My dragon tapped me on my shoulder again and this time

I had to look him in the eye. Fortunately, I have met a few courageous fellow dragon fighters who support me along with the few good friends I have. Slowly but surely, it became less vital to hang on to the fiction of normality and I made room for the damaged parts inside me. I learned to share my inner world, to relate it to the outside world. I was taught how to listen to my body. Nausea is a message, hyper-arousal a response and exhaustion means I have to rest. I learned to register when my senses become over alert and how my body pumps up to 'go to war'. I explored what makes me feel safe. I learned about trusting others even though I cannot hide my vulnerability. I learned to tolerate the voices inside my head. When they get angry, I try to slow down and ask for extra help and a helpful place to stay for a while. Instead of listening to the voices I try to enjoy music. I am discovering what kind of music I like. Instead of harming myself I should comfort myself, but this is still very difficult for me to do. Comforting myself triggers more pain and grief than self-harm. It is as if it cracks the stone in my stomach, which hurts a lot.

The stone in my stomach seems to be the source of the little girl's voice. Although I am afraid of her outrage, grief, shame and fear I am also curious about this little girl inside me. What is she like? I look at other girls and try out their colours, perfumes, dresses and make-up. I got myself a bear and a little pink doll. I sometimes like to sing, I like picture books about animals and watch everything grow in my garden. Through the damage and all the scars a little person becomes visible who I think I could like. It is a start, but I guess I still have a long way to go before I will be able to embrace her and the body she is in.

Me and my body: implications for understanding

In this chapter I have tried to illustrate the relations between trauma, dissociation and psychosis from the perspective of experience. In psychiatric practice, psychosis and dissociation seem to be viewed as being mutually exclusive. In my experience they are different but not separate. Trauma can connect them. Both dissociation and psychosis can be personal ways of reacting to overwhelming life circumstances. Dissociation, once, early in life, a necessary survival strategy, later becomes the prelude or perhaps even the cause of psychosis. To illustrate this I started by describing psychotic experiences, which can easily be seen as symptoms of what is called schizophrenia when you isolate them as mere symptoms. My next step was to put these experiences back in the context in which they could become real, thus making them meaningful. This step reveals how apparently abnormal behaviour can be very logical once seen in its original context.

Healing and help: implications for practice

I have illustrated part of my personal journey of discovery. Healing becomes possible when the content of what is generally considered as psychotic phenomena is taken seriously and is related to painful truths in the past. Dissociation is an important mechanism to survive and isolate unbearable and overwhelming emotions. It is an important coping mechanism for traumatic experiences during childhood. However, it can also be the cause or the basis of the development of psychotic symptoms. These symptoms conceal meaningful relational aspects experienced in harsh circumstances. They can be translated into what really happened in the past. Yet so far, this has not been common practice in psychiatry. Depending on co-morbidity, those labelled dissociative have a chance to get some kind of therapy. Those people identified as psychotic, however, are denied the opportunity to explore the significance of having had a painful past that can be addressed. I am convinced that this practice should and can be changed.

References

Boevink, W., Kroon, H., Van Vugt, M., Delespaul, P. and Van Os, J. (in progress). A Recovery Program of/for Persons with Severe Mental Illness: A Dutch Multi-Center Cluster Randomized Trial and a Conventional Randomized Controlled Trial'.

Chapter 14

The subjective experience of the link between bad things happening and psychosis

Research findings

John Read

Traditional research

All research into the causes of psychosis inevitably involves the people who experience it. The extent to which their views are heard, however, varies considerably. For example, probing people's brains and chromosomes tells us nothing about the individual's experiences or understandings thereof. But even in studies that do take account of what has happened in people's lives, the very nature of traditional 'scientific' research means that only those hypotheses that the researcher considers important are investigated. Furthermore, the voices of individuals are, inevitably, lost beneath totals, averages and statistical comparisons between groups. Nevertheless, quantitative research analyzing the differences between groups of people can be quite convincing, scientifically, when determining whether X causes Y.

For example, research using a range of scientific methodologies has recently established that many social factors are significant risk factors for psychosis. These include: mothers' well-being during pregnancy; insecure attachment in childhood; early loss of parents; witnessing inter-parental violence; dysfunctional parenting (often intergenerational); childhood sexual, physical and emotional abuse; childhood emotional or physical neglect; bullying; war trauma; rape or physical assaults as an adult; high levels of racist or other forms of discrimination; and heavy marijuana use early in adolescence (Larkin & Morrison 2006; Moskowitz *et al.* 2009; Read *et al.* 2008; Read & Gumley 2008)

Another example of an important finding from traditional 'quantitative' research is that disclosures of abuse by 'psychiatric patients', including those diagnosed as 'schizophrenic', are reliable (Fisher *et al.* 2011; Read *et al.* 2008). This is important given the tendency of some professionals to assume that abuse disclosures by people who experience psychosis are symptoms of their 'mental illness' (Read *et al.* 2007) and that such disclosures, perhaps including the first-person accounts described elsewhere in this book and later in this chapter, should not be believed.

The content of 'symptoms'

The closest this kind of research gets to giving a voice to people who experience psychosis is in studies which report on the content of their psychotic 'symptoms' and whether they are related to the bad things that have happened in their lives. Marius Romme and Sandra Escher, long-time champions of giving voice hearers a proper voice in research and clinical endeavours, were among the first to find that the content of the hallucinations of adults who were abused as children are often strongly reminiscent of episodes of traumatic victimization (Romme & Escher 2006). Three studies have found that the content of just over half of the psychotic 'symptoms' of adults who were abused as children are obviously related to the abuse (Read *et al.* 2008).

Some papers include examples. For instance, a study of incest survivors records that a man who had been raped several times by an uncle at age seven heard voices telling him he was 'sleazy' and should kill himself; and a woman who had been sexually assaulted by her father from a young age and raped as a teenager had the delusion that 'people were watching her as they thought she was a sexual pervert and auditory hallucinations accusing her of doing "dirty sexy things" ' (Heins *et al.* 1990).

Public opinion

The idea that psychosis is caused by bad things happening is not surprising to the public. Studies in 16 countries find that when asked what causes 'schizophrenia' most people (including family members – see Chapter 22) place far more emphasis on social factors such as abuse and poverty than on faulty brains or genes (Magliano *et al.* 2009; Read *et al.* 2006). The few studies that have specifically studied the causal beliefs of people diagnosed as psychotic or schizophrenic consistently find that they too favour psychosocial explanations (Read *et al.* 2006). For example, the factors espoused as 'likely/very likely causes' by Germans diagnosed with psychoses were: 'recent psychosocial factors' – 88 per cent; 'personality' – 71 per cent; family – 64 per cent; and 'biology' – 31 per cent (Angermeyer & Klusmann 1988). A USA study of beliefs about 'schizophrenia' found that 66 per cent of people who had received the diagnosis, but only 18 per cent of clinicians, cited 'the way he was raised' (Van Dorn *et al.* 2005). In London only 5 per cent of people diagnosed as 'schizophrenic' believed that their problems were caused by a 'mental illness' and only 13 per cent cited 'biological causes', compared with 43 per cent citing 'social' (McCabe & Priebe 2004). A recent Italian study found that 76 per cent of people diagnosed with 'schizophrenia' mentioned at least one social cause (most frequently family conflicts, and psychological traumas and losses), with only 10 per cent citing a biological cause (Magliano *et al.* 2009).

Research into subjective experience and first-person accounts

In addition to traditional 'numbers' research, there are also approaches to studying psychosis where the person's lived experience is placed centre stage.

These include researchers interviewing people and offering short quotations from the interviews to illustrate the researcher's conclusions, as well as individuals telling their own stories in their own way without a mediator.

Interviews by researchers

Space permits just three examples of studies in which people who have experienced psychosis have either been interviewed, or listened to, about their understandings of psychosis without a predetermined hypothesis. This is a biased sample as I had the privilege of being the research supervisor for all three of the projects, and all three researchers are far from ordinary psychologists – each bringing quite extra-ordinary talents to their work. (Each of them has contributed a chapter to this book focusing on a specific aspect of their research.)

Vanessa Beavan surveyed 154 New Zealand voice-hearers from the general population with a questionnaire, and then interviewed 50 of them (Beavan 2007). Among her major findings were that voices vary enormously on all dimensions studied – including wanted/unwanted and positive/negative, that the content of voices are personally meaningful to the voice-hearer, and that it is this meaning that is the biggest determinant of whether the voices are distressing (Beavan & Read 2010). Over half of the questionnaire respondents (58 per cent) reported a significant event taking place just before hearing voices for the first time, and for the majority of these (81 per cent) the event was negative:

> I was very close to my adoptive grandmother. There was no illness, nothing, she died in her sleep. . . . But that night I remember her coming to me and waking me up and she was in the doorway and I can remember her saying 'everything will be okay. I'm here for you.'

Of the 50 voice-hearers who told their stories to Vanessa in person, 26 (52 per cent) talked about childhood trauma – most commonly sexual abuse (20 per cent), physical abuse (20 per cent), emotional abuse (16 per cent), traumatic loss (10 per cent) and serious illness (10 per cent). For example: 'I think the voices started as a safety mechanism. I had a mother who was psychologically abusive, though not so often. But very emotionally abusive.'

Vanessa found, however, that trauma was just one of a complex range of causal explanations. When the questionnaire respondents were asked to tick one or more of 16 possible explanations, traumatic or stressful life events was only the fourth most endorsed (32 per cent). The most commonly endorsed were 'spiritual experience' (43 per cent) and 'the voices come to support me in times of need' (37 per cent). As in the studies of people diagnosed as 'schizophrenic' summarized earlier, few (10 per cent) ticked 'I have a brain disorder or disease.'

Jim Geekie received permission from 15 of his clients at a New Zealand First Episode Psychosis service to record and analyse the parts of their therapy sessions that related to the sense the clients made of their experiences. Five types of causal explanations emerged. For example, all 15 talked about 'Psychological Factors', the most common of these being 'anxiety, fear and worry' (8) and 'stress' (8): 'I didn't know that it [psychosis] was something that happens and it can mend. Bit like a broken bone kind of thing. Just due to too many, in my case I think, due to too many pressures.'

A second type of causal explanation, discussed by 12 of the 15, Jim called 'Development and Experience'. While only three talked about specific examples of sexual or other abuse, eight identified past experiences in a general sense, such as 'my upbringing'. Nine made comments which Jim categorized as 'Isolation', in which the general notion was that loneliness created a vacuum which was filled by the psychosis: 'And through desperate loneliness I created all that.'

Yet again the biological explanations deployed by most psychiatrists were of relatively little interest, with only three mentioning the brain and two heredity. Causal explanations, however, were just one of seven areas talked about (Geekie & Read 2009). One of the other six, 'Storytelling and Authoring', discussed by 12 of the 15, addressed the importance of developing and telling one's own account of what has happened and why.

Melissa Taitimu, a Māori Clinical Psychologist, interviewed 57 Māori about their understandings of what western mental health experts call 'schizophrenia' (Taitimu 2007). As well as 16 *tangata whaiora* (people seeking wellness/users of mental health services) she talked with Māori mental health staff and with *kaumatua* and *kuia* (elders). Among her many fascinating findings, most of which were in stark contrast to current psychiatric constructions, was that for many Māori the question about causes made little sense. The experiences were so integral to their everyday life that they did not need to be analyzed or pathologized. The most common framework for understanding 'extra-ordinary experiences' such as hearing voices was a spiritual one, including messages from ancestors, *matakite* (gift), *makutu* (curse) and several types of *mate Māori* (disorders). Like Vanessa and Jim's studies (in which the majority of participants were Europeans), Māori 'held multiple explanatory models'. Of the 57, 30 talked about drug and alcohol abuse as a cause, and 21 mentioned verbal, physical or sexual abuse.

What these three studies collectively illustrate is the wealth of information that emerges when you give people a chance to tell their own story. Besides confirming the 'numbers research' which showed that stress, loss, loneliness and abuse are very often causal factors, many other types of explanations emerged. It could be argued that the most important finding of all, albeit an obvious one, is that the causes are different for each person, depending on their personal life history and cultural context.

Telling one's own story

Scientific journals find little space for first-person accounts. One notable exception is *Schizophrenia Bulletin*, the journal founded by the remarkable dissident psychiatrist Loren Mosher in 1969, which for many years published regular first-person accounts. These, however, typically describe the impact of the 'illness' on people's lives rather than what was going on in their lives that drove them mad in the first place. In 2006, however, following the publication of several of the studies documenting the relationship between child abuse and psychosis mentioned earlier, the journal bravely published a powerful article by the author of Chapter 13 of this volume, Wilma Boevink:

> I don't think that abuse itself is a strong cause for psychosis. It hurts, but it is rather simple. I think that the threat and the betrayal that come with it feed psychosis. The betrayal of the family that says, 'you must have asked for it,' instead of standing up for you. That excuses the offender and accuses the victim. And forces the child to accept the reality of the adults. . . . You are forced to betray yourself. That is what causes the twilight zone. What makes you vulnerable for psychosis.
>
> (Boevink 2006)

The other exception is the recently launched *Psychosis: Psychological, Social and Integrative Approaches*, the journal of the International Society for the Psychological Treatments of Schizophrenia (www.isps.org). I have the honour of being its first Editor. Following an overwhelming vote of ISPS members in favour of including first-person accounts, every edition thus far has done so. For example:

> I often wonder when it began, this ascent into madness. Was there a date, a time, a word spoken? Was it an event or place that precipitated the ascent? Rather a kaleidoscope of bumps and bruises and harsh words which blend and melt into each other. . . . The family was staying with relatives and I was invited into my uncle's bed for 'cuddles'. After several occasions we 'got caught' and I was slapped and beaten by my aunty while she raged at my uncle.
>
> (Lampshire 2009)

It is hard to find a finer example of making space for people to tell their own stories than a recently published book called *Living with Voices: 50 Stories of Recovery* (Romme *et al.* 2009). This is a mixture of minimally edited interviews and people writing their own accounts. Despite the primary focus being on the process of recovery, the 50 people (from eight countries) were asked to comment on their understanding of the causes of their voice-hearing. All but seven (86 per cent) identified stressful or traumatic events or circumstances, the most common being sexual abuse (48 per cent) and emotional neglect (28 per cent):

> With me, there was never any confusion about the voice. I recognized it; it was the abuser's.

> I had been extensively bullied at school. . . . The typical themes for the voices are that I am stupid, ugly and worthless. The bullying seems to be carried on by the voices, although I didn't connect the two things at first.

Again, however, it is the diversity and variation behind the numbers and themes that are important for the individuals involved and their efforts to lead a full life.

Only a tiny proportion of books about 'schizophrenia' are by those who know most about what hallucinations and delusions are really like and what, for each individual, causes them. (However, at the time of writing the first three books on the website of the international bookseller Amazon, if you type in 'schizophrenia', are first-person accounts.) One exception is John Morrow who first published *How to Become a Schizophrenic: The Case Against Biological Psychiatry* in 1992.

> My parents tried to perform the duties of parenthood the best they could, but they had serious psychological problems of their own. Also I find it extremely difficult to condemn my parents for behaving as if I was going insane when the psychiatric authorities told them that this was an absolute certainty. . . . I find it hard to blame my mother for believing that I had inherited my great-grandmother's insanity . . . Psychiatry, with its pseudoscientific doctrines of inherited insanity and its incompetent practitioners with their self-fulfilling prophecies, together with my parents' gullibility and other personal limitations had in effect driven me insane.
>
> (Morrow 2003)

The trauma of not being heard

We must also acknowledge, albeit only in passing, the many first-person accounts of the traumas involved in being 'treated' by a mental health system that often doesn't listen, from John Perceval in 1832 to Kate Millett in 1990 (Bateson 1962; Millett 1990). Israeli psychologist Renana Elran is about to publish an analysis of such analogies throughout history (Elran, 2009).

Our collective capacity to acknowledge the awful things that we humans sometimes do to one another, to children in particular, is crucially important if we are ever to break the intergenerational cycle of violence and neglect. Our capacity to deny the truth, and thereby avoid all the associated emotions, is understandable. For those who have been abused or neglected, such denial is forgivable. For those who claim to be experts and healers in the field of human distress, however, such denial is unacceptable.

Professional experts have a long tradition of ignoring the views of their patients about the causes of their 'symptoms'. One of the 'grandfathers' of modern psychiatry, Eugen Bleuler, wrote the following in his famous monograph that introduced the term 'schizophrenia' to the world:

> People who speak of their delusions and their weird behaviour during the attack as being pathological phenomena . . . are not without reason easily considered as cured; whereas the opposite is thought of as being a rather certain sign of

continuing disease . . . They [schizophrenics] do not always locate the illness where the observer sees it to be. They realize, for example, the poor state of their nerves, the senselessness of their behaviour, but they insist that both are quite understandable reactions to stimuli and irritations of their environment.

(Bleuler 1911/1951: 257)

Believing that one's difficulties are caused by life events is still often seen as proof that you are mentally ill. A current research scale, measuring 'insight', scores the item 'Denies mental illness and sees any problems as arising entirely from external sources' as the strongest possible example of 'poor insight' (Liddle *et al.* 2002).

There is a small but growing number of first-person accounts of the failure of mental health services to ask about trauma or abuse and to respond humanely when people do talk about it. As was the case in relation to the causes of psychosis, there are also many 'scientific' studies on this issue – showing that the majority of mental health service users are never asked about any bad things that might have happened when they were little (Read *et al.* 2007). A poignant example of a first-person account of this sad fact is provided by Boevink:

In psychiatry my twilight zone was extended. There a distortion of reality was forced on me once more. Nobody ever asked me what had happened to me. Nobody ever asked me: what was it that drove you mad? I was observed, diagnosed, and treated as a disturbed person, but nobody ever looked at the association with my life history.

(Boevink 2006)

In my workshops for mental health professionals about how to ask about child abuse (Read *et al.* 2007) I do present the research about how commonly people diagnosed as 'schizophrenic' or 'psychotic' were abused as children, about the long-term effects and about how rarely service users are currently being asked. But I always include the following quotes, from a survey of service users (mostly with diagnoses indicative of psychosis) about whether it is a good idea to ask about abuse (Lothian & Read 2002):

There were so many doctors and registrars and nurses and social workers and psychiatric district nurses in your life asking you about the same thing, mental, mental, mental, but not asking you why.

I just wish they would have said, 'What happened to you? What happened?' But they didn't.

Implications for understanding

Perhaps the implications of all this for enhancing understanding are rather obvious. Research, whether quantitative or qualitative, can address subjective experience and can, as I hope has been shown here, make important contributions to our understandings of psychosis in general and, more specifically, how trauma is related to psychosis. The vast reservoir of knowledge held by those with first-hand lived experience remains largely untapped. This is beginning to change. Quantitative and qualitative researchers alike are gradually learning to alter their focus. When the research into first-person accounts is actually conducted by people with first-hand experience of what they are researching we are likely to see some fascinating advances in our understandings (Sweeney *et al.* 2008).

Implications for practice

The implications for those trying to understand and support people with experiences of psychosis seem even more obvious. Providing the opportunity to tell one's story and have it heard, really heard, is paramount. When listening to the stories we must try hard – and it *is* hard – to suspend our pet theories (biological, psychological, social, spiritual or whatever), and just listen. This can be healing all by itself. And the listener may learn something in the process.

In relation to trauma, we must actively invite the person to include in their story – if they wish – the worst that life has thrown at them. We must ask about abuse and trauma. Not because everyone has been abused, and not because everyone who has experienced significant traumas needs trauma-related therapy (although some do), but because not asking conveys that it is not safe to tell.

These two sets of implications are, of course, linked. The understandings we gain from research, qualitative and quantitative, should inform our practice. Indeed, my belief in the combined power of quantitative research and first-person accounts was recently reinforced in London at a clinical training workshop. In 2008 the UK National Health Service introduced new guidelines that all mental health service users should be asked about child abuse. I was invited to present the first training workshop, to 100 psychiatrists. The other main speaker was Jacqui Dillon, chairperson of the UK Hearing Voices Network – part of the growing international voice-hearers' movement (www.intervoiceonline.org). As Jacqui told her life story (Dillon 2010), I sat, with tears in my eyes, watching the reactions of the psychiatrists. Although I knew that all the numbers I had thrown at them meant that Jacqui's story could not be dismissed as a rarity, I had little doubt which of the two talks they were most likely to remember.

The final words about implications go to two experience-based experts:

> I invite readers to reflect on their practice and confront their ability to share people's distress without being overwhelmed by the desire to 'fix it'. In the busy clinical environment is there sufficient time allowed for clients to tell their complete story? What are the consequences if that isn't allowed to happen?
>
> (Lampshire 2009)

Hearing voices, self-harm, eating 'disorders' and dissociation, when viewed objectively, are frequently classified as symptoms of serious mental illnesses and disordered personalities that require treatment, eradication and cure . . . By tracing the roots of so-called 'symptoms' back to their origins in traumatic childhood events and having the courage to bear witness to painful truths, a more accurate, humane and respectful picture emerges which reframes 'symptoms' as essential survival techniques.

(Dillon 2010)

References

Angermeyer, M. and Klusmann, D. (1988) 'The causes of functional psychoses as seen by patients and their relatives. I: The patients' point of view', *European Archives of Psychiatry and Neurological Sciences*, 238: 47–54.

Bateson, G. (ed.) (1962) *Perceval's Narrative: A Patient's Account of his Psychosis 1830–1832*. London: The Hogarth Press

Beavan, V. (2007) *Angels at our Tables: New Zealanders' Experiences of Hearing Voices*. PhD, University of Auckland, New Zealand.

Beavan, V. and Read, J. (2010) 'Hearing voices and listening to what they say: The importance of voice content in understanding and working with distressing voices', *Journal of Nervous & Mental Disease*, 198: 201–205.

Bleuler, E. (1911/1951) *Dementia Praecox of the Group of Schizophrenias* (J. Zinkin, Trans.). New York: International Universities Press.

Boevink, W. (2006) 'From being a disorder to dealing with life: An experiential exploration of the association between trauma and psychosis', *Schizophrenia Bulletin*, 32: 17–19.

Dillon, J. (2010) 'The tale of an ordinary little girl', *Psychosis: Psychological, Social and Integrative Approaches*, 2: 79–83.

Elran, R. (2009) 'The beast within: A metaphor of madness in autobiographies of schizophrenics 1920s–1940s'. Paper presented at Second Global Conference: Madness – Probing the Boundaries. Retrieved from www.inter-disciplinary.net/probing-the-boundaries.

Fisher, H., Craig, T., Fearon, P., Dazzan, P., Lappin, J., Hutchinson, G. et al. (2001) 'Reliability and comparability of psychosis patients' retrospective reports of childhood abuse', *Schizophrenia Bulletin*, 37: 546–553.

Geekie, J. and Read, J. (2009), *Making Sense of Madness: Contesting the Meaning of Schizophrenia*. New York: Routledge.

Heins, T., Gray, A. and Tennant, M. (1990) 'Persisting hallucinations following childhood sexual abuse', *Australian and New Zealand Journal of Psychiatry*, 24: 561–565.

Lampshire, D. (2009) 'Lies and lessons: Ramblings of an alleged mad woman', *Psychosis: Psychological, Social and Integrative Approaches*, 1: 178–184.

Larkin, W. and Morrison, A. (eds) (2006) *Trauma and Psychosis: New Directions for Theory and Therapy*. London: Routledge.

Liddle, P., Ngan, E., Duffield, G., Kho, K. and Warren, A. (2002) 'Signs and Symptoms of Psychotic Illness (SSPI): A rating scale', *British Journal of Psychiatry*, 180: 45–50.

Lothian, J. and Read, J. (2002) 'Asking about Abuse during Mental Health Assessments: Clients' Views and Experiences', *New Zealand Journal of Psychology*, 31: 98–103.

McCabe, R. and Priebe, S. (2004) 'Explanatory models of illness in schizophrenia: Comparison of four ethnic groups', *British Journal of Psychiatry*, *185*: 25–30.

Magliano, L., Fiorillo, A., del Vecchio, H., Malangone, C., De Rosa, C., Bachelet, C. *et al.* (2009) 'What people with schizophrenia think about the causes of their disorder', *Epidemiologia e Psichiatria Sociale*, *18*: 48–53.

Millett, K. (1990) *The Loony Bin Trip*. New York: Simon & Schuster.

Morrow, J. (2003) *How to Become a Schizophrenic: The Case Against Biological Psychiatry* (3rd ed.). New York: Writers Club Press.

Moskowitz, A., Schafer, I. and Dorahy, M. (2009) *Psychosis, Trauma and Dissociation: Emerging Perspectives on Severe Psychopathology*. Chichester, UK: Wiley-Blackwell.

Read, J. and Gumley, A. (2008) 'Can attachment theory help explain the relationship between childhood adversity and psychosis?', *Attachment: New Directions in Psychotherapy and Relational Psychoanalysis*, *2*: 1–35.

Read, J., Hammersley, P. and Rudegeair, T. (2007) 'Why, when and how to ask about child abuse', *Advances in Psychiatric Treatment*, *13*, 101–110.

Read, J., Haslam, N., Sayce, L. and Davies, E. (2006) 'Prejudice and schizophrenia: A review of the "mental illness is an illness like any other" approach', *Acta Psychiatrica Scandinavica*, *114*: 303–318.

Read, J., Fink, P., Rudegeair, T., Felitti, V. and Whitfield, C. (2008) 'Child maltreatment and psychosis: A return to a genuinely integrated bio-psycho-social model', *Clinical Schizophrenia & Related Psychoses*, *2*: 235–254.

Romme, M. and Escher, S. (2006) 'Trauma and hearing voices'. In W. Larkin and A. Morrison (eds) *Trauma and Psychosis: New Directions for Theory and Therapy* (pp. 162–191). London: Routledge.

Romme, M., Escher, S., Dillon, J., Corstens, D. and Morris, M. (eds) (2009) *Living With Voices: 50 Stories of Recovery*. Ross, UK: PCCS Books.

Sweeney, A., Beresford, P., Faulkner, A., Nettle, M. and Rose, D. (eds) (2008) *This is Survivor Research*. Ross, UK: PCCS Books.

Taitimu, M. (2007) *Nga whakawhitinga: Standing at the crossroads. Maori ways of understanding extra-ordinary experiences and schizophrenia*. PhD, University of Auckland, New Zealand.

Van Dorn, R., Swanson, J., Elbogen, E. and Swartz, M. (2005) 'A comparison of stigmatizing attitudes toward persons with schizophrenia in four stakeholder groups: Perceived likelihood of violence and desire for social distance', *Psychiatry: Interpersonal and Biological Processes*, *68*: 152–163.

Part VII

Hearing Voices

We now move on to chapters which explore the subjective experience of a range of experiences traditionally considered to be the more obvious 'symptoms' of psychosis. We begin with two chapters looking at the subjective experience of hearing voices.

Debra Lampshire's personal account of her relationship with her voices (and more generally with what she refers to as the 'enticing siren' of madness) locates her experience firmly within the social arena and the struggles which can be associated with feeling and being accepted in a not always welcoming social world. Once again, in Debra's tale, we see how learning to listen differently to her experiences along with acquiring a greater sense of agency and control contributed to her coming to accept her own flawed self and to again face the challenge of living with and among other human beings. Like Egan Bidois in his earlier chapter, she stresses the cathartic value of coming to terms with the 'why' of her experience, and in doing so she demonstrates that her voices are not meaningless, but they serve an important function, reflecting her sensitivity to the 'wounded world' we all inhabit.

Vanessa Beavan reviews research, including her own, into the subjective experience of hearing voices. Yet again, we are reminded that subjective experience has been largely neglected in this area; at the same time Vanessa demonstrates that careful consideration of subjective experience can enhance our understandings and appreciation of the experience concerned. We see that Debra Lampshire's assertion that such experiences are meaningful is shared by other voice-hearers. Vanessa's chapter also reminds us that so-called 'psychotic' experiences, such as hearing voices, lie on a continuum with ordinary experiences and that many who happen to hear voices are not troubled by the experience and never seek, nor need, help from mental health services.

Chapter 15

The sounds of a wounded world

Debra Lampshire

Come: see real flowers of this painful world – Basho

When a person takes the time to chronicle his or her life, a person begins to extract, interpret, analyze and dissect moments, brief moments in time. For life is made up of moments. We search and invest hours in examining their relevance, impact and long-lasting effects. It is during this process of reflecting that one realizes that there are so many moments that constitute a life, many of which don't fit into determinable categories. Generally, most of life's moments are made up of mundane, mechanical, automated and ordinary undertakings of little interest to anyone. Although for me personally they are the moments I most cherish, for they embody success for me, affirmation that I have overcome oppression. When I am on occasion invited to talk about my life, it is not those exquisite moments I am required to impart. It is those other moments; those indiscreet, compelling, extraordinary moments of madness. So, in writing this I speak to you not of my life but of moments in my life, extraordinary moments compiled of immeasurable pleasure and indescribable pain. Yes, they may be defining moments, but like all moments they pass and I extract what I need before consigning them to memory and then joyously and with a sense of true relief I recommence my ordinary life.

Madness can be an enticing siren, calling from many ragged shores with a promise of tranquillity hidden amongst the rocks; unfortunately, we are just as likely to find ourselves shattered and impaled on the rocks as we are to find a safe and serene harbour. Once heard, though, those alluring siren calls are not easily forgotten and can be craved for, desired even, their duplicity forgotten amid the attraction of false rhapsody.

I have succumbed to that charm many times, only later to witness my own demise fabricated in notions of grandeur, supremacy and bestowed mystical powers. It is hard to express the sensation of rising above the limitations of mortals to have within your grasp the intoxicating vigour of obtaining all knowledge, all power, and all magic. This is the false rhapsody, this is the 'drug', this is the madness. Whilst you are embroiled in that moment, the world is changed, you are changed: everything is possible, everything is probable, everything is within your capabilities. There is nothing wrong; it is others who are not privileged enough to have access to such wonders. Surely, I have entered the realms of angels and the Gods. This is divine, I have been ordained, anointed, deified. These are the *rare* moments of madness, these are the monumental moments stored in memory along with the ecstasy of promise. The desire to return and explore the meaning of such profound experiences entices and occupies our thoughts during times of reflection, anguish and grief.

More common are the moments of madness in which a poisoned crown has settled on you. You discover your apparent anointment has turned into an unsustainable euphoria that envelops and ultimately suffocates reason, security and any sense of connection. It is only when the enchantment subsides that the costs become more apparent. The losses mount, the shame multiplies and the desolation is complete.

So frequent have been my excursions to this madness that it can feel as if I am returning to a borrowed world, a world I view as alien but identified as normal by some, a world of which you are not a part, only an occasional interloper. This world is meant for some and you feel scrutinized constantly to ascertain your eligibility. Society mandates who are and who are not desirable entities. Just like going though foreign borders, the rejection is often public, humiliating and indefensible. A cloak of shame descends as faceless, nameless others determine your future. Every ordinary moment is dispelled and one is judged entirely on those rare, extraordinary moments.

For several decades my extraordinary moments were given over to voices, voices that others couldn't seem to hear. The ascent was gradual, beginning when I was a child. My earliest and my fondest memories are of hearing a maternal voice. She would come to me at night, soothing me and inviting me to sleep whilst she watched over me, protecting me and ensuring I would come to no harm. I was a poor sleeper when I was young, with recurrent nightmares which would awaken me, terrified and screaming. My family were very sound sleepers, so it was not unusual for my pleas for help to go unattended. I had yet to learn the skills of self-soothing, so would remain awake and alert until the small hours, when daylight would remove all possibility of ambush. The maternal voice was a welcome companion and her role in speaking to me was calming and reassuring, and the stroking of my forehead was of enormous comfort to me. She is the only voice I have retained my whole life and her role remains that of defender and protector. I am still prone to nightmares and awaking terrified and screaming, but maturity has taught me the skill of self-assurance. I still hear her voice but I also feel her presence and her embrace and that is sufficient.

Over time the range and character of my voices developed. The newer additions became critical, jeering, intrusive and malevolent, causing me a great deal of distress. The distressing voices became the norm and quite quickly overpowered the positive voices and became a staple in my diet of verbal spam. My behaviour became more bizarre, my thinking more confused and my day-to-day life more difficult to navigate. I began to retreat, surrendering more and more to the voices, compelled to do their bidding and forgoing all other ventures, thereby abandoning any prospect of living a life of my own choosing. My surrender was complete and absolute. I stayed inside my house for 18 long years, waiting and listening, ready to heed their whims and trials. I developed fanciful beliefs. I believed that I was a messenger from God and that I was being tested by the voices to ensure I was a worthy recipient of this message of peace and loving kindness. I failed every task allotted to me but the voices always gave me another chance to redeem myself, threatening: 'We will give you one more chance and one more only.' How fortunate was I to be shown such mercy, such grace. I must try harder. I must endeavour to be what they wanted, what the world needed. The world's salvation rested with me. I and I alone held the responsibility of world peace in my hands for the sake of humankind. I couldn't afford to get it wrong!

I became obsessed with this notion, constantly fed by the voices until one day I realized that I wasn't The One. The realisation was slow – just small nagging doubts that were quickly overwhelmed by evidence presented by my voices. But the evidence became less convincing, the waiting time too long. I was fatigued by waiting. The blossom of the idea wilted and one by one the petals fell till all that remained was a hint of the idea. I could no longer carry the burden and could no longer pretend that I was worthy when clearly I was not. I had to face the fact that as much as I wanted to save the world I could not. I was not 'The Chosen One', I was just me. Holding onto the position of 'The Chosen one' was exhausting and with great sorrow I watched it slip from my grasp. I no longer had the strength to hold fast. So, when had 'being me' ever been good enough? I would have to resign my position of 'special' and resort back to my customary position of failure: unworthy, inadequate and a disappointment to those who had demonstrated any faith in me. The position was familiar, so I opened the door and returned to being the unwanted guest who I had let in. I gave up. I gave up because I had to. But more importantly, I gave up because I chose too. I no longer had the energy; passion was replaced by apathy, reality knocked down the door of my refuge. I stopped caring if I was right. Deciding to give up was easy and, in this instance, a sensible choice. It allowed me to give up on the fantasy and brought me crashing back to this earthly realm.

The loss of the dream consumed me and a rage built in me, smouldering and gnawing away at my essence. I did not wish to accept I was condemned to live in this 'real world'. Surely, I was made for better than this, but it seemed not. I was about to embark on my final journey, the descent into normality. I would have to pack up my theatre of fantasies and extend a flailing hand to a humanity which, my experience had shown, is discerning about requests for inclusion. The magnetism of madness can be strong. My retreat into madness was a response to rejection. Madness had been a place where I controlled all the outcomes. I gave myself the happy ending, the charmed existence; I could be all that I wanted. I didn't have to work at it, I just was. I was liked and admired. I was respected and adored. These moments, though, became fewer, the outcomes less predictable, the residual effects less convincing, less satisfying. I was confronted with the truth, the callous irrefutable truth: I was not special or gifted. I just was.

My voices have taken me on many journeys and filled an empty life and refreshed an idle brain. They made me laugh, cry, rage and feel. They protected and tormented, they maligned and praised me, they entertained and subdued me, but most of all they controlled me. They had become so central to my existence that the prospect of living without them seemed incomprehensible. They resided with and within me. There was no privacy, no respite and I was never lonely. They became as natural and tedious as breathing. A day without them was unthinkable – desired perhaps, but nonetheless unlikely. I loved and loathed them. I was totally committed to this relationship of lover, friend, enemy and ultimately abuser. However, I knew I would have to change this relationship and instead cultivate a relationship in which I would feel in control. I could never conceive of a life without voices. The idea was abhorrent to me, but if I was to work from a relational perspective, I could hold onto the good friends (voices) and monitor and modify the negative friends (voices). To sustain our relationship I had to demand some respect and consideration. I had never demanded anything of my voices, but now was the time. I realized with huge relief that I did not have to get rid of my voices. They were not the conductor of my life – I was. I may not have been up to the responsibility of saving the world but I had to try to save myself, the imperfect, flawed self. My true self had to take responsibility for who and what I was. I had to become my own rescuer, healer and supporter. I contracted to make myself human again, no longer incommunicado with humanity.

I could still recall moments of experiencing uncontaminated happiness before I had departed this world to dwell with my madness. I recalled the thrill and satisfaction that I gained from engaging with my fellow humans. So, I decided I would not eat at the table for the solitary. I would feast with the hordes at the same trough which holds the dilemmas, limitations and delights that all humans face. I would need to muscle my way in, but I would no longer settle for the crumbs of this unlived life.

I would have to prise apart the bars that separated me from society and enter not because I wanted to, but because I was entitled to. I had falsely believed I had to justify my existence. I was wrong. I had to have the courage to accept myself – as I was. I had to have the courage to listen to my own voice and my own heart and my own mind.

I started to truly explore the content of my voices and separated their attributions from my own. I tended to them in the same way I wished to be treated. I was less inclined to respond extremely emotionally and more inclined to become objective in my dealings with them. I took on the role of adult rather than submissive child. As I began to untangle the role of the voices, I discovered their strategies and mechanics and was then able to circumvent the mayhem in my life. I discovered that their repertoire of tactics was limited and I was able to manoeuvre myself into a position of power, a power I obtained in increments, gradually gaining my strength through successes and the occasional failure. I befriended those voices who allowed it and coached those who did not. I changed my relationship with the voices, dealing with the ones which were unhelpful by neither arguing nor denying but by acknowledging and discerning for myself their authenticity. I evaluated the content and gauged the level of distress I experienced in accepting the information. I realized I could choose to accept this content or not. That was my prerogative. I placed parameters around our relationship so we could coexist. I came to understand the role of the voices in my life, and I also came to pity them for they were as trapped and reviled as I had been. They revealed themselves as incompetent communicators, distorting and misinterpreting situations, often overreacting to perceived threats. The voices were unable to act on the information themselves, they needed me to do so and I soon realized that they were impotent without me. In fact they were nothing without me. Their need for me was so much greater than I imagined. When I embarked on this venture what I hadn't anticipated was the void the culling of the voices would induce. Mental health services are fixated on the elimination of the voices without comprehending the cost to the voice-hearer. No one prepares you for the emptiness and the destruction of what has been a way of surviving. I may have lost a tormentor, but I also lost a way of being.

Implications for understanding

Far from feeling liberated I felt diminished by the loss of my voices. Such is the savagery that comes from deconstruction, from tearing away at the things that at one time had been so meaningful and powerful. To actively engage in a process that diminishes you seems counterintuitive and just plain stupid. It is not so surprising then that I surrendered to madness, because madness welcomes and embraces so much of the attributes denied by living an ordinary life.

I have experienced many years of hearing voices. I do not consider them an indicator of madness but a way of coping with living within a wounded world. I have the ability to hear the inaudible cries of this damaged world. I am able to see, smell and feel the heart-rending scars, some fresh, some old but always painful. I can bear my own pain and my own catastrophes. What I find hard is to tolerate the anguish so discernible in others. I respond and react to the pain of others. I can sense it, smell it, taste it, and feel it. It is their pain I cannot endure without bearing witness to it.

Some subscribe to the view that I am a product of my environment, but I see myself more as a reflection of society's abdication from listening to the overt and covert pleas of those who embody human sensitivities. I represent what happens to a person in that kind of society. I am a barometer of society's health as much as my own. I represent the parts of our world we most despise, a mirror of our most feared quality which is the capacity to 'lose control'. Society withdraws from those we call 'other'. We circumvent our responsibility by labelling their sensitivities as 'madness'. We apportion blame, ignore and dismiss this 'other'. Now invalidated and denounced as superfluous to society's needs, we are subsequently viewed as burdensome, troublesome creatures relegated to invisibility: we are 'least'.

Mental health treatment is often regarded as the 'science' of delving into those dark recesses in people's minds, digging deep to extract the hidden malignancies that aggravate and erode people's moral fibre. In times past we have sent canaries down into the pits to determine if the environment is safe for miners. Canaries in cages are vulnerable to changes in the atmosphere. Being unable to escape, they are sacrificed for the benefit of others. I contemplate sometimes the idea that those of us who have been labelled mentally ill serve a similar role in our society. But, rather than 'canaries of the mines' we are 'canaries of the mind', perceptive to the cruelties perpetrated by an ignorant society. The canary's demise is a precursor to running away to hide, grateful that it was one of less value that was lost. Miners would never ignore the silencing of those birds' delightful song. Perhaps there is something for us to learn from their example.

The fabric of our lives is embroidered into a tapestry of great vibrancy, intricacy and richness upon which we feel compelled to gaze and show admiration. Starting with a clear canvas, each thought and experience, each moment, contributes a stitch and that which emerges is a masterpiece of possibilities, a wish for entrance to a benevolent world. Practices intent on categorizing and eliminating unrecognized protective behaviours or our uniqueness have a way of tugging at the threads holding individuals together and unravelling all that they have worked on, designed and crafted over years. I watch it unravel and am told I should be grateful. It is a sad, sad thing to watch such a creation being destroyed. It is a loss. It is spirit-breaking and soul-destroying watching your beliefs and all you held to be true disintegrate before you. This has been my life's work and now I'm informed it is inferior. Consider the effect on the heart, on the mind: my self-belief is all but lost, my abilities to live in this environment successfully are challenged. Like a cloth attacked by moths, holes appear, opened up by well-intentioned others, but leaving all that was once connected separated. I begin the darning process one hole at a time so that the cloth can regain its former strength, if not its former glory. But no longer is the cloth of my design.

Of all life's treasures, the one thing I value most is freedom. What I crave and desire most is freedom from torment, emotional pain and isolation. Freedom to be who I am, wherever I am, with whoever I am. This is the Holy Grail. I had believed that freedom was ordained, a state of nirvana imparted haphazardly to those who deserved it. But, when I explored it further, I came to understand that it is a state that requires constant vigilance and active work towards gaining and maintaining; it is to be fought for and revelled in. It is to be found in the most unexpected places, to be eked out and, most importantly, it needs to be exercised so it becomes accessible and companionable. I thought my freedom had been stolen, extracted by people and services alike, but it had not. I had abandoned it, given it up. My most precious possession. I decided to reclaim it, for with great fortune, I was to discover, it is never truly lost.

Implications for practice

When the world treats you unfairly, you come to believe you are deserving of it. You come to expect it and begin to feel comfortable with it. You allow yourself to become a victim. When we are children our lives are constructed by others: parents, extended family, teachers, friends, society at large. But such facades are incredibly fragile. As we mature we have the opportunity to deconstruct, renovate and redesign. The fact is, the basic structure stays intact. For some, those foundations have been assaulted by trauma, abandonment, bullying, abuse, neglect and emotional distancing. These happenings are too significant to be dismissed or reassigned, too momentous to be entirely forgotten. But, they can be repatriated and assimilated as learnings, a way of having a deeper understanding of the 'whys' in one's life. I, like most people, have spent a lot of my time endeavouring to make sense of the world and when I understood that past experiences have an impact in the present, the 'whys' emerged. Having a context can assist in normalizing and validating that which can appear incomprehensible. Coming to terms with the 'whys' is very cathartic; recognizing the 'whys' but not allowing them to determine or control your future: that is autonomy.

Autonomy is about choice and you can have a choice about how you construct your own life. You may have to acknowledge the injustices that have been done to you, but when you confront them and realize that they do not define who you are, you are no longer the victim. You may not be responsible for the things that have happened to you but you are responsible for how you let them colour your world. The role of victim may have been placed on you by others but only you can unshackle yourself from it. Now that's freedom.

With freedom comes responsibility. Things changed for me because I took responsibility for myself and my actions. Perhaps society needs to do the same. To claim our roles as citizens we may need not just to look at those who appear 'least' but also to work towards creating an environment which allows all to flourish. This is no small task. It begins with the individual and extends to the wider community. Human beings' capacity to harm is well-documented and so frequently touted as the norm. This is a myth. The world I have discovered is dominated by goodness. Acts of kindness are daily occurrences so ordinary in fact that they warrant no mention. Cruelty is out there without doubt, but it is not ordinary and so its effects are extremely damaging for those who have endured it. Cruelty can be subtle and insidious, eating away at you for many years, and for some of us it culminates in this thing that gets called mental illness. It is difficult for society as a whole to accept such inhuman behaviour towards others, so it is simpler to label the injured party the problem – therefore 'least'. I reject the construct of 'least'. I have adopted the role of seeker. I work actively towards immersing myself in endeavouring to be the person I want to be every day, for every day presents new challenges. There are days when I get it horribly wrong, but I take solace in the fact that I continue to get another chance. Perhaps those demons from long ago were a clue. It was not them who could give me another chance: it was me. In my own mad way I was holding onto the hope of better things; even amongst the ruins of chaos, goodness survived.

A life of banality is not what I had imagined nor aspired to for myself. I make no apology for being a voice-hearer who is alert to those primal screams. I am wired to hear them; it seems I have little choice. My choice is whether I allow them to control me and the life I would choose for myself. Perhaps it is I who has finally gained insight!

Come: see real flowers of this painful world – Basho

Chapter 16

Myriad voices, myriad meanings

Review of the research into the subjective experience of hearing voices

Vanessa Beavan

Introduction

Despite a long history of voice-hearers' perspectives being ignored and invalidated, there has been a shift in recent years towards creating a forum from which they can be heard. Some voice-hearers are speaking out for themselves (Cockshutt 2004; Dillon 2010), some are being invited to express their views as research participants (Beavan 2011; Jones *et al.* 2003), and, more recently, voice-hearers are working as equal collaborators in research and publications (Romme *et al.* 2009).

In this chapter I will review the research into voice-hearers' subjective accounts of their experience. This will include voice-hearers from both clinical and non-clinical samples, as experiences from both groups appear to have much in common (Beavan 2011). Further, there is compelling evidence that it is more accurate and more helpful to view psychotic-like symptoms as occurring on a continuum of human experience, found within both clinical and non-clinical populations (Van Os *et al.* 2000).

Hearing voices is a private experience and as such cannot be adequately understood without reference to the descriptions and definitions provided by voice-hearers themselves. 'Objective' research into brain activity and behavioural responses, or data from questionnaires using standardized language, can and do provide important information. However, such approaches have been criticized as reducing a meaningful experience to a meaningless symptom, discounting the context and having little relevance to informing therapeutic interventions (Romme *et al.* 2009).

In the discussion that follows, I have organized the information around six themes that have been identified by voice-hearers as key components of their subjective experience (Beavan 2011). It is by no means a comprehensive review, but aims to give the reader a flavour of the myriad ways in which voices manifest and the effects they have on people's lives.

Voice content

Voice content can vary greatly, both between and within individuals. Voices can be encouraging and soothing, saying such things as 'You will manage' and 'It's not your fault.' They can be abusive, calling the person hurtful names or criticizing their behaviour. Sometimes voice content is mundane, sometimes incomprehensible. Some voice-hearers refer to music and noises such as laughing or gun shots as voices (Close & Garety 1998).

While voice-hearers may describe their voices as predominantly positive or negative, few report hearing exclusively good or bad things. This is true in both clinical and non-clinical samples (Belofastov 2004; Johns *et al.* 2002), although there is some evidence to suggest that a predominance of negative voice content may differentiate the two groups (Beavan & Read 2010; Close & Garety 1998; Honig *et al.* 1998).

Whether positive or negative, voice content tends to be meaningfully connected to the person's life (Beavan & Read 2010; Romme *et al.* 2009). In particular, a strong relationship has been found between past experiences of trauma and voice content (Read *et al.* 2003). Examples might include a sexual assault victim hearing sexually toned insults or a widow being comforted by her recently deceased husband.

Voice identity

Research evidence suggests that the vast majority (70–80 per cent) of voice-hearers can identify at least some of their voices (Beavan 2007; Close & Garety 1998). Voices come in many guises and may be attributed to persons living or dead, gods or spirits, and even animals. They tend to have a characterized identity, such as 'an angel', 'demons', 'my mother', or 'the birds'. Even when the person is unsure of who their voice is, they are usually able to recognize it and distinguish it from other voices, for example, 'that very critical female voice' or 'the red voice'.

Many people report that the voices sound like people they know or remind them of people they know (Beavan 2007). Leudar and Thomas (2000) found that most of their participants reported hearing voices of people that were known and significant to them. Further probing revealed that in many cases the voice was experienced as *like* a particular someone, not thought to actually *be* that someone.

Spiritual voices seem to be common in both clinical and non-clinical populations, with many people experiencing both benevolent and malevolent spirit voices. Several general population studies found that about half of their participants had at least some voices that were attributed to gods or spirits (Beavan 2007; Romme & Escher 1989).

Voice-hearers also commonly identify their voices as a part of themselves, though different from thoughts or inner dialogue. One study (Beavan 2007) found that a third of the participants had at least one voice they referred to as part of themselves. All reported being able to distinguish these voices from their self-talk. In their study of 50 voice-hearers with a diagnosis of schizophrenia, Hoffman *et al.* (2008) found that 80 per cent were able to differentiate their voices from their usual verbal thoughts 'most of the time' or 'always'.

For some voice-hearers the task of identifying a voice is easy, because the voice identifies itself directly. This was the case for 16 per cent of Birchwood and

Chadwick's (1997) clinical sample of 62 voice-hearers. For the majority of voice-hearers the task is somewhat more difficult, and the individual may have to infer the identity of their voices based on qualities of the voice, such as gender and tone (Leudar & Thomas 2000). Voice content seems to be the most helpful clue, used by almost 70 per cent of Birchwood and Chadwick's sample to identify voices. For example, critical or threatening voices may be identified as belonging to evil spirits or unseen enemies while encouraging and guiding voices may be identified as belonging to God or spiritual guides.

Relationship between voice-hearer and voices

Voice-hearers tend to develop relationships with their voices. Usually the person's experience of each relationship will be congruent with who they identify the voice to be and what the voice says. For example, people who hear angels complimenting and encouraging them tend to feel supported by and reverent towards those voices (Beavan 2007; Watkins, 1998).

Frequently, the relationships a person has with his/her voices will mirror 'real-world' relationships in a literal sense (Birchwood *et al.* 2000). For example, a victim of sexual violence may hear the voice of her perpetrator (Fowler 2000) or a widow might hear the voice of her recently deceased husband (Grimby 1993). Other times, this will manifest in a more figurative sense. For example, a victim of bullying might hear demonic voices that intimidate and humiliate him.

At other times the relationship seems to serve a protective function for people who find themselves in difficult life circumstances. For example, some people report having warm and loving relationships with their voices, even when the voices first started within the context of abusive situations. In a recent general population study (Beavan 2007), many participants recounted how they would hear the voice of a parental figure soothing them in times of distress or protecting them by alerting them to dangers. Some participants reported that this was the most – or the only – loving relationship they had at that time. This suggests that in some cases the relationship a person develops with their voices may be fulfilling a need for love and protection that they cannot find in their 'real-world' relationships.

Emotional impact of the experience

Voice experiences impact on people's lives. Sometimes what the voices say has an immediate emotional impact. For example, common reactions are anger and anxiety in response to abusive or threatening voices (Cheung *et al.* 1997). Often people report feeling perplexed after their first experience and even veteran voice-hearers still sometimes experience confusion and helplessness (Beavan 2007). Other negative aspects of the experience include interfering with work and relationships, disrupting concentration, and inducing shame (Miller *et al.* 1993).

Although research often focuses on the negative impact of voices, some recent studies suggest that voices can also contribute positively to people's lives (Romme *et al.* 2009; Sanjuan *et al.* 2004). Positive aspects of voices include being relaxing and soothing, providing companionship, giving helpful information or advice, and defending or protecting the person (Miller *et al.* 1993).

In general population samples, positive experiences of voices appear to be more prevalent than negative experiences. For example, in his epidemiological study of almost 20,000 people, Tien (1991) found that the proportion of non-distressing voices was much higher than that of voices associated with distress or interference with functioning. Using a student sample, Bentall & Slade (1985) found only a very small minority of their voice-hearing participants reported being troubled by the experience. In his study of bereavement hallucinations, Grimby (1993) found that all of the widowers and the vast majority of the widows described their voices in a positive way.

Comparisons of clinical and non-clinical samples show that although most participants from each group describe both positive and negative voice experiences, participants in clinical samples are more likely to report distress (Beavan 2007; Close & Garety 1998; Honig *et al.* 1998). However, it seems that for many of these people, negative voices are comparatively less distressing than other difficulties in their lives (Belofastov 2004). Further, reactions to voices can change over time (Close & Garety 1998). This may be related to changes in the voices themselves, or in the person's ability to cope with them (Romme & Escher 1989).

Finally, it is important to mention the significant role that stigma may play in exacerbating a person's emotional distress in response to their voices. The following excerpts (from Beavan 2007) highlight this:

> I'm very wary of saying I've been diagnosed with anything to do with schizophrenia, anything to do with hearing voices, because there's a lot of people who would think I was something dangerous if I told them. There's so much prejudice around them. I'm very careful of what I say to people.

> It's social suicide to mention that you hear voices.

Escher (2005) argues that the generally accepted view of voices as a symptom of mental illness creates a taboo that reduces the freedom people have to talk about their experience. Indeed, voice-hearers commonly keep their experiences to themselves (Beavan 2007). However, when voice-hearers find themselves in a safe and supportive environment in which they are not judged negatively but instead are asked curiously about their experiences, they tend to talk freely and find this beneficial (Coffey & Hewitt 2008; Lakeman 2000).

The voices are real

Voice-hearers are overwhelmingly consistent in their assertion that voices are real (Beavan 2007; Garrett & Silva 2003). Indeed, one voice-hearer asserts that attempting to conform to the shared reality of those around him and thus pretend the voices are not real is to be delusional (Cockshutt 2004).

One of the most compelling reasons that people believe their voices to be real is that the voices are usually experienced as a sensation; that is, they are perceived as coming through the auditory sense organ (Aggernaes 1972; Barrett & Caylor 1998). Other aspects that contribute to the sense of reality include loudness, vividness and acoustic clarity (Leudar *et al.* 1997). Also important are the personifying qualities of the voices, such as age, gender, accent and emotional tone (Leudar *et al.* 1997; Nayani & David 1996). Finally, the characteristic of 'involuntarity' (Aggernaes 1972) increases the sense of reality. Most voice-hearers believe it is impossible to alter the experience by simply wishing it to change; that is, they have little sense of control over their experience (Aggernaes 1972; Garrett & Silva 2003; Barrett & Caylor 1998).

Explanatory models

Both within and outside of the context of psychiatric services, voice-hearers' own explanations of their experiences are often considered delusional and evidence of a lack of insight. Voice-hearers are therefore rarely asked for their opinion about the cause of their experiences. If an opinion is offered it is frequently ignored. However, voice-hearers do generate explanations to account for their experiences and these merit consideration.

Research to date suggests that voice-hearers (in both clinical and non-clinical samples) show a strong tendency towards psychological and spiritual explanations over biological ones (Angermeyer & Klusmann 1988; Beavan 2007; Jones *et al.* 2003; Romme *et al.* 2009). Examples of psychological explanations include the effects of interpersonal trauma, abnormal cognitive processes and dissociated parts of the self, all of which are supported by the scientific literature (Baker & Morrison 1998; Lataster *et al.* 2006; Nayani & David 1996).

Examples of spiritual explanations include having a direct line to God, possessing psychic abilities, and communication with ancestors as a culturally normal phenomenon. Some people understand their voices as part of being paranormally gifted and draw on literature or scripture to support this. Other people feel less certain about the origin of their voices but find that thinking about their life history and spiritual beliefs can help to increase their understanding of the experience (Thomas *et al.* 2004). One general population study reported that two thirds of participants felt that a spiritual explanation accounted for at least some of their voice experiences (Beavan 2007).

Examples of biological explanations include references to brain dysfunction and the effects of both prescription and recreational drugs. These tend to be the least endorsed types of explanation (Angermeyer & Klusmann 1988). Cockshutt (2004) asserts that the reason many voice-hearers find medical explanations alone of little value is because they ignore the reality of voices and invalidate the experience.

Implications for understanding

Research into the experience of hearing voices, from voice-hearers' own perspectives and in voice-hearers' own language, has significantly contributed to our understanding of this phenomenon. When attempting to understand a private experience whose very existence may contradict our own belief system, it is important to acknowledge and put aside our own assumptions about reality and to respect the experiencer's report as equally valid (Naudin & Azorin 1997).

Commonly, the experience of hearing voices is understood (by non-voice-hearers) as no more than a symptom of severe mental illness, and in particular, schizophrenia. This association may be due to an understandable exposure bias that has led many mental health professionals to use exclusively pathological models of voice-hearing (Boyd-Ritsher *et al.* 2004). However, research suggests that this is neither an accurate nor a helpful model for understanding the complex phenomenon of hearing voices and does not fit with subjective reports. The majority of voice-hearers do not require input from mental health services (Romme & Escher 1989; Tien, 1991).

Voice identity, voice content and the social and psychological functions voices might serve are aspects that are very much de-emphasized, if not completely neglected, when voices are seen as a pathological symptom (Boyle 2006). Considering these aspects is crucial, however, if we wish to respect the subjective experience of the voice-hearer. Non-pathological models promote normalization of the experience, reduce stigma, and encourage recovery through meaning-making and integration of the experience into a person's life journey. The research presented here suggests that voice-hearing may be best understood as a variation of normal human experience that, while at times distressing, is best understood within the context of other significant life experiences and relationships.

Implications for practice

First, it is vital that people working therapeutically with voice-hearers acknowledge that not all voices are problematic. That is, not all voices cause significant distress or significantly impair the person's functioning. This is true even for those voices that occur within the context of a significant mental health problem. A careful exploration of voice characteristics should help both the clinician and the voice-hearer to come to discern which, if any, of the voices would be appropriate targets for intervention. The clinician should never assume the voice-hearer wants to be rid of all (or any) of their voices, although, of course, this may be the case for some clients.

Second, regardless of the clinician's own ideas about the origins and meaning of voices, they must endeavour to acknowledge the reality of the client's experience.

Third, clinicians should ask about who the voices are and what they say. Many clients will likely make spontaneous connections between their current voices and their past or present life experiences and relationships. This will be particularly so for poignant life events such as trauma. In such cases, it may be helpful to spend time working through the trauma or refer the client on to a trauma specialist, as this seems to have positive effects on the voices, as well as on the person's overall well-being (Beavan 2007; Romme *et al.* 2009). Some clients may not be able or willing to make connections between voice content and life experiences because it is too painful a process, or because there may be no connection.

Fourth, clinicians and clients should aim to develop a shared formulation about voice experiences (Morrison 2003), perhaps, in the process, gently challenging those explanations that seem unhelpful, particularly in terms of the power and omnipotence attributed to the voices (Chadwick & Birchwood 1995). Beliefs about voices may offer clues to helpful coping strategies and/or the most prosperous avenues for therapeutic intervention. In particular, clinicians should not discount the potential importance of spiritual understandings. If clinicians feel unable to address these issues with clients, they should be encouraged to refer the client to someone who is spiritually competent, or at least support the client in the process of seeking out such a person.

Finally, the stigma around hearing voices needs to be acknowledged, addressed and challenged. Some clients might benefit from information that normalizes the experience or from attending a hearing voices group for peer support. Clients and/ or their families may like to join an organisation such as the Hearing Voices Network (www.intervoiceonline.org), which provides training, support and information through accessible media such as pamphlets and the internet with the goal of promoting acceptance and reducing discrimination.

References

Aggernaes, A. (1972) 'The experiential reality of hallucinations and other psychological phenomena', *Acta Psychiatrica Scandinavica, 48*: 220–238.

Angermeyer, M. and Klusmann, D. (1988) 'The causes of functional psychoses as seen by patients and their relatives. I: The patients' point of view', *European Archives of Psychiatry and Neurological Sciences, 238*: 47–54.

Baker, C. and Morrison, A. (1998) 'Cognitive processes in auditory hallucinations: Attributional biases and metacognition', *Psychological Medicine, 28*: 1199–1208.

Barrett, T. and Caylor, M. (1998) 'Verbal hallucinations in normals. V: Perceived reality characteristics', *Personality and Individual Differences, 25*: 209–221.

Beavan, V. (2007) 'Angels at our tables: New Zealanders' experiences of hearing voices'. Unpublished PhD thesis, University of Auckland, New Zealand.

Beavan, V. (2011) 'Towards a definition of "hearing voices": A phenomenological approach', *Psychosis: Psychological, Social and Integrative approaches, 3*: 63–73.

Beavan, V. and Read, J. (2010) 'Hearing voices and listening to what they say: The importance of voice content in understanding and working with distressing voices', *Journal of Nervous and Mental Disease, 198*: 201–205.

Belofastov, A. (2004) 'Listening to voices: A grounded theory analysis of verbal auditory hallucinations'. DPsych thesis Victoria: Monash University, Australia.

Bentall, R. and Slade, P. (1985) 'Reality testing and auditory hallucinations: A signal detection analysis', *British Journal of Clinical Psychology, 24*: 159–169.

Birchwood, M. and Chadwick, P. (1997) 'The omnipotence of voices: Testing the validity of a cognitive model', *Psychological Medicine, 27*: 1345–1353.

Birchwood, M., Meaden, A., Trower, P., Gilbert, P. and Plaistow, J. (2000) 'The power and omnipotence of voices: Subordination and entrapment by voices and significant others', *Psychological Medicine, 30*: 337–344.

Boyd-Ritsher, R., Lucksted, A., Otilingam, P. and Grajales, M. (2004) 'Hearing voices: Explanations and implications', *Psychiatric Rehabilitation Journal, 27*: 219–227.

Boyle, M. (2006) 'Developing real alternatives to medical models', *Ethical and Human Psychology and Psychiatry, 8*: 191–200.

Chadwick, P. and Birchwood, M. (1995) 'The omnipotence of voices II: The beliefs about voices questionnaire (BAVQ)', *British Journal of Psychiatry, 166*: 773–776.

Cheung, P., Schweitzer, I., Crowley, K. and Tuckwell, V. (1997) 'Violence in schizophrenia: Role of hallucinations and delusions', *Schizophrenia Research, 26*: 181–190.

Close, H. and Garety, P. (1998) 'Cognitive assessment of voices: Further developments in understanding the emotional impact of voices', *British Journal of Clinical Psychology, 37*: 173–188.

Cockshutt, G. (2004) 'Choices for voices: A voice-hearer's perspective on hearing voices', *Cognitive Neuropsychiatry, 9*: 9–11.

Coffey, M. and Hewitt, J. (2008) ' "You don't talk about the voices": Voice-hearers and community mental health nurses talk about responding to voice-hearing experiences', *Journal of Clinical Nursing, 17*: 1591–1600.

Dillon, J. (2010) 'The tale of an ordinary little girl', *Psychosis: Psychological, Social and Integrative Approaches, 2*: 79–83.

Escher, A. (2005) 'Making sense of psychotic experiences'. *Department of Psychiatry and Neuropsychology*. Maastricht: Maastricht: University, Netherlands.

Fowler, D. (2000) 'Psychological formulation of early episodes of psychosis: A cognitive model'. In M. Birchwood, D. Fowler and C. Jackson (eds) *Early Intervention in Psychosis*. London: Wiley.

Garrett, M. and Silva, R. (2003) 'Auditory hallucinations, source monitoring, and the belief that "voices" are real', *Schizophrenia Bulletin, 29*: 445–457.

Grimby, A. (1993) 'Bereavement among elderly people: Grief reactions, post-bereavement hallucinations and quality of life', *Acta Psychiatrica Scandinavica, 87*: 72–80.

Hoffman, R., Varanko, M., Gilmore, J. and Mishara, A. (2008) 'Experiential features used by patients with schizophrenia to differentiate "voices" from ordinary verbal thought', *Psychological Medicine, 38*: 1167–1176.

Honig, A., Romme, M., Ensink, B., Escher, S., Pennings, M. and Devries, M. (1998) 'Auditory hallucinations: A comparison between patients and non-patients', *Journal of Nervous and Mental Disease, 186*: 646–651.

Johns, L., Hemsley, D. and Kuipers, E. (2002) 'A comparison of auditory hallucinations in a psychiatric and non-psychiatric group', *British Journal of Clinical Psychology, 41*: 81–86.

Jones, S., Guy, A. and Ormond, J. (2003) 'A Q-methodological study of hearing voices: A preliminary exploration of voice hearers' understanding of their experiences', *Psychology and Psychotherapy: Theory, Research and Practice, 76*: 189–209.

Lakeman, R. (2000) 'Helping people cope with voices'. *Mental Health Nurses for a Changing World: Not Just Surviving*. Broadbeach: Queensland, Australia.

Lataster, T., Van Os, J., Drukker, M., Henquet, C., Feron, F., Gunther, N. and Myin-Germeys, I. (2006) 'Childhood victimisation and developmental expression of non-clinical delusional ideation and hallucinatory experiences: Victimisation and non-clinical psychotic experiences', *Social Psychiatry and Psychiatric Epidemiology*, *41*: 423–428.

Leudar, I. and Thomas, P. (2000) *Voices of Reason, Voices of Insanity: Studies of Verbal Hallucinations*. London: Routledge.

Leudar, I., Thomas, P., Mcnally, D. and Glinski, A. (1997) 'What voices can do with words: Pragmatics of verbal hallucinations', *Psychological Medicine*, *27*: 885–898.

Miller, L., O'Connor, E. and Di Pasquale, T. (1993) 'Patients' attitudes towards hallucinations', *American Journal of Psychiatry*, *150*: 584–588.

Morrison, A. (2003) 'Cognitive therapy for people with psychosis'. In J. Read, L. Mosher and R. Bentall (eds), *Models of Madness: Psychological, Social and Biological Approaches to Schizophrenia*. Hove, East Sussex: Brunner-Routledge.

Naudin, J. and Azorin, J. M. (1997) 'The hallucinatory epoche', *Journal of Phenomenological Psychology*, *28*: 171–195.

Nayani, T. and David, A. S. (1996) 'The auditory hallucination: A phenomenological survey', *Psychological Medicine*, *26*: 177–189.

Read, J., Agar, K., Argyle, N. and Aderhold, V. (2003) 'Sexual and physical abuse during childhood and adulthood as predictors of hallucinations, delusions and thought disorder', *Psychology and Psychotherapy: Theory, Research and Practice*, *76*: 1–22.

Romme, M. and Escher, A. (1989) 'Hearing Voices', *Schizophrenia Bulletin*, *15*: 209–216.

Romme, M., Escher, S., Dillon, J., Corstens, D. and Morris, M. (2009) *Living with Voices: 50 Stories of Recovery*. Ross-on-Wye: PCCS Books in association with Birmingham City University.

Sanjuan, J., Gonzalez, J., Aguilar, E., Leal, C. and Van Os, J. (2004) 'Pleasurable auditory hallucinations', *Acta Psychiatrica Scandinavica*, *110*: 273–278.

Thomas, P., Bracken, P. and Leudar, I. (2004) 'Hearing voices: A phenomenological-hermeneutic approach', *Cognitive Neuropsychiatry*, *9*: 13–23.

Tien, A. (1991) 'Distributions of hallucinations in the population', *Social Psychiatry and Psychiatric Epidemiology*, *26*: 287–292.

Van Os, J., Hanssen, M., Bijl, R. and Ravelli, A. (2000) 'Strauss (1969) revisited: A psychosis continuum in the general population?' *Schizophrenia Research*, *45*: 11–20.

Watkins, J. (1998) *Hearing Voices: A Common Human Experience*. Melbourne: Hill of Content Publishing Company.

Part VIII

Delusional beliefs

Along with hearing voices, delusional beliefs are commonly considered to be archetypal symptoms of 'psychosis', and are often referred to in clinical literature as 'bizarre' or 'un-understandable'. The two chapters which follow challenge both of these assumptions, demonstrating that if we attend more to the person's experience and life history, we see that the beliefs are understandable and meaningful as well as being closely related to other ordinary experiences, such as the common human tendency to read meaning into others' behavior.

John Wraphire provides us with a rich and detailed description of his experience, allowing us to enter into his world and get a sense of what it felt like to be him at that time. Like Debra Lampshire in her chapter, he identifies his social sensitivity and his experiences of rejection as contributing to his social isolation, which in turn allowed his reading of meaning into others' behavior to become amplified and distorted, although certainly not un-understandable. He identifies contact and support from others as being pivotal in his recovery; as in previous accounts, we also see his increased sense of agency – as manifested in his decision to come off medication and leave mental health services – as being important contributors to his coming to live a life of his own choosing.

Michelle Campbell and Anthony Morrison's overview of research into the subjective experience of delusional beliefs provides further support for the position that psychotic experiences, including delusional beliefs, are meaningful, and can be seen to be so if one attends to the life experiences and concerns of the individual. Like many of the previous chapters, themes of sense of identity, relationships with others and the experience or fear of negative evaluation by others in social situations are identified as among the primary concerns of those who experience delusional beliefs.

Chapter 17

Deluded loner

John Wraphire

Introduction

This chapter will explain the delusions I experienced between the ages of 16 and 20. I will explain exactly what my delusions were, what may have caused them and how they were treated.

Early life

I had quite a happy early childhood. I had supportive parents, friends, and I enjoyed school. But my parents weren't doing so well together. One night I heard them yelling and breaking plates. Another night I saw my parents with policemen in the bathroom. Dad was standing naked with patches of blood over his body. When I was five my parents separated. Dad moved into an apartment. Mum had to sell the house, and over a ten-year period she moved five times. I lived at dad's place on weekends and at mum's on weekdays. I attended three primary schools because mum moved often. Mum didn't like the company of other children so I was usually alone at mum's place. I preferred dad's place because I could play with children in the neighbourhood.

When I was seven dad suffered a serious fall while drunk and paralyzed his left side. Dad could no longer use his left leg or hand well. My best friend and I thought it was unfortunate that dad could no longer take us bike riding. We thought his accident made him grumpy. Dad drank alcohol almost every night, which would often make him irritable. It was rare for a weekend to pass without dad and I arguing. On numerous occasions dad told me, 'You've got your brains in your bum' or, 'You've got no common sense.' His words never lowered my confidence in my intellect; they just made me avoid him.

As a child I was socially sensitive. I have a memory of being laughed at by two men when I was around eight. I guessed they were laughing at my shorts, so I never wore those shorts again. It may have been the first time that I was conscious about my appearance. I never discussed my sensitivity with my parents as I didn't believe they could help me.

One night, when I was 14, dad – in one of his silent and serious moods – passed me his half-eaten plate of chips. He didn't tell me what he wanted, so I had to guess. I guessed he didn't want the rest of his chips, so I put them back in the bag I was eating from. At this he called me a 'selfish bastard'. I had had enough, and without explaining to him the misunderstanding, I left and decided never to see him again. As a result, I no longer saw my best friend, who I'd known for eight years.

I now lived at mum's place full-time. In my bedroom I watched television, ate my meals and used my computer, so I didn't spend much time with mum. Mum used to come home from one of her jobs, angry to see I had yet again not washed the dishes. After yelling at me, mum would do the dishes loudly. Every loud clang was a message to me: 'I'm angry that you haven't done the dishes.'

In the later years of secondary school I lacked confidence socially. I couldn't think of much to say, so I was often quiet. I thought I was a loner with no friends, and I guessed that others thought this too. I didn't want others to think this of me, so I pretended to be confident. I couldn't ask people what they thought of me, as that would reveal my weakness, so I listened to them and I looked at their body language to find out.

One day I wasn't feeling confident about my appearance. My hair gel hadn't flattened my hair the way I wanted. A man in a passing car looked at me, then combed his hair back with a hand. At that moment I believed he was telling me 'your hair looks bad'. I believed he felt his own hair as messy when he saw my hair, and combed it back to satisfy his need to flatten it. Looking back now, I still believe he reacted because of what he saw. An observer watching someone eat a sour lemon may salivate. A supporting observer of a rowing team may also rock his own body in time with the rowers. His reaction was no coincidence. I knew what he was thinking. My mistake was that I believed he knew that I knew that his reaction revealed what he was thinking. I now believe he was not particularly aware of his reaction and therefore didn't intend to send a message.

I used to come home after difficult, lonely days at school and listen to the album 'Division Bell' by Pink Floyd. I particularly liked the song 'Keep Talking' which I played for hours. I think my repeated listening made me further isolate myself from other students. Some of the lyrics were: 'I sit in the corner, and no one can bother me . . . my words won't come out right . . . but I can't show my weakness.'

A loner with no friends

In one class, when I was 16, I sat still and silent while other students talked and laughed with each other. With nothing to say I made my face expressionless and stared at the table in front of me. I listened and watched with all my peripheral vision for any signs of what they were thinking about me. One person said: 'He's like a rock.' One person stuck up for me, saying: 'Don't talk about him like that.' On other occasions: people said: 'I don't know [why he's so quiet], he was fine at camp', 'He's got no friends' and 'He's such a loner.' People were saying what I believed about myself. Although expressionless, I was full of pain. I began avoiding classes where I might be teased. I am certain I did not sense hallucinations, although I think I occasionally misheard people's words as what I expected they would say about me. I dreaded going to school. I told myself that age 16 was the hardest year of my life.

I decided to leave secondary school and enrol into tertiary school. All the new students were beginning as strangers, so I felt socially equal with everyone. It was an opportunity for me to make friends, but before long classmates would talk and laugh with each other, while I sat silent and alone. They spent break times together, while I spent break times playing video games.

I believed that the more often people saw me on my own, the more likely they would think, 'He is a loner.' I came to call these people 'acquaintances'. I felt more comfortable with strangers, because strangers hadn't seen me numerous times and therefore realized I was a loner. Strangers became acquaintances when they saw me numerous times on my own and would then be likely to think, 'He is a loner.'

As a Caucasian in a multi-racial city, I felt comfortable with people of certain races and uncomfortable with others. I was more comfortable with non-Caucasian, non-Westernized, very young or very old people, as I felt they did not judge me. I described these people as being 'in their own world'. The people who I believed judged me were usually Caucasian or Westernized and between the ages of 15 and 40. I would call these people the 'white middle class'. These people, including myself, had a habit of comparing their strengths and weaknesses against others. I described these people as being 'socially aware'. I further categorized these people as sympathizers or perpetrators. Sympathizers knew I was a loner but didn't try to hurt me. Perpetrators knew I was a loner and tried to hurt me or couldn't avoid hurting me because it was their habit to compare themselves against myself.

Interpreting body language and sounds

A scene from a Mr Bean episode nicely demonstrates some of people's actions that I used to interpret as messages. In this scene, Mr Bean, about to make a purchase, looks around at all the people in the shop, clears his throat to get their attention, and with an expression of pride displays his credit card for everyone to see. All his actions were a message for others: 'Look at me, I'm so great, I have a credit card.' In my case, I interpreted even more subtle human actions as messages, such as the sound of a person moving a chair, a person moving a body part in my direction, a brief glance at me, a cough, or even the sound of swallowing. I generally interpreted these actions, much like Mr Bean's throat-clearing sound, as the suggestive statement 'I'm better than you'. I will refer to these actions as 'suggestive actions'.

Additionally, I came to associate certain external sounds with certain ways to compare myself against others. To give some examples, I associated the sound of birds chirping with attractiveness, the sound of cars passing or keys jingling with financial wealth, and the sound of a train passing with employment status. If I was with another who I thought was judgemental of me, and we could both hear birds chirping, I thought it reminded us both of attractiveness and I thought we were both comparing our attractiveness against each other. I will refer to these sounds as 'third-party sounds'. I thought all socially aware people made these associations. I thought everyone thought the same way I did.

My delusions often involved both a person's suggestive action and a third-party sound. One example is when I was in a classroom with one young male classmate. I thought he was arrogant and liked to feel dominant. We heard people outside (this is the third-party sound), which reminded me I was a loner. I believed that the classmate was also thinking I was a loner, so I felt ashamed. The classmate then cleared his throat (this is one suggestive action) and glanced at me (this is another). These suggestive actions carried the message: 'I have friends like they do, but you don't' or 'You're a bit of a loner, aren't you?' The suggestive actions also confirmed what I guessed he was thinking.

Another example is when I was in a classroom with one female student and I heard people outside talking about unattractive people (third-party sound), which made me compare my attractiveness with the female student's. I began to think I was more attractive than her and I believed she was thinking the same thing. At this moment I dared not make any suggestive action (sound, movement, silence or stillness). A suggestive action would reveal that I was thinking: 'The people outside are talking about unattractive people, and you're unattractive yourself.' So I avoided coughing, glancing at her, turning my head in her direction (if I was within her vision). If I was typing I would keep typing at the same speed and volume, even if I had nothing left to type in my work. If I was still I would try to remain still. If I happened to be shaking my leg I would keep shaking my leg at the same rhythm. If I happened to be silent, I would continue my silence. I tried to keep my sounds and movements constant, and not irregular or outstanding and suggestive. If a few seconds had passed and I'd not made a suggestive action, I could then continue my work without offending her.

Students often said I had no friends. Every time the word 'friend' was spoken I was reminded of my lack of friends. I became afraid of the word 'friend'. I also developed a physical reaction to this word. In class I tried to be very still and appear confident, but whenever the word 'friend' or even the sound 'fr' was spoken I would uncontrollably jolt out of my stillness. I wondered if classmates saw me physically react and if they knew why.

When I was 18, after another year of constant difficulty, I left tertiary school without finishing. By now I had made one friend – someone I had met via email. I had become religious after six months of religious teachings. I decided to follow one instruction in particular from the Bible: 'Have no fear . . . because your Father has approved of giving you the kingdom. Sell the things that belong to you . . . Make . . . a never-failing treasure in the heavens' (Luke 12: 32–33).

Still living with mum, I discarded all possessions from my bedroom, including my childhood toys, and years of school workbooks. I erased five years of data from my computer. My room became empty. I minimized my possessions to a backpack, a change of casual and formal clothes, and the Bible. I slept on a sun bed and I lived in my cupboard to reduce the ability to communicate by sound with my neighbour. Because he was African, the sound of passing cars or of a toilet flushing (third-party sounds) reminded me that Caucasians have been technically advanced. If a car passed and I then made a sound, the sound would carry to him the message: 'Whites have been more technically advanced than you.' Eventually I began using my computer and the internet again. The internet allowed me to communicate with people without being judged by them. I lived in the cupboard for around three months, coming out only for food and the bathroom. On my 19th birthday dad phoned me. I decided to resume communication with him for the first time in five years.

Mum grew angry about my lifestyle and after an argument I left home. I decided I'd be homeless and work in fast-food restaurants for food and money. Wearing layers of clothing, with my Bible and computer in my backpack, I caught a bus to the city centre. I sat next to a man sleeping and began reading the Bible. I tried to appear confident, but the well-dressed people on this cold Friday night pitied me, and I felt ashamed. At midnight I phoned dad and caught a bus to his place. After eight days and another argument with dad I went to mum's for three days, during which I found my own place to live.

In my first rented place I arranged my room to minimize my ability to hear and send sounds. I positioned my mattress on its side against the wall next to me. The bed base was turned upside down, diagonally positioned above me with one end on a table behind me and the other end on the ground near my feet. I slept on a camping mat underneath the bed base. The landlord's bedroom was next to mine, and I believed I was communicating with him by sound. Because he was Māori, the sound of motorbikes passing (third-party sound) reminded me of gangs. If a motorbike passed and I then made a sound, the sound would carry to him the message: 'Many gangsters are Māori, and you are Māori.' After a few months I moved into a sleep-out, which I again set up to minimize my ability to hear and send sounds. Because I considered one tenant unattractive, the sound of chirping birds reminded me that I thought she was unattractive, and I thought she and other tenants thought the same. If I or another tenant were to then make an irregular sound, the sound would carry to her the message: 'Birds are attractive, but you're not.' Because I thought all people on the property were poor financially, there was no relative weakness, and so sounds following the sound of passing cars couldn't mean 'I'm rich but you're not.' Because we were all unemployed, there was no relative weakness, and so sounds following a passing train couldn't mean 'I have a job but you're unemployed.'

Because sounds happened almost all the time and because people were often within earshot, the exchanges of messages were frequent. People were constantly comparing themselves against me. People's thoughts were no longer private. People often revealed the cruel things they were thinking about me. I had been communicating with people in this way for around three years. I knew if I couldn't hear or see people then I couldn't receive their messages. I contemplated damaging my hearing and sight to achieve this, though I never did. One night, alone in my sleep-out, lying on my camping mat under my bed base, with my computer on my lap connected to the internet, I made my television sound static noise at maximum volume, and I wore ear muffs and a blanket around my head. Finally I couldn't hear any other person or sound. I felt great peace of mind.

Seeking help

Increasingly I queried the accuracy of my beliefs. I wondered how other people could deal with all the non-verbal communication. I told my family doctor: 'I think I may be paranoid.' I had recently learned the word 'paranoid' and related it to my experience. She said: 'Because you think you are paranoid, there is a problem.' She asked: 'Do you hear voices?' I said that I didn't, but she stated on the psychiatric referral that I 'may hear voices', so as to raise the urgency of the assessment. The next day I was visited by two nurses and a psychiatrist who interviewed me for an hour. Three days later I was told I had schizophrenia. I became very uncertain about my thoughts and senses. I learned that schizophrenia was misunderstood and feared, so I didn't tell people my diagnosis. I began regular sessions with a psychiatrist, a psychologist and an occupational therapist. I also began taking medication.

Anti-psychotic medication

I took mainly haloperidol and risperidone. The medication caused unpleasant reactions including tiredness, shaking arms and weight gain. The most bizarre reactions were absence of semen during orgasm, difficulty reopening my eyelids while blinking, and difficulty reopening my jaw while chewing food. It used to take me 30 minutes to eat a bowl of mixed vegetables. The most unpleasant reactions were the panic attacks. My psychiatrist encouraged me to move into residential rehabilitation. I worried what living there would be like, but after a pleasant visit I decided to add myself to the waiting list. I spent my days waiting at mum's place, lying on my bed, looking at the cracks in the ceiling, listening to a Christian radio station. My shaking arms prevented me from falling asleep easily, so I used to wait for the evening to take the medication, so I could become tired enough to fall asleep and escape the conscious day.

Residential rehabilitation

After a month of waiting, I moved into residential rehabilitation. The residents followed a program of activities including cleaning, food shopping, cooking, outings, counselling and therapeutic workshops, all of which I enjoyed. I formed many friendships with the residents and staff. We residents seldom discussed our experiences. We simply accepted each other as housemates and got on with the lives we now had.

During the panic attacks I felt like my thoughts were accelerated and my emotions were amplified and I was hypersensitive to what people were thinking about me. Every panic attack I had started when I was with people, and usually stopped when I was alone. During an attack I felt a strong need to be alone so that the attack had a chance to stop. Sometimes I'd have an attack during sessions with my psychologist or psychiatrist. One day an attack began while I was cycling to my friend's house. I thought everyone was thinking I was a loner with no friends. I kept my head lowered in shame. I remember how clearly and in so much detail I could see the ants on the pavement. I travelled at speed hoping I would hit a car and somehow derail the panic attack. Panic attacks felt horrible and I had no control over them. After months of attacks I told the residents and staff that I was considering suicide. I considered kneeling head first in front of a freight train after midnight. One night I made a private, thorough plea to my then God to end the attacks. Surprisingly, the next morning I had no attack, but I waited in fear for their return. Strangely, they never returned.

Leaving the mental health system

Now 20, I told my psychiatrist I wanted to come off medication. Coming off medication successfully was unheard of. I'd heard people can get worse when they stop medicating. She cautioned that if my 'voices' became worse I would need to be put on stronger medication. I told her that I'd never heard voices, so I then realized that my psychiatrist had mistakenly understood that I had been hearing voices. My medication was tapered off. I waited for any bad reaction. To my relief I began to feel much better. My energy levels rose greatly and all the unpleasant effects of the medication disappeared. I felt so fortunate to be off medication.

At 21 I moved into a second rehabilitation residence with less staff supervision and more independence. At 23 I left the mental health system altogether. Over the following decade I gained a degree and an enjoyable career. However, most of my friends are still in the system. Four have died, two of them by suicide. I now mistrust much of the mental health system and believe that its motive seems to be to produce money, not to produce health, having seen the documentary *Psychiatry: An Industry of Death*.

Nowadays, I am a lot more confident than I used to be. My friends like me and they even think I'm funny. However, I'm still tense when with acquaintances. I'm not good at chit-chat, which seems to be the way people become friends, so I think I'm missing opportunities to make friends. I avoid informal gatherings such as parties, but I enjoy formal gatherings, such as sport or an educational class. I feel very different to most people, and I like to spend my free time alone or with my partner. I am still teased on occasion for being different or for being alone, usually by groups of teenagers. To their surprise I now confront them and ask why they teased me. I tend to call myself an introvert, but it's more helpful to realize that I am the confident person I want to be when I am with my friends or family.

Implications for understanding

I think that the cause of my social difficulties was having few friends. Had I spent more time with my family, I would have gained more social skills, friends and confidence from an early age. My lack of communication with people caused my beliefs about people to become inaccurate and unverified.

Being diagnosed with schizophrenia was unhelpful. Schizophrenia is unspecific and it did not identify my unique experience. The most accurate way to identify my experience was to identify my specific delusions. My experience cannot be further summarized. It cannot be simplified into one word and it cannot be identified in one hour. It's hopeless to treat schizophrenia, but it's quite possible to change beliefs. Additionally, schizophrenia is misunderstood and feared, and is associated with hallucinating, which I did not do.

The medication made me tired all day, gave me twitches and made me want to end my life. The medication could never have changed my delusions into accurate beliefs. Medication helped in no way and was the worst thing I did for myself.

Implications for practice

Residential rehabilitation was most helpful as the activities and the friendships I formed there occupied my mind and replaced my delusions. The sessions with my psychologist allowed me to talk about and make sense of my delusions. Interestingly my delusions were replaced long before I made sense of them. Over the years my various social, spiritual and intellectual achievements have given me greater confidence. People now see me as the confident person I've wanted them to see.

My delusions are now a memory. Had I not sought help I may have ended my life. However, I value my experience because it was a unique and strange experience of life, which no one else has the ability to experience.

Chapter 18

Subjective experiences of delusions and paranoia

Michelle L. C. Campbell and
Anthony P. Morrison

Introduction

The following chapter will review research that has examined people's experiences of delusions, with a particular focus on paranoia, and conclude with some emerging ideas about the implications of these studies for understanding delusions and paranoia and how this knowledge could improve clinical practice.

The subjective experience of delusions

It is beginning to be acknowledged that exploring the subjective experience of delusions is an important area of study. For example, Rhodes & Jakes (2000) examined people's experience of delusions in terms of motivational themes. From their experience of providing cognitive therapy, these authors explain that the content of people's delusions seems to relate in various ways to aspects of their life and concerns. They interviewed 14 participants all of whom had received a diagnosis of a psychotic disorder. They asked participants about personal problems and goals and about their delusional beliefs. First, a list of 6 motivational categories was created (social connection, competence, experiential, material, direction and evaluation). Essentially, this study highlights the importance of life experiences in making sense of the content of delusions and to emphasize this point Rhodes & Jakes quote Jung (1914: 162): 'These symptoms immediately became comprehensible when considered from the standpoint of the individual's previous history.' A similar notion has been expressed by Laing & Esterson (1970:12): 'Our question is: are the experiences and behaviour that psychiatrists take as symptoms and signs of schizophrenia more socially intelligible than has come to be supposed?'

Rhodes & Jakes also refer to the idea that most psychological distress relates to unmet fundamental human needs (Gilbert 1989). For example, it is explained that persecutory delusions are an expression of a feeling of being an outsider to the group, which relates to people's fundamental need for affiliation. Gilbert concludes that it is beneficial to consider key aspects of delusions as symbolizing the actual problems and aims of the individual. Thus, the subjective aspects of the experience of delusions are strongly emphasized.

More recently, Rhodes *et al.* (2005) carried out a qualitative study analyzing the content of delusional beliefs. They conducted semi-structured interviews with 25 people who had received a label of 'severe mental illness' in order to investigate the range of manifest themes of delusions. Delusional themes identified in participants' discourse were categorized into six domains: negative self, negative interactions, special self, identity and relationships, specific mental experiences, and entities. Participants tended to have specific sets of themes. For any individual these themes could be drawn from diverse domains. For example, one participant expressed themes in the domains of special self, entities, and identity and relationships. It is notable that no two participants had the same pattern of theme domains. This suggests that people's experiences of delusions do not fall into neat sets according to type of delusions. Rather, individuals' delusions tend to have complex, interconnected themes from different domains. The authors also emphasize how different two of the participants' persecutory delusions are, even though they fall into the same category (i.e. persecution). The authors conclude that people express various themes in their delusional beliefs and that, most importantly, these sets of themes usually interconnect to form a meaningful whole. The idiosyncratic nature of people's delusional beliefs is highlighted and it is suggested that mental health professionals would usefully appreciate this in their interactions at work.

Drinnan and Lavender (2006) explored the relationship between religious beliefs and religious delusions using semi-structured interviews that aimed to allow participants to talk openly and reflectively about their experiences. All seven participants were involved with mental health services. An overarching theme of 'negotiating identity' was established and four sub-themes seemed to be related processes. They highlight the role of early life experiences in the formation of the content and nature of delusional beliefs. It was noted that all participants had religion in their background but, importantly, their religious delusions were heavily influenced by other factors such as difficult family experiences. A central point highlighted by participants was that they often felt their religious ideas were dismissed by mental health professionals. It seems that this understandably led them to feel reluctant to discuss these issues. This is a point that mental health professionals must pay attention to in order to improve practice and enhance the efficacy and acceptability of the care offered.

Research examining subjective experiences of paranoia

Two published studies (Boyd & Gumley 2007; Campbell & Morrison 2007) that have focused on the subjective experience of paranoia will be considered in detail.

Boyd & Gumley's study

These authors interviewed ten people who had experiences of persecutory delusions, using a standard definition (Freeman & Garety 2000). All ten participants had experienced severe mental health problems. These interviews focused on what the word paranoia meant to these individuals. The data gathered was analyzed using a 'social construction' version (Chamaz 1990) of grounded theory methodology (Glaser & Strauss 1967).

To summarize their findings the authors proposed a core process of 'fear and vulnerability'. The sub-categories of 'confusion and uncertainty' and 'self under attack' were considered to contribute to the core process and it was these processes which appeared to lead to the development of 'safety systems'. *Figure 18.1* illustrates how these themes of paranoia were found to interact.

From the interview data 'fear and vulnerability' appeared to be the most important theme. For example, when Participant 6 was asked about what the word paranoia means for him he replied: 'It means fear.'

Within the sub-category of 'confusion and uncertainty' Boyd & Gumley note that these feelings are a core aspect of the subject's experience of paranoia. Certain factors (voices, fall outs, drugs, and sleep deprivation) were found to make these feelings worse. For example, for some participants voices eroded their trust in the self and others and increased their uncertainty. Participant 9 stated:

> But you can hear voices sometimes, sometimes the voices add to the paranoia. Voices can add to it and add it on and if you're daft enough to go with the voices they can antagonize it and they can make it worse.

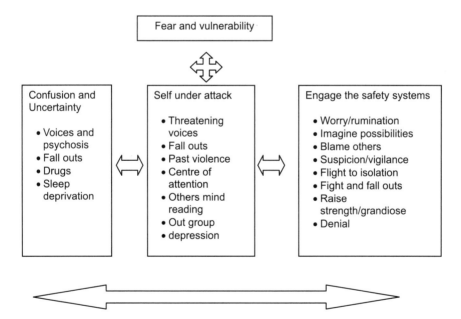

Figure 18.1 Diagram to show how the themes of persecutory paranoia interact.
Source: Boyd & Gumley (2007).

With regard to the sub-category of 'self under attack' the authors note that an important aspect of the experience of paranoia is to feel as though one is under attack. The source of this attack was varied, as noted in *Figure 18.1*, but often the attack was internally generated, such as when an individual thinks that others are saying critical things about them. For example, Participant 7 said:

> I thought they were listening all the time [laughing]. When I think about it it's quite funny. As if that's all people have got to do with their time. But I thought everyone was that interested in my life, I thought I was all they had to think about.

Within the sub-category 'engage the safety systems' the authors explain that participants were repeatedly placed in situations which left them feeling confused and uncertain. They also felt under attack and therefore fearful. In response to this people activated their safety systems, which include various processes as outlined in *Figure 18.1*. These systems appeared to have a positive effect in the short term but were ultimately self-perpetuating. For example, Patient 9 talks about the effect staying in the house and not coming out had on his paranoia:

> Makes it worse. Better being out talking because then you know what's going on. Better the devil you know than the devil you don't know. If you're not talking to the devil you don't know what is going on and then you start imagining and your imagination can run riot.

Boyd & Gumley (2007) conclude that paranoia evolves as a mechanism to keep oneself safe in dangerous situations. They emphasize that the participants were often responding to genuinely frightening experiences. The authors highlight the usefulness of using social constructionist grounded theory in their endeavours as this approach recognizes that knowledge is created by social processes, that knowledge and social action interact (Burr 1995). This approach necessitated that the researcher understood the participants' reality through using their language, by accepting their experiences as valid and by working collaboratively to develop a shared understanding of paranoia. This is a therapeutic endeavour in itself.

Campbell and Morrison's study

The primary aim of the study was to explore people's subjective experience of paranoia (Campbell & Morrison 2007). Secondary aims included comparing the responses of those who had received a psychiatric label with those with no psychiatric history and exploring people's beliefs about paranoia and experiences of trauma. A qualitative semi-structured interview design was adopted. Twelve participants took part in the study. Six had received a diagnosis of a schizophrenia spectrum disorder and experience of paranoia; the other six had no psychiatric history. The non-clinical group did have experience of paranoia as identified on the Peter's delusions inventory (Peters *et al.* 2004).

Interviews lasted 60-90 minutes and focused on the following: the content of the person's paranoid thoughts; the person's beliefs about their paranoia; the person's thoughts about the function of their paranoia; whether the person had experienced any trauma in their lifetime and whether the individual made any links between these experiences and their paranoid thoughts. The transcripts were analyzed using interpretative phenomenological analysis (IPA). The aim of IPA is to explore participants' views of the world (Smith 1996) and, as far as possible, to adopt an insider's perspective (Conrad 1987). Simultaneously, IPA recognizes that research is a dynamic process in which the researcher has a role to play by providing his or her own interpretation of the data gathered (Smith *et al.* 1999). So, the analyst attempts to make sense of participants' attempts to make sense of their own experiences.

After analyzing the data, four main themes emerged: the phenomena, beliefs about paranoia, factors that influence paranoia, and consequences of paranoia (see *Table 18.1* for a summary of all themes and sub-themes identified).

Each superordinate theme will be described and examples of some of the master themes and their sub-categories will be given, using quotes to illustrate the

Table 18.1 Emerging themes in people's subjective experience of paranoia

Theme 1: The phenomena	Theme 2: Beliefs about paranoia	Theme 3: Factors that influence paranoia	Theme 4: Consequences of paranoia
Content of paranoia Perception of harm Intention of harm Type of harm Acceptability of belief	**Positive beliefs about paranoia** Re-evaluation Protection	**Unusual perceptual experiences** Control Promote paranoia	**Emotion** Anxiety Fear Anger
Nature of paranoia Confusion Dynamic process Origin of paranoia	**Negative beliefs about paranoia** Control Conflict	**Biased information processing** Loose association Personalizing	**The self** Self-perception Self-esteem Splitting of self
Insight into paranoia Causes Remoteness from reality		**Past experience** Severity Impact	**Behaviour** Defence Controllability Harm to self
		Factors that alleviate Safety Re-appraisal Setting limits Medication	

richness of the data. Reference will also be made to the similarities and differences observed between the clinical and non-clinical groups.

'The phenomena' describes what the interviewees experience when they refer to paranoia. The content of paranoia was the first master theme in this category. Central to the content of people's paranoid thoughts was the notion of harm. This was similar for the clinical and non-clinical groups as both perceived current or future harm as central to the experience of paranoia. Interestingly, both groups acknowledged to some extent that they had only weak evidence to support this.

> In the past five years it has been experiences of believing that people are talking about me. Sort of, if you walk in on a conversation and people laughing and believing it's about me.
>
> (Claire, non-clinical group)

An important difference between the clinical and non-clinical groups was the type of harm envisaged. The non-clinical group often talked about less intense harm whereas the clinical group often spoke about serious physical or psychological harm:

> I can be suspicious, you know, about what people might say behind my back because I just don't know.
>
> (Jacob, non-clinical group)

> Well I suppose it was like the big brother thing but I had no consent . . . I thought everything was a big plot and people were just watching me.
>
> (Tara, clinical group)

The nature of paranoia was the second master theme in this category. The experience of confusion, for example, was described by both groups as part of their experience of paranoia:

> I mean you want to trust people, I want to be friendly with everybody and not upset anybody but it is hard sometimes because for no reason people don't like you and I think well why? What have I done?
>
> (Sandra, non-clinical group)

The third master theme in this category considers how both groups gave some thought to how reality-based their paranoid ideas were. Here, the two groups differed with regard to the extent that they acknowledged how removed their ideas could be from reality. The non-clinical group tended to acknowledge explicitly that their ideas could be remote from reality whereas the clinical group tended to talk more about the strangeness of their ideas.

> Sometimes it could be a complete figment I think.
>
> (Jacob, non-clinical group)

I thought even the taxi driver knows me ... and I thought he is being especially nice to me because he knows he is on the telly, you know it is really, really strange.

(Tara, clinical group)

The 'beliefs about paranoia' that participants expressed could be divided into two sub-categories: positive beliefs about paranoia and negative beliefs about paranoia. This is consistent with recent cognitive conceptualizations of paranoia (Morrison 2001; Morrison *et al.* 2005). One of the central differences between the two groups was that the clinical group spoke about their negative beliefs about their paranoia mostly in the context of the fact that they believed they were powerless in relation to their paranoid thoughts, whereas the non-clinical group spoke about their beliefs about being able to take control over their paranoid thoughts.

Well it is a feeling that you are not really in control of your life when people are sort of plotting against you, or that sort of thing. You don't really have any control [text omitted] over your life.

(Ralph, clinical group)

One of the main similarities between the groups with regard to positive beliefs about paranoia was that both felt that paranoia could protect them from future danger or harm:

I think sometimes that other people might think that I am being a bit funny but I have got to protect myself.

(Sandra, non-clinical group)

If I, say I was in the pub for instance, and an argument was getting aggressive, I would go, you know.

(Andy, clinical group)

'Factors that influence paranoia' could affect participants' paranoia either for better or for worse. For example, the first master theme in this category was unusual perceptions and both groups talked about their unusual perceptions worsening their paranoid thoughts either by providing evidence for their ideas or by adding to the content.

Well in the evidence I, ummm, I was hearing voices.

(Andy, clinical group)

Both groups also talked about the influence their past experiences had upon their paranoid ideas:

I am suspicious of what people do behind closed doors in a sense, you know James had this completely other life [text omitted] when it comes to anything beyond friendships I am instantly suspicious of men's motives and I think it has really coloured my view of men in that sense.

(Collette, non-clinical group)

Similarly, with regard to alleviating factors both groups talked about the importance of feeling safe. However, this was done differently by the two groups. The non-clinical group spoke about themselves in safe contexts, i.e. as having achieved a feeling of safety in some aspect of their life, whereas the clinical group talked about their desire to feel safe and seemed to indicate that this feeling was missing from their lives; this feeling appeared completely missing when their paranoid thoughts were at their worst.

I don't get scared on the streets on my own, I do feel quite safe. I take it for granted that I am quite tall and I don't think . . . I am an easy target.

(Collette, non-clinical group)

The mind can't relax for me but it is only when I get home that I feel safe, but then I still don't feel safe, sometimes [I think] that they know where I live and they are going to knock on my door.

(Chris, clinical group)

The 'consequences of paranoia' were highly varied, but a predominant theme across groups related to anxiety and fear:

I am scared of them hurting me, distrusting me. I would rather not know people and not know that they have talked about me rather than let someone in and trust them and then to find out that they have done something.

(Sandra, non-clinical group)

The findings of this study are supportive of the notion of a continuum of paranoia (Strauss 1989; Van Os *et al.* 2000) where fears about negative social evaluation are at the lower end and paranoid ideas are at the top end. Both groups spoke about their experience of paranoia and many similarities in content were observed. For example, all participants spoke about paranoid thoughts relating to the prediction of harm coming to them and many participants spoke about the confusion that ensues when one experiences paranoia. Importantly, all participants spoke about the negative consequences of anxiety and fear in relation to their ideas; some also spoke about the notion of being 'split' or 'in two minds' with regard to their paranoid thoughts. Despite these negative consequences, based upon this research into subjective experience it appears that the function of paranoia relates to an attempt to protect oneself from predicted harm by, for example, being 'on the look out' or avoiding dangerous situations. Factors that seemed to worsen paranoia included unusual perceptual experiences and negative past experiences. Significantly, negative past experiences seemed to provide evidence for paranoid thoughts and to influence the content of these ideas.

There were also some noticeable differences between the groups. One of the most striking differences was the issue of control. The clinical group felt controlled by their ideas whereas the non-clinical group spoke about ways in which they gained control over their thoughts. This may relate to another important difference between the groups: how safe people felt. In general, the non-clinical group spoke about having achieved feelings of safety, which served to reduce their paranoid thoughts, whereas the clinical group spoke about how difficult it was for them to achieve a feeling of safety. Another difference between the groups related to the intensity of harm that was anticipated. The non-clinical group tended to refer to less intense harm whereas the clinical group spoke about serious physical and emotional harm. Furthermore, participants differed in the degree to which they thought their ideas were reality based with the clinical group being more likely to speak about the 'strangeness' of their thoughts than their possible distance from reality.

This analysis is rich with examples of experiences of paranoia from people's daily lives, which highlights that paranoia is a multifaceted and complex but understandable and meaningful experience.

Implications for understanding

With reference to delusional beliefs in general, it is strongly indicated that people's life experiences have a major impact upon the content of their ideas. It is through asking people about subjective experiences that this becomes apparent. When the full impact of life experiences on delusions is acknowledged it is understandable that people do not simply hold one type of delusional belief but express ideas from various domains (Rhodes *et al.* 2005). For example, a person having paranoid ideas in the negative-self domain as well as the special-self domain may appear contradictory but this is explicable when we consider that a person's early life may have encompassed these conflicting themes. The constellations of people's delusional ideas are highly idiosyncratic, yet still meaningful and interconnected. It seems that delusional beliefs relate to the fundamental concerns in a person's life (Rhodes & Jakes 2000) which are likely to be associated with unmet fundamental human needs (Gilbert 1989). Research which focuses on the subjective experience of delusions is able to capture these issues because its focus is on individuals' personal meanings.

From the research studies that examine the subjective experience of paranoia specifically, it seems that persecutory delusions are a psychological defence mechanism, the ultimate aim of which appears to be to protect the individual from harm. However, whilst paranoia helps people to anticipate threat and be alert for danger, this comes at a cost; some of the negative consequences of paranoia are anxiety, fear and a restricted life. Thus, the mechanism which aims to protect (paranoia) becomes a cause of additional psychological harm (e.g. reduction in functioning, low self-esteem).

Implications for practice

With regard to delusional beliefs generally, it would be beneficial if mental health professionals try to fully understand people's whole delusional framework. It seems that such an endeavour will aid clinicians and researchers to better understand and appreciate a person's psychological pain as well as their aims for recovery. In addition, acknowledging the influence of people's life experiences in the development of their delusional framework is likely to be a validating and therapeutic process. This matter would need to be sensitively approached with the client, given that part of the function of delusional beliefs may be to shield the person from acknowledging the distress associated with early experiences. It would be useful for clinicians to acknowledge the impact of people's life experiences in the development of their delusions, as often this may provide clues about how to intervene and provide acceptable support.

The research exploring the subjective experience of paranoia reinforces the notion of these ideas functioning as a defence mechanism. With reference to paranoia specifically, it seems that fear and vulnerability are central. Therefore, clinicians and supporting family members could usefully make it a priority to help people gain feelings of safety in their immediate environment. Establishing what can be done to support people to do this is an important first step. If basic issues of safety are compromised it is futile to intervene to reduce people's paranoia. Mental health services would be able to offer a superior service if clinicians acknowledged the function of psychotic experiences for the individual and incorporated this knowledge into their interactions with service users. Further, a relevant factor in people experiencing paranoia was the feeling of being out of control, so assisting people to increase their feelings of agency will help to counteract these feelings. Any interaction with people who experience psychosis could be seen as an opportunity to achieve this. For example, this may be about enabling someone to say 'no' – e.g. to refuse treatment – or helping them to have a voice in meetings or in relationships. Interpersonal interactions with those with psychosis are essential if we are to work alongside these individuals to help them achieve their goals. If clinicians, family members, friends and co-workers approach these interactions in a compassionate manner we will considerably improve the likelihood of recovery for those diagnosed with psychosis.

References

Boyd, T. and Gumley, A. (2007) 'An experiential perspective on persecutory paranoia: A grounded theory construction', *Psychology and Psychotherapy: Theory, Research and Practice, 80*: 1–22.

Burr, V. (1995) *An Introduction to Social Constructionism*. London: Routledge.

Campbell, M. and Morrison, A. P. (2007) 'The subjective experience of paranoia: Comparing the experiences of patients with psychosis and individuals with no psychiatric history', *Clinical Psychology and Psychotherapy, 14*: 63–77.

Chamaz, K. (1990) 'Discovering chronic illness: Using grounded theory', *Social Science and Medicine, 30*: 1161–1172.

Conrad, P. (1987) 'The experience of illness: Recent and new directions', *Research in the Sociology of Health Care*, *6*: 1–31.

Drinnan, A. and Lavender, T. (2006) 'Deconstructing delusions: A qualitative study examining the relationship between religious beliefs and religious delusions', *Mental Health, Religion & Culture*, *9*: 317–331.

Freeman, D. and Garety, P. A. (2000) 'Comments on the content of persecutory delusions: Does the definition need clarification?' *British Journal of Clinical Psychology*, *39*, 407–414.

Gilbert, P. (1989) *Human Nature and Suffering*. Hove: Erlbaum.

Glaser, B. G. and Strauss, A. L. (1967) *The Discovery of Grounded Theory: Strategies for Qualitative Research*. Chicago: Aldine.

Jung, C. G. (1914) 'The content of the psychoses'. In *The Psychogenesis of Mental Disease*. London: Routledge and Kegan Paul.

Laing, R. and Esterson, A. (1970) *Sanity, Madness and the Family*. London: Tavistock Publications.

Morrison, A. P. (2001) 'The interpretation of intrusions in psychosis: An integrative cognitive approach to hallucinations and delusions', *Behavioural and Cognitive Psychotherapy*, *29*: 257–276.

Morrison, A. P., Gumley, A., Schwanneauer, M., Campbell, M., Gleeson, A. and Griffin, E. (2005) 'The beliefs about paranoia scale: Preliminary validation of a metacognitive approach to conceptualising paranoia', *Behavioural and Cognitive Psychotherapy*, *33*: 1–12.

Peters, E., Joseph, S., Day, S. and Garety, P. (2004) 'Measuring delusional ideation: The 21-item Peters *et al.* Delusions Inventory (PDI)', *Schizophrenia Bulletin*, *30*: 1005–1022.

Rhodes, J. and Jakes, S. (2000) 'Correspondence between delusions and personal goals: A qualitative analysis', *British Journal of Medical Psychology*, *73*: 211–225.

Rhodes, J., Jakes, S. and Robinson, J. (2005) 'A qualitative analysis of delusional content', *Journal of Mental Health*, *14*: 383–398.

Smith, J. A. (1996) 'Beyond the divide between cognition and discourse: Using interpretative phenomenological analysis in health psychology', *Psychology and Health*, *11*: 261–271.

Smith, J. A., Jarman, M. and Osborn, M. (1999) 'Doing Interpretative Phenomenological Analysis'. In M. Murray and K. Chamberlain (eds) *Qualitative Health Psychology: Theories and Method*. London: Sage.

Strauss, J. S. (1989) 'Subjective experiences of schizophrenia: Toward a new dynamic psychiatry: II', *Schizophrenia Bulletin*, *15*: 179–187.

Van Os, J., Hanssen, M., Bijl, R. V. and Ravelli, A. (2000) 'Strauss (1969) revisited: A psychosis continuum in the normal population?', *Schizophrenia Research*, *45*: 11–20.

Part IX

Negative symptoms

Another of the typical characteristics of psychosis (specifically associated with the diagnosis of schizophrenia) relates to a group of experiences referred to as 'negative symptoms'. Essentially, these refer to the loss of a range of experiences, with particular emphasis given to the apparent loss of the experience of emotions. The two chapters in this section explore these so-called negative symptoms, both convincingly showing that if we take into account the subjective experience of the individual concerned, we are forced to question our assumption that how someone appears to us on the outside is a good indicator of how the individual feels from the inside: those who are deemed to be experiencing negative symptoms are in fact troubled by intense, overwhelming emotions, not by the absence of them.

Eleanor Longden's personal account of her experience not only provides us with clear evidence of the stark contrast between how she felt (overwhelmed by emotion) and how she appeared to others ('vacant and disinterested') but also shows us that having one's subjective experience so invalidated by those around can exacerbate the underlying problems of isolation, feelings of powerlessness and uncertainty about the self. Failing to consider the subjective experience of the other risks not only missing important aspects of what is going on for the person, but also inadvertently acting in ways which aggravate the person's predicament by replicating the circumstances which contributed to this in the first place.

James Le Lievre and colleagues' chapter on research carried out in this area focuses on James' qualitative research into the subjective experience of negative symptoms. In addition to providing further evidence of the presence of intense emotions, they also identify important aspects of the processes involved in reaching the state of 'negative symptoms', including being not acknowledged by others and feeling confused in interpersonal relationships.

Chapter 19

Negative symptoms
More, not less

Eleanor Longden

Ten years ago, when I was 18, I went mad. 'Gone mad' is what people sometimes say, as if madness is a direction or a place; a discrete destination. But that is not what madness is, for when you go mad you don't actually go anywhere, you remain exactly where you are. And a different person arrives instead. The doctors called it schizophrenia; I referred to it by other names, which better expressed my misery and confusion. I struggled artfully with my psychosis and revelled in the whole frenzied repertoire: the voices, the visions, the bizarre intractable delusions and that cruel, infinitely prolonged living death of anguish and isolation that tortures you beyond endurance and bleeds you, through exhaustion, hopelessness and loss of self-respect, into a shadow of your former self. My face, whenever I could bring myself to look in the mirror, was pinched and pallid. As white as a sheet. And I felt flat, pale, worn. I felt threadbare. But what will I do when I'm so worn, so white?

In some ways, of course, I was one of the lucky ones. I had a loving family, a tenacious resolve to recover, and a chance meeting with a sensitive, creative psychiatrist who valued me and my potential and who saw beyond the degraded, hopeless exterior and reached out to the person in pain beneath. Together, they guided and negotiated me out of my dark, subconscious world. The voices became thinner, greyer and harder to hear. I no longer stepped sideways out of my own time (only to wake and find that the world had gone on without me). In a way it was startling to realize how starkly attractive madness could sometimes be – how coolly watchful, reasoned and commanding. I flattered myself that I had been beautifully mad, like something from a poem.

But shockingly – ironically – a fresh horror now began: because finally I was sane enough to realize how mad I had been. I was surrounded by the wreckage of my life and it clung to me, funereal and weighty, carved into my memory like a brand. It felt as if I was stumbling, blindly snatching handholds and seeking salvation, but then suddenly all hope would be lost and I'd pitch down helplessly, loudly and clumsily, without grace or restraint, gathering speed and shock and grazes. My life lay behind me in a vast expanse of wasteland, the colour of hell-flames, blazing in my mind like a Sodom at which I dared not look back. That was my subjectivity and my reality and I couldn't even express it, because it was too overwhelming. I couldn't let myself start to cry, because I'd never be able to stop; couldn't get angry or I'd scream forever. You become too tired to stay awake (that gasping, grinding fatigue), yet too restless to sleep (because what dreams might come?). You're irritable, miserable, hopeless and lifeless and no amount of comfort is ever enough. I had a silent, suspended misery about me; at other times I felt black and sluggish and lethal. Even when I smiled I still looked sad. *Nothing* was a word I associated with myself.

Truly, though, it's hard to explain; descriptions of despair are only ever approximations. Sometimes you need to move away from the imprecision of words, to the silences hidden between speech.

And so, slowly, unwittingly, I began to withdraw. Maybe I was just removing myself from things; maybe that was my idea of freedom, to purchase some cheap brand of absolution. (Cheap: an intriguing word – most assistance in my life was costly and medical and unexciting.) The possibility of escaping from the world in this way (so simple and painless, so effective) began to consume me, lingering above my head like the raw-boned, rangy haloes of medieval saints. And so I went for hours, then days, without speaking. I huddled in corners, softly crooning to myself. I muttered my name over and over to reaffirm that I was still there: Eleanor, Ele-a-nor-nor. (*Nor must madness unwatch'd go.* Mad? Am I? Apparently so.) I felt the weight of my own emptiness, lost in the blackness within my own body, and I began to fantasize about finding my missing half, a twin who would heal and complete me and make me whole. I felt utterly alone, my thoughts veering frantically between jarring screams and despairing whimpers. Occasionally it seemed as if I had forgotten *how* to think. At other times I felt frenzied and terrified, gazing at the world through smoked glass in which everything was shadowed and grotesque. My despair was a dark fragment like a bruise, a patch of syrupy, fleshy blackness pulsing inside me like a living thing. From the outside? To onlookers I appeared silent, dry-eyed and impassive. And in a way I admired myself; I got through the days.

But then memories began to surface, memories which had been buried for years, partly banished by the numbing, sweaty nubs of sulphur-yellow pills. Memories of being pillaged then discarded, bruised and dripping – *please don't hurt me, please, please*. No wonder I was mad. The fear and horror prevented me from moving, and my body would stiffen and empty itself of feeling. *If I can just stay still*, I thought, *I'll survive. I'll be safe and I'll be free.* Animation could hurt my chances, and I intended to last, albeit desolate and infused with grief. Ironically, considering I'd suffered greatly at university, I constructed a memory of a garden I used to visit whilst a student and still sane. I'd gone there partly because it was always empty, but mostly because I'd loved its untamed beauty and the earthy, pagan wildness of its sudden twists and niches. It was a Tennyson garden, a skewered fairy tale with rumours of the future in it. I'd loved its gently curving cavities, the way the path unfurled, and how the air suffused and shivered as if in fever. But most of all I loved the roses. They were coarse and wild, unlike the blowsy, pampered blooms that grew in the main gardens, where the earth was tilled and as straight as a hair parting. I'd felt that if I held a mirror above them it would mist over with their breath. They dotted through the bushes in clusters of small red explosions. Like Aztec hearts, the garden laughed with roses. And so, because reality was so shocking and painful, that's where I would go. It was my background noise, my sickness and its cure.

Gradually, I became aware of the doctors conferring: my 'illness', it would seem, had taken a new and vicious turn. My affect was 'grossly abnormal, profoundly disrupted'. I was too vacant and disinterested, too depersonalized: there was, they said, disturbing evidence of 'negative symptoms'. A crisis hospital admission was legislated. Hauled onto a strange ward, I studied the peeling, institutional corridors and the sad, drab faces of the other patients, their colours fading like tropical fish drying out on a beach. I could hear a nurse saying what a shame it was, how I was pretty, intelligent (seemingly) and had let it go to waste. 'She's from a good home,' said one. I felt guilty, as if I had committed a crime. Even here, I wouldn't fit in – I wasn't even mad in the right way. A tired-looking doctor came in and jerked my forehead back with his hand. I tried to focus on his face but it was impossible; one moment he had a ghastly skull's smile, then his features would soften and disperse as if soaked in water. 'Completely psychotic,' he said. 'Look at her pupils, they're fixated. Come here,' he instructed the others, 'take a look.' They all leaned in to inspect my feverish, twitching eyes, and I could sense the dislike and pity in their faces as they picked away at my psyche, as if I had deliberately betrayed myself and rubbed a genie's lamp for accomplishment and beauty, then chosen insanity and degradation as the third, final wish. My story seemed as archaic and outmoded as a folktale, the kind of story that should never happen now, not in these days of modern medicine. One of the rare catatonic schizophrenics! Occasionally I tried to smile, or even laugh. My cheerfulness was a performance, a clutch at normality, but they did not smile back so I stopped. 'It would be better for her if she had cancer,' said the consultant, glancing up from her notes. 'At least it would be easier to cure.' My mother was advised not to visit me, although she was desperate to. She sent me cards with bright, loving messages, which the nurses mislaid and forgot to pass on. Where had they gone, the people I could love? They might as well have vanished – as I had. I was also a missing person.

Sat in the smoking room, I gazed once more at my fellow patients. They looked like birds whose wings had been clipped, or wrecked, broken butterflies with pleading eyes. Maybe we were wishing the pain would stop, even though we knew wishing did not apply. Maybe we were longing to hear someone call our names, because that way we would no longer be renounced and unclaimed. Perhaps we would have tried to claim each other, had we had the energy, if we had not been so numb and so absorbed. How diffident we were! As pale and abstracted as bad thoughts, keeping our eyes to the ground and observing the world in short gasps, like sips. Yet we were still flesh and blood, as framed and free as the elements, and charting our dark inner space. We were relentless and craving, we saw into the future, we saw the interminable, we saw the immortals.

'No,' said the consultant. 'You see nothing. Nothing at all.'

One of the first things I did on the ward was set fire to my arm. I did it with a cigarette lighter and a bottle of bleach and at the time I wasn't even sure why I'd done it, except that it was an absolution of a kind, a charred and blistered scream. It was the second time in my life that I'd opted for such flagrant self-immolation, and any sympathy the staff may once have felt was swiftly replaced by irritation. 'People like you!' hissed the nurse, 'You make a mess of yourselves and expect us to clean it up.' With a neat flick of her forefinger she opened a sinister-looking yellow bottle, poured its contents onto my singed flesh and began to scrub. The skin slid off and soon there were puddles of blood on the floor. I began to sob in a dry, desperate sort of way, and tried to explain that this was my stigmata. My voice sounded like a phantom, like something dying: a thin, keening gasp of exhausted pain. 'So you can talk when you want to,' said the nurse triumphantly. She swaddled the oozing mess in gauze and pushed me out of the door. 'You'll live,' she said.

Later. 'Did the voices make you do it?' asked another nurse as I sat, swathed in bandages and cowed in misery and humiliation in the office. 'No,' I replied in a flat, monotone voice. 'It was because I didn't know what else to do.' But I couldn't really begin to explain what it had been like. I didn't have the words for it. *How that sinuous wound opened and darkness welled up. And I cried through it, my body cried for me.* 'I was desperate,' I said feebly. It was hard to talk, as if my mouth was too full of teeth. The nurse doled out a smile and said, 'I see,' although she clearly didn't. What she was really thinking is, 'How could you do this to yourself? How *could* you . . .?' with an implication that trailed off unfinished. But I could tell from her insouciance and cool indifference that what she really thought was, '*Could I end up like you?*' as if my madness was labile and therefore contagious. I was an invalid, or at least one who has been invalidated. No identity. No point. I felt like I was 80 years old – I was 18.

The doctors were polite but sceptical and disinterested – and intent, it seemed, to sacrifice me on an eerie altar of science. This left me fearful and wordless, burning in obliterating, outraged silence, and after that I resolved to tell them nothing more. My story would be secret and without sound, and I would keep my sorrow to myself. How to sort through the skeins of my ravelling mind? '*She doesn't want to live in the real world*,' said the nurses. But what kind of criticism was that, when reality was so painful and inadequate, so fragmented and pointless and endless? I vowed I would shift within the awareness of myself, in this world just beyond reality. And I would go on, I would persevere, be silent, suspended and obscure. I would wrap myself in discretion like a fog and fight my psychic civil war alone. My mind would be its own secret province, an uncharted territory known only to me. I would fling back my shoulders, charge, meet these medical adversaries unaided and alone. Drum roll, curl of smoke and fire. My yearnings would be pinned to the war that I'd heard being waged on the brink of the unknown; for I also wanted to know, and to join the combat, to live and die as part of the fighting host, without reservation, without commentary. A voluptuous mindlessness. And then I wanted to run away to the edge of infinity, tear out to the horizon and meet myself on the other side. Because I knew that very slowly they were killing me (even though they would never let me die) and I wanted an invisible wreath of vengeance on my grave, garlanded with roses. I was a dreamer in a fluid body, dreaming that I was awake – even though in dreams of this place I was always lost. I couldn't strive for myself any longer, for I knew now what I couldn't learn before: that there is never only one, of anyone, and this was my life on a blended web of yarn, good and bad together. I had been so used by others that I hadn't known how to experience my own self. This realization was my brief moment of escape. A fleeting look, a feeling, a shuddering sigh. And yet, and yet. I knew that it was no good, not really. According to them, this was not creative, nor a search for identity, nor even catharsis. For they had told me so, they had shown me: '*You have paranoid schizophrenia.*' And out of all the moments, that was the worst.

I played with the psychiatric paradigm, and came to realize that I had no choice. Hope? Or was it despair? One or the other. But in reality I did not have the courage to feel hope. It would have been avoidance, escapism. It would have been bad luck. I felt that I would rather have been out of life than let myself be torn and mutilated by this birth that I couldn't possibly survive. Me, the doctors, we were destructive opposites like matter and anti-matter, like black and white. Us and them. Matter exists only spiritually to represent some idea and body. But it does. Matter. And this means I am damaged, it means I am unfit. (Unfit for what? I don't know. They didn't say.) And so I submitted to this version of events, submitted to what was happening to me, let go of my will and suffered the loss of myself. I wanted to believe that there was more to me than this, more than met the eye. But to them the eye could be deceived through posture, positioning and iconography, through distilled light and discerning shafts of vision. What you see is what you get (except it never was), and to them little was revealed when we sat eye to eye. The all-seeing I. Hollow. Unclean, you might say. I suppose you might say that.

In the end the surliness and stillness which led me to resist the doctors' probing and refuse medication earned me a place in 'The Annexe'. This chamber was little more than a padded cell, and I was aware of being watched through the grille in the door. This silent observer would have seen a girl crouched on the floor, her matted blonde hair coiling across the tiles, her eyes flickering yet fixed on nothing. No affect, they would have said. No emotion. The air in the annexe was thick and curdled, with heavy, reeking sediments sinking in the corners, and my mouth tasted metallic from the blood in it. What I'd hoped for was sudden realizations and resurrections. Not this silence. Not like this. I'd wanted to believe that this was a story I was telling, a story that had happened to someone else. *Dear You, I'll say . . . whoever you are. And I know that you will listen to my story, just as one day I will hear yours when we meet.* Who was I telling it to? No one, yet everyone. The same person as children do, when they write their names in the snow.

Suddenly, there on the Annexe floor were roses. But they were not as I'd remembered. These things were monsters, a slaughterous shade of red and shining with the same wetness as blood. I was drowning in their crimson faces. The thorns ripped my skin, already bruised and inflamed from the doctor's needles. My head filled with blackness and the sound of silence, and the last thing I remembered was the sigh of the rose petals as they drifted down and enveloped my breaking heart.

Implications for understanding

When first exploring the positive–negative dichotomy in the repertoire of 'schizophrenia' symptoms, clinicians sought to characterize the degradation and diminution – the loss – of normal functioning and subjective life. Since then, researchers have refined and honed that repertoire to clinically capture the patient's (lack of) emotional responsiveness and experience. Thus, affect is inappropriate, or 'blunted', or impoverished. Such individuals are socially withdrawn. They exhibit signs of alogia, avolition, anhedonia. They are without feeling.

Based on the experience of myself and others, I would propose that the opposite is nearly always true. The paradox is that we are not devoid of emotions, we are overwhelmed and crushed by them. Studies actually suggest that psychotic patients report comparable, and in some cases greater, emotional experiences than non-clinical controls (see Kring & Germans 2004). The discrepancy is in how this is expressed. Frequently, 'a paucity of affect' relates only to the articulation of one's feelings, not the feelings themselves. This incongruity is driven by the misguided assumption that objective assessments of emotion, as made by psychiatric professionals, accurately correspond to the subjective life of the individual under scrutiny (Sass 2000). This is an important issue, because a diverse and meaningful emotional life has traditionally been denied individuals designated 'schizophrenic'; emotion is either dismissed as disturbed and disorganized, or else presumed to be entirely absent. Yet the notion that emotionality communicates one's humanity reinforces the cultural conclusion that those with psychosis are less than fully human (Jenkins 2004). I vividly remember being inspected by a junior doctor for signs of 'blunted affect' (I would later learn that he was undertaking an exam and my consultant had deemed me a suitable case study for 'negative symptoms'). He was a nice man in many ways, replete with eager, clumsy kindness. But the detached, clinical authority with which he attempted to dissect my emotional life was genuinely shocking. After a cursory inspection, he delivered his verdict with a triumphant flourish – 'extreme poverty of emotional and cognitive responsiveness' – while the consultant nodded her approval. Had he (or anyone) taken the time and trouble to discuss this with me, I would have told them I felt like I was being ripped apart from the inside. Ironically, I had spent the time before this interview drawing a picture of a girl (clearly identifiable as myself) in a Munch-like attitude of frenzied, screaming despair. The nurse who came to escort me to the psychiatrist's office found these tortured scribblings grotesque and morbid, and told me as much. 'It's just as well,' she said pitying, 'that you're going to see a doctor.'

Implications for practice

Professionals should be mindful of the grave risks in presuming they can reliably judge internal states simply by observing them; any assumptions should be respectfully compared with the subjective account of the person themselves. Exposure to well-meaning yet overbearing and arbitrary assessments of my emotional state was infuriating, disorientating and deeply disempowering. Instead, clients should be invited to share their subjective experience (whether verbally, in writing, or though expressive arts), and have it received with respect, humility and compassion.

For some individuals, withdrawal functions as a preventative coping strategy. Those who have 'shut down' emotionally are likely to be experiencing extremes of fear, despair and fragmentation. My own experience of this reflected a fundamental need to disconnect from a world with which I had ceased to identify or desire to know. Or, at other times, it protected me from the shocking, unsettling impact of voices or flashbacks. In clinical terms, staff should attempt to understand the nature/cause of the client's experiences and focus on how to help them feel physically and emotionally safe (Watkins 1996). A crucial aspect of this is ensuring that care is continuous by using the same workers, all operating in a consistent, congruent way. A parade of different faces, telling you different things, and with often wildly contradictory opinions on your prognosis and the nature of your distress, does not help to create safety and security. This is one of the reasons I am greatly in favour of crisis houses as opposed to hospitalization, due to their potential for preventing further fragmentation (Mosher 2008). Such places embody the traditional idea of 'asylum' – a sanctuary offering safety, protection and refuge. Organized around consumer-orientated principles, such as peer-support and empowerment, these healing atmospheres not only avert many of the perils of hospital admission (forced admission, traumatic treatment, lack of control/collaboration), they also foster a safe space in which sharing and exploring one's subjectivity becomes more feasible and inviting.

Supporting someone who has shut down emotionally is not an easy task, yet something as simple as a willingness to tolerate and respect their withdrawal is key. Constructive, hopeful and optimistic messages are important. Conversely, punishing, punitive approaches (in which experiences are trivialized or condemned) are soul-destroying. They can also be dangerous. Trying to forcibly impair someone's coping strategy is like compressing a spring – it considerably ups the stakes, and I do not believe workers have a right to do this unless they have something better to offer. Similarly, the focus on language-based interventions (from structured psychotherapy to simply haranguing for responses to conversation) is often inappropriate and restricted. I remember a helpless sense of 'How do I express the inexpressible? How do I talk about my fear, when to articulate that I'm afraid is, in itself, frightening?' If someone is extremely detached or depersonalized, mindfulness or grounding techniques (e.g. Chadwick *et al.* 2005) may be of some benefit for calming and re-orientating them. It's easy to spend too much time in your head. Getting back into your body can be much more consoling. Needless to say, patience on the part of professionals is an important requisite in this process, as is the ability to tolerate reticence and refusal; it may take a long time before someone is ready to express their subjectivity and share their story.

Conversely (and particularly in institutional settings), low industry and motivation may be better explained by external factors, such as a lack of stimulation, or infantilizing, disempowering care. I once spent three months on a ward in which the only available activities were a stack of board games and a CD player, but my requests for more to do were always met with the response that I 'wasn't well enough'. Encouraging and supporting self-sufficiency is therefore crucial. Similarly, the crushing impact of neuroleptics means that many 'negative symptoms' are often better explained as side effects of anti-psychotic medication (Barnes & McPhilips 1995). It may be helpful in the short-term of emotional crisis to soothe the person through sedation, but in the long term I believe it diminishes recovery prospects, simply because coping with emotion is not learned.

References

Barnes, T. and McPhillips, M. (1995) 'How to distinguish between the neuroleptic-induced deficit syndrome, depression and negative symptoms in schizophrenia', *International Clinical Psychopharmacology*, *10*: 115–121.

Chadwick, P., Taylor, K. and Abba, N. (2005) 'Mindfulness groups for people with psychosis', *Behavioural and Cognitive Psychotherapy*, *33*: 351–359.

Jenkins, J. (2004) 'Schizophrenia as a paradigm case for understanding fundamental human processes'. In J. H. Jenkins and R. J. Barrett (eds) *Schizophrenia, Culture and Subjectivity: The Edge of Experience* (pp. 29–61). Cambridge: Cambridge University Press.

Kring, A. and Germans, M. (2004) 'Subjective experience of emotion in schizophrenia'. In J. H. Jenkins and R. J. Barrett (eds) *Schizophrenia, Culture and Subjectivity: The Edge of Experience* (pp. 329–348). Cambridge: Cambridge University Press.

Mosher, L. (2008) 'Soteria and other alternatives to acute psychiatric hospitalization: A personal and professional view', *Journal of Critical Psychology, Counselling and Psychotherapy*, *8*: 184–196.

Sass, L. (2000) 'Schizophrenia, self-experience and the so-called 'negative symptoms'. In D. Zahavi (ed.) *Exploring the Self: Philosophical and Psychopathological Perspectives on Self-Experience* (pp. 149–182). Amsterdam: John Benjamins Publishing.

Watkins, J. (1996) *Living with Schizophrenia: An Holistic Approach to Understanding, Preventing, and Recovering from 'Negative' Symptoms*. Melbourne: Hill of Content Publishing.

Chapter 20

The subjective experience of negative symptoms

Characteristics of emotional withdrawal

James A. Le Lievre, Robert D. Schweitzer and Alan Barnard

According to the diagnosis of schizophrenia in the DSM-IV-TR (American Psychiatric Association 2000), negative symptoms are those personal characteristics that are thought to be reduced from normal functioning, while positive symptoms are aspects of functioning that exist as an excess or distortion of normal functioning. Negative symptoms are generally considered to be a core feature of schizophrenia. However, negative symptoms are not always present in those diagnosed, and a diagnosis can be made with only negative or only positive symptoms, or with a combination of both.

Negative symptoms are said to include an observed loss of emotional expression (affective flattening), loss of motivation or self directedness (avolition), loss of speech (alogia), and a loss of interests and pleasures (anhedonia). Positive symptoms include the perception of things that others do not perceive (hallucinations), and extraordinary explanations for ordinary events (delusions) (American Psychiatric Association 2000). Both negative and positive symptoms are assessed through observation and interview with the patient and generally do not closely consider the patient's subjective experience.

However, aspects of negative symptoms, such as affective flattening, are highly contended. Within conventional psychiatry, the absence of emotional expression is assumed to coincide with an absence of emotional experience. Contrasting research findings suggest that patients who were observed to score low on displayed emotional expression scored high on self ratings of emotional experience. Patients were also observed to be significantly lower on emotional expression when compared with others (Aghevli *et al.* 2003; Selton *et al.* 1998). It appears that there is little correlation between emotional experience and emotional expression in patients, and that observer ratings cannot help us to understand the subjective experience of the so-called negative symptoms.

This chapter will focus on research into the subjective experiences of negative symptoms. A framework for these experiences will be used from the qualitative research findings of the primary author (Le Lievre 2010). In this study, the primary author found that subjective experiences of the negative symptoms belonged to one of the two phases of the illness experience: 'transitioning into emotional shutdown' or 'recovering from emotional shutdown'.

The chapter will expand on the six themes from the phase of 'transitioning into emotional shutdown'. This phase describes the experience of turning the focus of attention away from the world and onto the self and the past, thus losing contact with the world and others (emotional shutdown). Transitioning into emotional shutdown involves: 'not being acknowledged', 'relational confusion', 'not being expressive', 'reliving the past', 'detachment', and 'no sense of direction' (Le Lievre 2010). Detail will be added to this framework of experience from other qualitative research in this area. We will now review the six themes that constitute a 'transition into emotional shutdown' and corresponding previous research findings.

Not being acknowledged

The first theme of 'not being acknowledged' is a summary of the many and varied ways in which participants diagnosed with schizophrenia experience others as negating their needs, independence and existence (Le Lievre 2010). Aspects of this theme include the experience of others: not listening; being disinterested; interrupting; ignoring; misinterpreting; drawing irrelevant conclusions; or not conforming to expectations.

Perhaps the best known contributor to the idea of not being acknowledged for people diagnosed with schizophrenia is R. D. Laing. With anecdotal evidence, Laing (1965) referred to the experience of not being acknowledged as disconfirmation, which he hypothesized led to ontological insecurity and ultimately to ontological annihilation. Laing suggested that disconfirmation was not just others disagreeing with the ideas of the person; it involved others disconfirming the existence of that person. Laing provided an example of a person who explained the impact of being disconfirmed in an argument: 'At best you win an argument. At worst you lose an argument. I am arguing in order to preserve my existence' (Laing 1965: 43).

With ontological insecurity from constant disconfirmation from others, Laing (1965) explained, a person diagnosed with schizophrenia would continue to want a connection with others, to be acknowledged by others, and to be assured that he or she exists. At the same time he or she paradoxically needs to be separate from and beyond the reach of others, due to the potential threat of being invalidated and ontologically annihilated.

The tension experienced by people diagnosed with schizophrenia between wanting to involve themselves with others, but feeling rejected and marginalized, is supported by Corin and Lauzon (1994). The experience of 'not being acknowledged' for diagnosed people has also been experienced in medical settings. Diagnosed people said that they did not feel listened to by clinicians who had a biomedical approach (Chadwick 1997). Clinicians working from a biomedical approach were reportedly experienced as seeing their clients in more objective and materialistic terms, as opposed to more subjective, experiential or heartfelt terms (Chadwick 2007). Whether or not diagnosed people's experience of 'not being acknowledged' by clinicians resulted in differences in therapeutic outcomes is not argued here. However, in one study, the distance resulting from not being acknowledged by the clinician led to the majority of service users experiencing their psychiatrists as less helpful than nurses, social workers and other service users (Rogers *et al.* 1993).

The process of not being acknowledged has been referred to as invalidation in recent studies and is described as the process of having one's interpretation of events or experience brought into question, not supported, ignored or rejected (Geekie & Read 2009). The experience of invalidation is said to result in a sense of questioning one's own judgement. Invalidation is reported to apply to an individual's experience of self and his or her social world.

The diagnosed person's sense of helplessness and insignificance is reportedly increased through a medical system that does not acknowledge their wish to be more involved in their own recovery (Strauss 2008). Strauss stated that 'the lack of being taken seriously by others can have a strongly negative impact on course and outcome' (Strauss 2008: 202). One service user reported that medical staff were 'doing things to her', that she did not feel respected and that the lack of acknowledgement from the medical staff resulted in her own lack of identity (Deegan 1993).

Relational confusion

Having not been acknowledged when they expected to be, participants in Le Lievre's (2010) research experienced confusion about the state of their relationships with others. The individuals in this study became confused and bewildered about why other people appeared to be competing against them, rather than acknowledging and supporting them (Le Lievre 2010).

The concept of relational confusion extends the work of Sullivan (1927), Blankenburg (2002), and Binswanger (Spielberg 1972). Sullivan (1927: 116) suggested that diagnosed people became perplexed and wrote that 'the patient becomes more and more entangled in contradictions, alternative notions and illusions' when looking for explanations of events in the world. Blankenburg (2002) suggested a loss of natural self evidence or a loss of the 'common sense' orientation to the world, which involved a loss of the frameworks which a person ordinarily uses to make sense of the world. Binswanger (Spielberg 1972: 226) suggested a breaking apart or 'splitting up experience into rigid alternatives' and a 'cover up of intolerable alternatives'.

Where Sullivan (1927) referred to 'alternative notions' and Binswanger (Spielberg 1972) referred to the patient's experience of 'rigid alternatives', the study by Le Lievre (2010) would suggest that the alternatives experienced by patients may often be between the other as a supportive friend, or not a friend at all. Where Binswanger (Spielberg 1972: 226) suggested a 'cover up of the intolerable alternatives', the Le Lievre (2010) study would suggest that unconsciously covering up the intolerable alternative of the other not being a friend would render unsupportive behaviour unexplainable and very confusing.

Not being expressive

Relational confusion remained unresolved in the study by Le Lievre (2010) when the participants were not willing or able to express their concerns to others. Participants reported not being expressive due to a number of reasons, including: not understanding others; a lack of knowledge; a desire to avoid conflict; feeling dulled down from medication; and not knowing what they wanted to achieve through their expression. Not being expressive was experienced by these participants as being detrimental to their mental health.

The theme of not being expressive has recently been described as 'bottling it up' (Geekie 2007). Davidson *et al.* (2001) also support the theme of not being expressive through their descriptions of a person diagnosed with schizophrenia who was unable to express him/herself to resolve family problems. One supporting example by Davidson *et al.* (2001) involved a person who was unable to buy and share gifts with their family. As a result, that individual chose to be absent from family gatherings to avoid the situation, rather than express her dilemma with her family.

The theme of not being expressive is consistent with Davidson and Stayner's (1997) position that people diagnosed with schizophrenia suspend their efforts to express themselves to avoid a negative experience, in an attempt to preserve whatever self-esteem remains. The diagnosed person's self-esteem is described as being under attack from others, in a similar sense to Laing's (1965) process of disconfirmation. Remaining quiet denies the other any chance to attack the individual's utterances, and hence keeps an aspect of the person hidden and preserved.

At the depth of difficulties in expression and coinciding isolation, any remaining opportunity to communicate with others is thwarted by the side effects of medication (Davidson *et al.* 1998; Lindstrom 1994). Medication is said to numb the sensations from social activity so that society's call to interact is barely heard. If the call for expression is heard, responses are slowed down by medication so that one's attempt at dynamic interaction becomes untimely and ineffective (Tooth *et al.* 2003).

Reliving the past

With relational confusion and no clarification through expression, participants in the study by Le Lievre (2010) questioned themselves through a reflective process of reliving the past in an attempt to find clarity. Trying to understand one confusing event sometimes led to the memory of another confusing event, and multiple interpretations of each event until participants felt overwhelmed. It was at the point of being overwhelmed by interpretations of confusing interactions that several participants spoke of how voices would comment on the situation in question. Here, the negative symptoms lead to positive symptoms, which is a reversal of the assumptions within conventional psychiatry.

Previous research has suggested that patients diagnosed with schizophrenia were hyper-reflective, and reflected on the past in an automatic or involuntary way to resolve confusion (Sass & Parnas 2007). Parnas and Handest (2003) suggested that during the reflective process, individuals would create multiple interpretations. Multiple interpretations were thought to increase the likelihood of finding a reasonable understanding of the confusing interaction.

Reliving the past has been supported by Larsen (2004), who described several informants in his studies who explained that the psychotic episodes and becoming isolated from others afforded them the time required to consider the past and make important decisions in life involving love relationships and other significant life situations. On one occasion, an informant explained that deliberately taking a break for a week to go away and consider the past and important decisions for the future eliminated the need for a psychotic episode and hospitalization, which was the course taken on previous occasions. Here, the process of withdrawing from others and reflecting on the past, which is associated with the negative symptoms, is considered to be a valuable process and can occur voluntarily while well or involuntarily during psychosis.

Detachment

With an experience of relational confusion and a need to relive the past, participants in the Le Lievre (2010) study experienced emotional detachment from others and a subsequent need for physical isolation to avoid being questioned by others. Detachment from others is experienced as a part of the reflective process, and isolation was experienced as a way of protecting one's self from others. Sadly, this is also experienced as a very lonely time. Detachment could increase to the point of complete emotional shutdown from others, which participants described as coinciding with their hospitalization with psychosis (Le Lievre 2010).

Eugene Minkowski made early inroads into understanding the experience of detachment for people diagnosed with schizophrenia (Sass 2002; Spielberg 1972). Based on his qualitative investigations, Minkowski argued that it was not the higher intellectual capacities that were lacking from people diagnosed with schizophrenia, but a more basic and fundamental sense of connectedness, or original unity with people, which would normally provide the dynamism of subjectivity. Minkowski proposed that it was this loss of vital contact that created a disturbance in the structure of the self and was the *trouble generator* (Sass 2002).

Being detached from the world has also been referred to as an altered sense of presence or immersion in the world (Parnas & Handest 2003). As a person experiences increasing detachment between self and the world he or she begins to experience a lack of excitement from the things in the world (Corin & Lauzon 1994), otherwise known as anhedonia. With detachment, a diagnosed person was said to become preoccupied with metaphysical understandings and existential re-orientations in an attempt to make meaning of their experience (Moller & Husby 2000).

Although many people diagnosed with schizophrenia have a profound desire to be connected with others, in the study by Davidson & Stayner (1997) they were described as being unable to do so effectively, and eventually suspended their efforts in order to preserve self-esteem. Davidson & Stayner's (1997) research suggests that eventually, partly through the absence of energy, and partly to save what is left of their self-esteem, the person stops trying to connect with others. One of their participants stated:

> For us, giving up was a way of surviving. Giving up, refusing to hope, not trying, [and] not caring: all of these were ways of trying to protect the last fragile traces of our spirit and our selfhood from undergoing another crushing.
> (Davidson & Stayner 1997: 10)

The cumulative effect of failure to connect, subsequent withdrawal, and the hope of connecting with others was described as a fading light at the end of a tunnel by a participant who explained that 'with each uncommunicated experience the darkness grows'(Ruocchio 1991: 358).

Detachment and disconnection appear to be similar ideas to the notion of fragmentation. Fragmentation has been described as the loss of the sense of connectedness that usually exists between self and world, and the loss of connection between different aspects of experience which can apply to an individual's sense of self, the interpersonal world and the material world (Geekie & Read 2009).

No sense of direction

When participants in the study by Le Lievre (2010) relived the past, they expressed not only a general sense of detachment, but also no opportunity to focus on the future, hence they experienced no sense of direction. Without a focus into the future, participants described the experience of having a jumbled up life. They also explained a lack of desire to focus on the future, as the extraordinary aspects of past experiences had been so much more engaging and challenging than the present or the future appeared to be. Participants reported that they could not find a way to describe or conceptualize their peak experiences of new meanings and understandings of things in the world, and were thus felt unable to utilize those indefinable horizons in the present or the future.

While other research was not found to compare with Le Lievre's (2010) finding of participants having no sense of direction, no meaning and no purpose, this finding is contrasted with the notion of 'spirituality' (Randal & Argyle 2006). It has been suggested that a 'spiritual emergence' is experienced when an individual finds a greater meaning for their life (Randal & Argyle 2006). However, it has also been suggested that when too many alternative meanings are generated, an individual can go beyond a spiritual emergence, and spiral into even greater turmoil, or a 'spiritual emergency' (Grof 1989).

Summary of 'transitioning into emotional shutdown'

Participants in Le Lievre's (2010) qualitative study reported a primary experience of not being acknowledged. Not being acknowledged created a fragile sense of self. To preserve this fragile sense of self, participants revealed less of themselves by reducing their level of emotional expression, conventionally considered to be 'flattened affect'. They could not understand why they were not acknowledged and became confused about the state of their relationship with the other. Participants typically did not express their confusion and reported being quiet in order to prevent a further lack of acknowledgement. This act of self preservation may be seen as being akin to the negative symptom of 'alogia', which is the characteristic of having reduced speech.

Participants began to relive the past, in an automatic (or hyper-reflexive) way, in an attempt to understand what had gone wrong between themselves and others. The reflective process necessarily created detachment from other people and the world. With detachment came a loss of involvement and excitement ('anhedonia'). With a focus on a past moment of confusion, and a longing for the intensity of experience that came with their extraordinary realizations during the height of their psychotic episodes, participants were not involved with the present or the future, which reflects the negative symptom of 'avolition'.

Implications for understanding

Conventional research involving people diagnosed with schizophrenia has resulted in the development of concepts such as 'negative symptoms'. Seeing these characteristics as 'symptoms' of a biological entity and illness creates a search for meaning only at a cellular level.

Approaching the subjective experience of the negative symptoms and their context through qualitative methods has afforded the emergence of many important psycho-social and spiritual understandings. These experiences have been interconnected through overarching themes that tell a meaningful story (Le Lievre 2010). The themes of not being acknowledged; relational confusion; not being expressive; reliving the past; detachment; and having no sense of direction describe the way in which the individual's focus of attention moves away from the world and others in the present, onto the past and the self. These themes allow others, including clinicians, to understand the subjective experience of the individual's social environment and the way in which they experience themselves responding to that environment.

Implications for practice

Research into the subjective experience of negative symptoms as experienced by people diagnosed with schizophrenia suggests that individuals experience themselves as reacting and responding to others, which includes becoming emotionally withdrawn when they experience not being acknowledged by others. It would be beneficial for mental health practitioners to be familiar with these findings based on research into subjective experience as this may help them to become more empathic, open, affirming and understanding of the experience of service users, no matter how different the service user's experience and understandings may be to the clinician's own experience and understandings. An empathic approach by clinicians is likely to encourage service users to tell their story, which may facilitate their own process of making sense of relational confusion.

Understanding, accepting and allowing the views of others does not imply that the clinician needs to have the same experience or understandings as their patients. In contrast, approaches based upon preconceived notions of how the world is to be experienced and understood, where those notions differ to the notions of others, is likely to be experienced as hostile. When the patient is not able to argue effectively or ignore the views of others, they are likely to find themself in an impossible position. Their sense of self will be at risk, and their safest option may be an emotional, social and physical withdrawal.

References

Aghevli, M. A., Blanchard, J. J. and Horan, W. P. (2003) 'The expression and experience of emotion in schizophrenia: A study of social interaction', *Psychiatry Research*, *119*: 261–271.

American Psychiatric Association (2000) *Diagnostic and Statistical Manual of Mental Disorders* (fourth edition, text revision). Washington, DC: American Psychiatric Association.

Blankenburg, W. (2002) 'First steps toward a psychopathology of common sense', *Philosophy, Psychiatry and Psychology*, *8*: 303–315.

Chadwick, P. K. (1997) 'Recovery from psychosis: Learning more from patients', *Journal of Mental Health*, *6*: 577–588.

Chadwick, P. K. (2007) 'Peer-professional first-person account: Schizophrenia from the inside: Phenomenology and the integration of causes and meanings', *Schizophrenia Bulletin*, *33*: 166–173.

Corin, E. and Lauzon, G. (1994) 'From symptoms to phenomena: The articulation of experience in schizophrenia', *Journal of Phenomenological Psychology*, *25*: 3–50.

Davidson, L. and Stayner, D. A. (1997) 'Loss, loneliness and the desire for love: Perspectives of people with schizophrenia', *Psychiatric Rehabilitation Journal*, 20: 3–12.

Davidson, L., Stayner, D. A. and Haugland, K. (1998) 'Phenomenological perspectives on the social functioning of people with schizophrenia'. In K. T. Muser and N. Tarrier (eds) *Handbook of Social Functioning in Schizophrenia* (pp. 97–120). Boston: Allyn and Bacon.

Davidson, L., Stayner, D. A., Nickou, C., Styron, T. H., Rowe, M. and Chinman, M. L. (2001) 'Simply to be let in': Inclusion as a basis for recovery', *Psychiatric Rehabilitation Journal*, *24*: 375–388.

Deegan, P. (1993) 'Recovering our sense of value after being labeled', *Journal of Psychosocial Nursing, 31*: 7–11.

Geekie, J. (2007). *The Experience of Psychosis: Fragmentation, Invalidation and Spirituality*. Unpublished thesis, University of Auckland, New Zealand.

Geekie, J. and Read, J. (2009) *Making Sense of Madness: Contesting the Meaning of Schizophrenia*. New York: Routledge Mental Health.

Grof, S. (1989) *Spiritual emergency. When Personal Transformation Becomes a Crisis*. Los Angeles, CA: Jeremy P. Tarcher.

Laing, R. D. (1965) *The Divided Self*. Ringwood, Australia: Pelican.

Larsen, J. A. (2004) 'Finding meaning in first episode psychosis: Experience, agency, and the cultural repertoire', *Medical Anthropology Quarterly*, 18: 447–471.

Le Lievre, J. A. (2010) 'The experience of emotional expression in the context of social relations for people diagnosed with schizophrenia: A phenomenological explication', Unpublished thesis, Queensland University of Technology, Australia.

Lindstrom, L. H. (1994) 'Long-term clinical and social outcome studies in schizophrenia in relation to the cognitive and emotional side effects of antipsychotic drugs', *Acta Psychiatrica Scandinavica*, 89: 74–76.

Moller, P. and Husby, R. (2000) 'The initial prodrome in schizophrenia: Searching for naturalistic core dimensions of experience and behaviour', *Schizophrenia Bulletin, 26*: 217–232.

Parnas, J. and Handest, P. (2003) 'Phenomenology of anomolous self-experiences in early schizophrenia', *Comprehensive Psychiatry*, 44: 121–134.

Randal, P. and Argyle, N. (2006) 'Spiritual emergency – a useful explanatory model? A literature review and discussion paper'. Spirituality and Psychiatry Special Interest Group. Retrieved from: www.rcpsych.ac.uk/members/specialinterestgroups/spirituality/publicationsarchive.aspx

Rogers, A., Pilgrim, L. and Lacey, R. (1993), *Experiencing Psychiatry: Users' Views of Services*. Basingstoke: Macmillan Press.

Ruocchio, P. J. (1991) 'The schizophrenic inside', *Schizophrenia Bulletin*, 17: 357–359.

Sass, L. A. (2002) 'Self and world in schizophrenia: Three classic approaches', *Philosophy, Psychiatry and Psychology*, 8: 251–270.

Sass, L. A. and Parnas, J. (2007) 'Explaining schizophrenia: The relevance of phenomenology'. In M. C. Chung, K. W. M. Fulford and G. Graham (eds) *Reconceiving Schizophrenia*. New York: Oxford University Press.

Selton, J. P. C. J., van der Bosch, R. J. and Sijben, A. E. S. (1998) 'The subjective experience of negative symptoms'. In X. F. Amador and A. S. David (eds) *Insight and Psychosis* (pp. 78–90). Oxford: Oxford University Press.

Spielberg, H. (1972) *Phenomenology in Psychology and Psychiatry*. Evanston, IL: Northwestern University Press.

Strauss, J. S. (2008) 'Prognosis in schizophrenia and the role of subjectivity', *Schizophrenia Bulletin*, 34: 201–203.

Sullivan, H. S. (1927) 'The onset of schizophrenia', *American Journal of psychiatry*, 7: 105–134.

Tooth, B., Kalyanasundaram, V., Glover, H. and Momenzadah, S. (2003) 'Factors consumers identify as important to recovery from schizophrenia', *Australian Psychiatry*, 11: 70–77.

Part X

Family perspectives

The final two chapters in our pairs of chapters relate to the experiences of family members of those who happen to experience psychosis. As in previous areas covered, we find that this is a neglected area of research, with family members' subjective experience rarely given the attention it warrants, with the consequence that little is known about family members' subjective experience.

Jay Neugeboren helps remedy this situation through his writings on his experience of his brother Robert's long-standing mental health difficulties. Jay's poignant story outlines his struggles both with his brother and with mental health services involved with his brother's care. We are moved by Jay's sense of frustration at not knowing how best he should go about relating to his brother as he – like the clinicians involved – is confronted with the uncertainty of how best to support a fellow human being who happens to be struggling. Ultimately, though, what comes through Jay's story is the warmth, love and humor the brothers share and Jay's persuasive conclusion that at the heart of good care (whether from family, friends or clinicians) is exactly what he is able to maintain with his brother: a loving relationship.

John Read and Lorenza Magliano's summary of research into families' experience finds that stories by family members are often replete with a sense of grief and loss and the stresses and burdens of caring, with families commonly complaining that they find services are not sensitive to their needs. When families are asked about their understandings of the causes of mental health difficulties, we find that, like individuals who experience such troubles, family understandings are multi-factorial and commonly identify adverse life events as significant. Both chapters demonstrate that to understand the experience of psychosis, it is critical that we learn to listen to the voice of subjective experience, whether that be from the individual concerned or from his or her family.

Chapter 21

I called you my brother

Jay Neugeboren

At 3am on a cool summer night – a few hours after my youngest son, Eli, has graduated from high school – I find myself cruising the deserted streets of Northampton, Massachusetts, searching for the 50-year-old man who is my brother. I have considered calling the police, but I know that if a policeman actually finds my brother and approaches him, Robert might, as in the past, panic and become violent.

My brother has spent most of his life, since the age of 19, in mental hospitals and psychiatric wards in and around New York City. The list is long: Hillside, Creedmoor, Elmhurst, Gracie Square, Bellevue, Kings County, Rikers Island, Mid-Hudson Psychiatric Center, South Beach Psychiatric Center, Bronx Psychiatric Center, and others.

Until the time of his first breakdown in 1962, Robert had been a delightful, popular, and gifted boy and young man – talented at dancing, acting, and singing, invariably winning the lead in school and camp plays. He'd had a love and gift for many things, including tennis, writing, painting, drawing, and chess. (He was in a chess club with world chess champion Bobby Fischer at Erasmus Hall High School in Brooklyn, but Fischer refused to play with him, because, Robert says, smiling, 'he said I played crazy.') He was a good if erratic student in high school, won a scholarship to college, and successfully completed his freshman year at the City College of New York.

He was, in short, a bright and idiosyncratic young man with a sense of life and humour all of his own, a person who until his first breakdown showed no signs, (except for those that, looking back, any of us might find in ourselves) that such a breakdown was at all likely, much less inevitable.

Robert's diagnosis has changed frequently through the years, depending largely upon which drugs have been successful in keeping him calm, stable, and/or compliant. He was 'schizophrenic' when enormous doses of Thorazine and Stelazine calmed him; he was manic-depressive (bipolar) when lithium worked; he was manic-depressive-with-psychotic-symptoms, or hypomanic, when Tegretol or Depakote (anticonvulsants), or some new antipsychotic or antidepressant – Trilafon, Adapin, Mellaril, Haldol, Klonopin, Risperidone, Clozaril, Olanzapine – showed promise of making him cooperative; and he was schizophrenic (again) when various doctors promised cures through insulin-coma therapy or megadose-vitamin therapy or Marxist therapy or gas therapy. At the same time, often in an attempt to minimize side effects, other drugs were poured into him: Artane, Benadryl, Cogentin, Kemadrin, Symmetrel, Prolixin, Pamelor, Navane . . .

During these years, Robert also participated in a long menu of psychotherapies: group therapy, family therapy, multifamily group therapy, psychoanalytically oriented psychotherapy, art therapy, behavioural therapy, vocational rehabilitation therapy, and so on. Most often, though – the more enduring his condition, the truer this became – he was treated solely with drugs, and received no talk therapy at all.

It is as if, I often think, the very history of the ways our century has dealt with those it calls mentally ill has, for more than 40 years now, been passing through my brother's mind and body.

Robert and I talk with each other most days and see each other often, and though our visits are not without their difficulties (why should we be different from other brothers?), visits in my home, with my children, had, up until the time of my son Eli's graduation, invariably been without incident.

'I've never seen Uncle Robert this way,' each of my three children said to me in the hours before and after Eli's graduation. 'Is he going to be all right? Can I help?' And then: 'And what about you, Pop – are *you* going to be all right?'

Robert spent the day and evening of Eli's graduation in and out of the house, withdrawing hundreds of dollars, ten dollars at a time, from automated teller machines; buying second-hand clothes at local thrift shops; leaving trails of clothing, coins, cigarette butts, small paper bags and crumpled, snot-filled tissues in virtually all the rooms of my (11-room) house; going from room to room and turning lights on and off; showing me pieces of paper upon which he had written indecipherable messages while demanding that I understand what they meant; and, whenever my children and their friends arrived home, hurrying from sight and hiding.

Eli returned home from his all-night graduation party at about 6am and Robert, who I had not seen since the night before, arrived not long after that, and ordered me to put him on a bus for New York. He looked ghastly (he had – inexpertly – given himself a haircut, and had shaved off his moustache) and seemed totally disoriented: his hands and arms were flapping uncontrollably, his body was hunched over, his eyeglasses were covered with a milk-white sticky substance ('Scum!' he declared), his movements were jagged, and he kept turning on me, ordering me around, screaming things that made no obvious sense.

Whether I did or did not reply, he became more and more enraged, telling me that I wasn't listening to him, that I never listened to him, and that if I didn't do what he said he didn't know what he might do. 'I want letters!' he kept shouting. 'I want letters!'

At the bus stop he scurried around, virtually on all fours, picking up cigarette butts and searching for money. He wore a wide-brimmed straw hat, a tuxedo vest over a T-shirt, tight white extra-short pants, bright knee-high red socks. He went to each of a half-dozen sidewalk newspaper kiosks and began putting quarters in them, taking out papers, and either stacking them on top of the kiosks or putting them in a mailbox. He went back and forth to a pay phone, dialling for information about people on Staten Island and yelling at the operator; he walked across the street to a parking lot and shouted questions at me; he wept and he screamed, and I found myself hoping the bus would come on time (or ahead of time), that he would be allowed to board it, and that he would somehow get back to his halfway house (located at a psychiatric centre) safely.

I had been in situations like this with Robert before, and though, as I said to my children, seeing Robert like this was not new for me, each time it happened it did still take me by surprise, and each time it happened, it seemed unutterably sad and heartbreaking.

How could it be that somebody who was so warm and loving, so charming, happy and seemingly normal one moment could become so angry, wild, and lost moments later? And how could it be that each time it happened – no matter the years gone by – it felt as if it were happening for the first time?

Though, with the years, I've learned to cope with these situations, and though Robert has actually reversed the path his life had been on (despite grim prognostications, he has come to be able to spend more time out of hospitals than in them, and has made more of a life for himself than most people ever dreamed possible), I still find myself going through litanies of familiar questions and doubts: Should I call the local police and have them take him to a hospital and deal with getting him back to New York City? Should I ask Robert where he was all night, and if he'd been drinking and/or doing drugs? Had I been remiss in not having talked with Robert during a period when he was stable about how we might navigate a future crisis, and had there been any way to do this that would not – my fear – have increased Robert's fears that I thought he *would* be having more breakdowns? Should I try to drive him the two hundred miles back to Staten Island? Should I call the hospital on Staten Island? And how should I respond to his outbursts of anger, his questions, his tears?

What could I do, I wondered, now as ever, that might ease his pain and confusion and minimize damage? If he was in free fall, as it were, was there anything that would help buffer the fall so that, instead of plummeting downward ten stories before he crashed, he could bounce down gently after, say, only falling a few steps? Should I say anything at all, and was there a right thing or wrong thing to say, or was it better to say nothing and to just leave him be?

In a situation like this, despite the many times I'd been here before, what I felt most of all was an overwhelming sadness and helplessness. Who knew if there was anything at all that might ease things, or make them less awful? Who knew, really, what to do?

What I did, finally, as before, was to act on my belief that, despite all, Robert still knew himself – even at a time like this – better than anyone else did, and that if he was determined to get back to Staten Island by himself, he would.

So I did what I usually do when things get bad for Robert. I tried, gently and firmly, to be as patient and direct with him as I could (telling him, for example, that I would call ahead to his halfway house to let them know he was on his way; asking again if he did, in fact, want me to drive him back to Staten Island) and, when he came near to me, I put my arms around him and told him I loved him, and talked with him about whatever came to mind – his meals (I'd packed him a lunch), the bus, the trip back, the weather.

While people waiting for the bus stared, or tried not to stare, or moved away, Robert stayed close to me: I was glad he'd been able to visit, I said, and I wished he wasn't having such a hard time again, and we'd talk on the phone that evening, and I was very glad he'd been able to be here for Eli's graduation and had seen Miriam and Aaron, and we would see one another again soon.

Robert navigated the eight-hour trip home – bus, subway, ferry, and bus – successfully. We spoke that night – he cried a lot, complained about the medications, and then he was off on flights of words that, because I knew the reference points, seemed more poignant than strange. 'I didn't embarrass you, did I?' he asked at one point. 'I didn't embarrass the children, I hope.'

The following morning, for the first time in a year, and for at least the 50th time in his life, he was hospitalized. When I called the doctor in charge of Robert's ward and he asked what I thought had precipitated Robert's break, I said that there were some immediate causes that seemed obvious, but that the real precipitant, it seemed to me, was simply the fact of his life – of the last 31 years of his life. If you'd been where Robert had been, suffered all the drugs, abuse, incompetence and pain he'd suffered, the wonder wasn't why he'd broken again, but why he hadn't, like so many others he'd known, died or killed himself or deteriorated completely.

But then I did name some of the things that might have precipitated this break. There was the graduation itself, and being with family. There were his desires and fantasies about living in my home with me now intensified because Eli would be going off to college and I would be living alone (but I'd been the single full-time parent of my three children for nearly a decade, and though Robert often asked about moving in with me, he himself had begun saying he didn't think it was a good idea). There was the fact that, a few weeks before, Robert's best friend had been moved from the home in which he and Robert had lived together for two years and into which Robert had been hoping to return (so where would he live now?). There was the fact that he had been out of the hospital for 11 months, and the healthier he was, the more boring the activities at the hospital's day centre became. There were the feelings aroused by being with me and my children – seeing Eli graduate (and at the age Robert was when he had his first breakdown) and seeing us move ahead with our lives while his life seemed, still, to be going nowhere.

Though I could, as ever, talk about what I thought had caused Robert's condition, long and short term, the more important question (or was I thinking this way in order to give myself heart, in order to find something good in a situation that was god-awful?) wasn't what had caused this breakdown, or any of the others, but what, given his life, had enabled him to survive, and to do more than survive

– to retain his generosity, his warmth, his intelligence, his pride, his humour, and his sense of self. This, it seemed to me, was, as ever, the true miracle and mystery.

I had, not long before, asked Robert if he ever had any sense of what made him go off the way he did sometimes – of what the difference was, of what made things change for him, or in him? He had been silent for a long time, and then had said, 'No answer.' These were, I said at once, afraid my questions might have hurt him, questions nobody seemed to know the answers to. 'So why should I know?' Robert said then. 'Am I different from anybody else?'

The doctor at the South Beach Psychiatric Center concluded that Robert's breakdown had been precipitated by alcohol and substance abuse. Robert had admitted that on the way up to visit me he had had a few beers and had inhaled amyl nitrite. The amyl nitrite ('poppers') was 'part of the gay lifestyle,' the doctor said, and was taken by homosexuals to increase sexual pleasure. The alcohol and substance abuse, he concluded, had clearly 'destabilized' and 'unhinged' the parts of Robert's brain that his medications – lithium and Depakote – had stabilized. The problem, therefore, was 'noncompliance'.

I had heard this from doctors before, and I responded with an obvious if rhetorical question: 'Okay, but what was it that caused the noncompliance?' If mental illness was as debilitating and awful a condition as it seemed to be (as surely it had been for Robert), and if the medications alleviated that condition, why would anyone ever stop taking the medications, or do anything to interfere with their beneficial effects?

As my father had once put it, to a doctor who refused to continue treating Robert because Robert had stopped taking his pills, 'So where, Doctor, is the pill to make him want to take the pills?'

When I visited Robert after his breakdown, on a locked unit at the psychiatric centre, on Staten Island, he was, as in previous hospitalizations there, on isolation: living, day after day, 24 hours a day, in a bare room in which there was nothing but a sheetless bed and an empty dresser. This was called, by the staff psychologist, Henry Grossman, 'reduced stimulation'.

When I had previously questioned, as gently as I could, whether being on isolation, and on heavy doses of Thorazine (the medication Robert hated above all others), and not being permitted to make or receive calls, or to have visitors, might not feel to Robert like punishment instead of therapy, Grossman had replied that this might temporarily be the case. 'But our experience,' he said, 'is that in retrospect patients come to appreciate the reduction of stimulation – the limits and boundaries that have been set for them.'

He also assured me that Robert was not just locked away in a room – that every hour on the half hour, for five minutes, Robert was taken to the bathroom and for a walk down the hallway. When I asked if Robert had had or would be receiving any therapy – if he was talking with anybody in any regular way about what he was going through – Henry's reply was abrupt: 'Robert cannot tolerate therapy.'

This seemed to me an absurd statement – Robert couldn't tolerate therapy? You mean you can't tolerate trying to work with him, I wanted to scream. Why are you a therapist if you don't want to work with patients, to listen to them? And when will Robert be able to 'tolerate' therapy – when he's well?

But it was the same old story, and I was in the same old quandary: if I complained too much, or confronted Robert's healthcare workers with their inadequacies, or sent off the long letters I often composed in my head (to *The New York Times*, to hospital and state officials, to doctors, etc.), I feared they would only take out their resentments of me upon Robert – that they would (as had happened before) simply talk with me less, care for Robert less, and/or ship him off to a ward where he would receive even less attention (and more drugs) than he was presently receiving.

A week later, on a warm summer day, because of my visit Robert has been granted courtyard privileges, and we sit at a picnic table. He opens the bag of food I've brought him for lunch, but his hands are shaking so badly that when he tries to eat an egg salad sandwich, the egg salad sprays everywhere. He is frustrated, apologetic, embarrassed. I talk with him easily, we joke back and forth, and after a short while I scoop up pieces of egg, tomato, lettuce, and bread, he takes his false teeth out, and I feed him with my fingers, placing the food directly into his mouth.

When he cannot tolerate his tremblings any longer, he walks away. He calls to me, and I sit next to him, and we talk about the ward, about Eli's graduation, and about our cousins. We have more than three dozen first cousins (both our parents came from large, extended families), and I fill Robert in on who is where and doing what, and which relatives I've seen or heard from. Suddenly Robert turns, leans down, and kisses the back of my hand several times, after which he begins weeping. 'Oh, Jay, Jay,' he cries softly. 'They're barbarians here. Barbarians, barbarians! Pavlovians.'

He presses his mouth to the back of my hand, and I take him to me, hold him. A few minutes later, we walk around the courtyard, and then he tells me that he likes to walk back and forth, in a diagonal, between two trees – they are about ten yards apart – and count the number of times he can do this. So we walk back and forth together, and I sing to him, and then he joins in – putting his arm around my waist, leaning on my shoulder – and we go back and forth again and again, loudly singing old camp songs, in English and Hebrew, that we remember from our childhood.

He eats some more, and then we walk again, side by side, our hands clasped behind us, mimicking two diplomats, trading stories and news. He clutches his dentures in one hand, a piece of bread locked in their bite, and when he puts the top bridge back in his mouth, I say something about his being on uppers. He giggles, inserts the lower bridge. 'And now you're on lowers,' I say, and add that I don't understand why, since he's on uppers and lowers, which probably balance each other, the hospital has to give him any other medications. 'It's how they make their profit,' he says.

When I call Robert after our visit, he is flying – repeating everything he says twice, rambling on about people living and dead as if they are with him on the ward, thanking me for visiting him and for the things I brought him, giving me lists of the foods he's eaten and the things he wants me to send him, talking about Adlai Stevenson and Bill Clinton (who is, he says, his son) and how the whole country is in a *very* big depression – and every few seconds he tells me that he has to hang up (though he never does). And then, when he finally takes a breath, and I tell him I love him, he talks to me in a way that is totally natural.

'Oh, Jay,' he says, 'don't you see? There's nothing better in my life than what's happening! You don't know. You don't know, Jay. You don't want to know. My life only goes so far . . .' He weeps freely, keeps talking. 'This life of working here and there in hospitals, or as a volunteer, and being here now, and doing nothing – isn't there ever going to be anything better for me? Please get me out of here, Jay. Please, please . . .'

When I tell him I called him the day before but nobody could find him, he asks me what I called him, and when I say, 'I called you my brother,' he laughs, says, 'That's an old one, Jay. That's an old one.'

Moved as I am by his plea for a life different from the one he has, I find that I am feeling relieved, and, even, mildly exhilarated. I am also feeling exasperated, yet again, with the treatment, and lack of treatment, he receives from the staff; when I talk with his new prescribing psychiatrist, his fourth since his hospitalization, I discover, for example, that this man – 'So why are you calling me?' are his first words to me after I identify myself as Robert's brother – has been prescribing and changing Robert's medications for a full week without having spoken with Robert.

But I am feeling better because the truth is that when Robert and I are together, no matter where, we're happy. Not always, and not without a pervasive sense of loss and sadness, but happy to be with each other because it seems good, in an often frightening and miserable life, to be known, and to be able to be near the person who knows you and is known by you.

Implications for understanding

When, through the years, people have asked what my hopes for Robert are, my answer has remained constant and simple: I hope he has more good days than bad. Despite his condition, and his life, he remains as complex and unique a human being as any of us, and the important thing to remember is that I am not his social worker, or doctor, or medication monitor, or nurse, or therapist, or case manager, but – first, last, and always – his brother.

Implications for practice

Several years ago, when Robert moved from South Beach to the Bronx Psychiatric Center, it was the consensus of the staff that he would never be able to live outside a locked ward. For the first time, however, he began taking Clozaril. Within six months, the Director of Psychology called to tell me that the results were, as I'd already seen in visits with Robert, wonderful, amazing, miraculous! Robert was calm, clear-headed, symptom-free, relaxed – and the hospital began preparing him for discharge. Then one morning Robert telephoned in a total panic: 'Alan's leaving, Alan's leaving!' he kept screaming. It turned out that his social worker, Alan, with whom he had an excellent relationship, had been transferred, overnight and without warning, to another hospital. The result: Robert decompensated completely, and it would be more than a year before the hospital would begin once again (this time successfully!) to prepare him for discharge. The question, then, is: why did the medication that worked so well on Monday, stop working on Tuesday? One answer: because Robert had been deprived of a relationship that had been a crucial, transformative one in his life.

A dozen years ago I went around the country interviewing hundreds of individuals who suffered from serious mental illnesses, had been institutionalized short and long term for these conditions, yet had been able to return to full, viable lives in this world (as physicians, lawyers, janitors, teachers, social workers, etc). While they varied in what they believed had made the difference – some attributing their recoveries to medications, some to doctors or social workers, some to religion, some to particular programs – they all, without exception, said that the crucial difference lay in a *relationship*: in the fortuitous presence in their lives of a person who cared for them, who believed in their ability to survive and come to a better life, and who was committed to caring for them for the duration (Neugeboren 1999).

Sir William Osler (1961: 105), the legendary Johns Hopkins physician, noted that 'it is much more important to know what sort of patient has a disease than what sort of disease a patient has.' What maximizes treatment are continuity of care – mental health professionals who know their individual patients well, and over time; judicious and minimal use of medications that are prescribed not merely on the basis of this-medication-for-this-symptom, but on the caregiver being able to put the patient's symptoms into the larger context of the patient's history; and an ongoing relationship that involves talk therapy of some kind so that the patient benefits from being listened to and attended to without judgment. When even one of these elements is missing, we severely compromise our ability to provide truly beneficial treatment for those, like Robert, who suffer the long-term ravages of serious mental illness.

References

Neugeboren, J. (1999) *Transforming Madness: New Lives for People Living with Mental Illness*. New York City: William Morrow.

Osler, W. (1961) *Aphorisms From His Bedside Teachings*. Springfield, IL: Charles C Thomas.

Chapter 22

The subjective experience and beliefs of relatives of people who experience psychosis

John Read and Lorenza Magliano

In search of relatives' stories

The traditional starting place when attempting to summarize a body of research is to search a database such as PsycINFO. Searching 'families' or 'family' and 'schizophrenia' or 'psychosis' produced 10,296 articles. A scan of the first 100 of these, however, revealed that none had asked the relatives themselves what they thought, or felt. They were mostly about genetics, biological abnormalities and psychiatric drugs. Refining the search using 'subjective experience' or 'first person' produced just 71 papers.

Fourteen first-person accounts

Thirty five of these 71 papers are 'First-person accounts' published in the journal *Schizophrenia Bulletin* between 1979 and 2004. Fourteen of the 35 are by relatives. All but one are deeply depressing stories about grief and loss, shame and stigma, and the stresses and burdens of caring:

> I'd wonder where the little boy I'd loved so dearly had gone.
>
> (Jaffe 1992)

> I remember thinking that his friends are going to college and my son is going into a mental institution . . . I cried all the way home.
>
> (Kagigebi 1995)

The grief seemed to be deepened by hopelessness about recovery, often based on the assumption of an irreversible illness:

> I looked up schizophrenia in our medical book. After reading their information I didn't see much hope.
>
> (Kagigebi 1995)

> She has a severely debilitating form of this devastating and demoralizing brain disease.
>
> (Smith 1991)

> He [family doctor] was an honest and wise man. He told us there is no cure for schizophrenia.
>
> (Piercey 1985)

This notion of an incurable disease led in turn to the belief that the burden of caring, and all the stresses involved, would also be endless:

> The nightmare goes on and on and on!
>
> (Kagigebi 1995)

The only story not saturated with sadness and pessimism was a daughter's about her mother:

> We can now respond effectively to Mom's symptoms ... Each family member has been touched by the family group process ... Nearly all our relationships have improved ... Locking up troubled people and chemically subduing them is more expensive, both economically and emotionally. It should be the last option, not the first. Mom's recovery process has been a remarkable experience for me.
>
> (Sundquist 1999)

Studies of relatives of people experiencing psychosis for the first time

The first ever review of 'qualitative studies of first episode psychosis' (Boydell *et al.* 2010) found 29 studies. Nine focused primarily or exclusively on family members. The majority of these studies addressed a topic of the researcher's choice, mostly relatives' experiences of seeking help or their observations about how the 'symptoms' developed. We focus on the two which seemed to give people a chance to talk about what *they* wanted to talk about.

The first (Sin *et al.* 2008) involved interviews with 15 British parents of young men, who reported a long list of things they did for their sons, and the sacrifices involved. This reflects the findings of much larger studies of family burden (Magliano *et al.* 2005). Many of the 15 parents spent a lot of time searching for 'normalizing activities' to meet the social, educational and occupational needs of their sons. This fits with the stated needs of people who experience psychosis (Byrne *et al.* 2010). The parents felt 'almost invisible to mental health services' and 'there was an overwhelming welcome from all the carers interviewed to the idea of orienting services to become more family/ carer oriented'.

The second study interviewed eight sisters and two brothers (Sin *et al.* 2005). All described being overwhelmed by feelings, ranging from resentment and blame to guilt, loss, shame and embarrassment. Nevertheless, many also talked about positive outcomes:

It has some good effect as well because it's made me open up to how people feel and be more aware.

We became closer. She's always welcome here [younger sister's house].

I think it made our family a lot more close-knit.

I think it's caused my parents to become more aware of what he [her older brother] needs and what we all need.

(Sin *et al.* 2005)

The researchers highlighted, again, that 'all of the siblings reported that they would appreciate an opportunity to talk about their experiences and how the onset of psychosis may have affected them. Sadly, most of them reported that such opportunity does not currently exist.'

Beliefs about causes

Clearly, the experiences of family members vary on several dimensions including optimism about recovery. Perhaps one of the major determinants of hope is what one thinks is troubling the loved one and what may have caused this (Aderhold & Gottwalz 2004).

Most relatives seem to adopt what researchers would call a 'multifactorial approach'. For example, when offered 30 possible causes, relatives selected from none to 27, with an average of eight (Esterberg & Compton 2006). This holding of multiple, even seemingly contradictory, explanations is shared by people who experience psychosis themselves (Geekie & Read 2009; Magliano *et al.* 2009).

Nevertheless, in 16 out of 22 studies about causal beliefs, relatives understand their loved one's problems more as reactions to adverse life events than as symptoms of a biologically based illness (see *Table 22.1*). For example, in a nationwide survey of over 700 relatives in Italy, 21 per cent endorsed 'heredity' as a cause, but 36 per cent endorsed 'psychological traumas' and 46 per cent endorsed 'stress' (Magliano *et al.* 2004). The findings for Indian family members were 'brain disorder' – 15 per cent, 'genetics/heredity' – 14 per cent, and 'stressors' (work and family) – 55 per cent (Srinivasan & Thara, 2001).

This international preference for psychosocial over biogenetic causal explanations is consistent with the views held by the public in general, and by 'patients' themselves (Read *et al.* 2006; Magliano *et al.* 2009). Some studies found that relatives rejected the 'medical model' even more strongly than other people. Austrian relatives were roughly twice as likely as the rest of the general public to believe that their loved ones' difficulties were caused by 'nervous strain', 'occupational stress' and 'unhappy family situation' (Grausgruber *et al.* 2007). In Italy, relatives were twice as likely to believe that 'schizophrenia' is *entirely* caused by psychosocial factors (Magliano *et al.* 2004). In this study, relatives who believed that 'schizophrenia' was due exclusively to biological causes (7 per cent) were more

Table 22.1 Family members' beliefs in predominantly biogenetic (BIO) or psychosocial (PS) explanations for their relatives' problems

Study	Country	n	Preference for biogenetic vs psychosocial causal beliefs
Alivisatos and Lykestos (1964)	Greece	273	PS
McGill et al. (1983)	England	36	PS
Lefley (1985)[1]	USA	84	BIO
Angermeyer et al. (1988)	Germany	84	PS
Karanci (1995)	Turkey	60	PS
Whittle (1996)	England	54	PS
Angermeyer and Matschinger (1996)[2]	Germany/ Austria	476	BIO
Phillips et al. (2000)	China	245	PS
Shibre et al. (2001)	Ethiopia	104	PS (sup)
Srinivasan and Thara (2001)	India	254	PS
Corcoran et al. (2003)	USA	20	PS
Magliano et al. (2004)	Italy	709	PS
Van Dorn et al. (2005)	USA	83	BIO
Kurihara et al. (2006)	Bali	39	PS (sup)
Esterberg and Compton (2006)	USA[3]	61	BIO
Grausgruber et al. (2007)	Germany	137	PS
Monteiro et al. (2006)	Brazil	15	PS (sup)
Corcoran et al. (2007)	USA	13	PS
Gladstone et al. (2007)	Canada	10	PS
Penny et al. (2009)	England[4]	11	PS
Wasserman et al. (2010)	USA	36	BIO

Notes
1 Relatives who were also mental health staff
2 Members of relatives' organizations
3 Afro-American
4 Pakistani
(sup) = supernatural/religious/spiritual causal beliefs that were stronger than either BIO or PS

pessimistic about the possibility that their loved ones would ever recover (Magliano *et al.* 2001). Several studies found that the greater the contact with mental health services, the more relatives came to believe in the 'medical model' (Esterberg & Compton 2006; Magliano *et al.* 2001).

Some studies also found that compared to the general population fewer relatives perceived 'schizophrenics' to be dangerous compared with the general public (Thompson *et al.* 2002; Grausgruber *et al.* 2007).

This strong preference for psychosocial causal factors might be surprising to readers who have googled 'schizophrenia' and found multiple websites, often American, claiming to speak for families (such as schizophrenia.com and nami. org). These drug-company sponsored organizations (e.g. the National Alliance for Mental illness) are, it seems, not representative of most family members when they proclaim that 'schizophrenia is a chronic, severe, and disabling brain disease' (schizophrenia.com).

Four of the five studies in which relatives prefer biogenetic causes were done in the USA, which has one of the most medical/biological mental health services in the world. Fourteen of the 15 studies conducted outside the USA found that relatives prefer psychosocial explanations.

Experiences of mental health services and views about treatments

We also found a range of views and experiences about specific types of services and treatments. For example, when Canadian relatives were asked 'What should be done?' 97 per cent supported more resources for work/recreation opportunities; 87 per cent wanted involvement of family and friends; 66 per cent endorsed drug treatment; and 18 per cent (compared with 42 per cent of the general public) supported mental hospitals (Thompson *et al.* 2002). In Italy, relatives are equally in favour of psychosocial treatments (46 per cent) and medication (48 per cent) (Magliano *et al.* 2004).

A recent book entitled *Experiences of Mental Health In-patient Care* (Hardcastle *et al.* 2007) included five stories by British 'carers'. They were overwhelmingly negative:

> Far from seeing her improve, this chaotic environment seemed to make her more frightened and indeed more ill.

> The staff seemed disinterested in my son's life before he was ill, or in the whole of his world outside of hospital.

> The staff were uninterested in her and had nothing to offer her . . . just drugs.

> . . . with the nursing staff in the office with the door shut, chatting together. No one offered me a cup of tea, or a word of comfort.

> I felt that I was invisible, as nobody seemed to notice me . . . Whenever I asked for information I was usually told that they couldn't tell me because of confidentiality. I didn't know what this meant, and it was never really explained to me.

This last point was echoed in a recent Italian study in which 96 per cent of relatives agreed with the relatives' right to be informed about the patient's mental condition, a view shared by 62 per cent of Italian 'patients' (Magliano *et al.* 2008). Readers may also be interested in three books that describe approaches that do place the family centre stage in treatment (Aderhold & Gottwalz 2004; Bloch Thorsen *et al.* 2006; Hakansson 2009).

There were two exceptions to all these negative experiences:

> He [the psychiatrist] was unfailingly kind and courteous, showing warmth, humanity and listening respectfully to my daughter and myself. He offered me the first glimpse of hope.

> The contact with the psychiatrist and the regular meetings to which we were invited were all so professional, structured and had an objective – how can we help Lorraine become well and feel better about herself. Both my wife and I welcomed the family therapy. It was such a help to air those pent-up emotions and understand them.
>
> (Magliano *et al.* 2008)

We noted earlier that British relatives tend to focus on 'normalizing activities' so as to meet the social, educational and occupational needs of their sons (Sin *et al.* 2008), and that Canadian relatives (97 per cent) place resources for work and recreational activities at the top of their wish list (Thompson *et al.* 2002). This is consistent with a study in five European countries, in which relatives stated that they used mainly social strategies to help their loved ones, especially social activities either inside or outside the family, and positive communication with them (Magliano *et al.* 1998). Belief in the importance of the latter is shared by the public (Read *et al.* 2006). For example, more than 90 per cent of both community members and health workers in India stated that the best ways to help were 'love and affection' and 'listening to understand' and rated 'close family member' and 'close friend' as 'helpful'. Only 6 per cent of the public and 15 per cent of the health workers rated medication as 'helpful'. Sadly, the researchers concluded that there was an 'urgent need for training' to teach the public they are wrong (Kermode *et al.* 2009).

Researcher bias

This difficulty that some researchers have in allowing people to state their beliefs or tell their stories without distorting them to fit their preconceptions is further illustrated by the book *Families Coping with Mental Illness* (Kawanashi 2006). Interviews with 50 relatives from Los Angeles and Tokyo echoed many of the themes identified above, including distress at the emergence of the loved one's difficulties, and strong reactions to hearing the diagnosis and to the hospitalizations and treatments that followed. These are reported respectfully, and even with a sense of awe at the resilience involved. However, the tone changes when it comes to a section entitled 'The Big Question: What Caused the Mental illness?' The author first informs the reader that there is only one true answer to this question, claiming (wrongly) that 'theories that emphasize how family interactions with the patient can cause schizophrenia have in fact no statistical scientific basis' (Kawanashi 2006:123).

Having thus set the scene we read that: 'Many point out how dysfunctional the family of the patient was, suggesting it may be the conflict-ridden family environment that caused their family member to become sick. They also refer to the parental personality and their way of raising children as possible factors that contributed to the onset of mental illness' (ibid).

> This child had only chaos during the first four years of life.

> Her father drank a lot – like an alcoholic – and I think he may have molested her.

> Because we came from such a dysfunctional home.

> Well, is he really mentally ill or is it because of such a damned awful childhood?
> (Kawanashi 2006)

These observations, sadly, are dismissed as mistakes, 'based as they are on daily impressions and mostly non-scientific interpretation' (ibid. 116).

There is a small but growing number of books written by family members themselves, including one by a sister (Hawkins 2010) and one by a brother (Neugeboren 2003), who has also written about what he thinks needs to change in the mental health system (Neugeboren 2001; 2009). Such books inevitably have an individual perspective on the various issues identified in this chapter, but it is at least their own perspective, not that of a biased researcher.

Implications for understanding

Family members have powerful, often heart breaking, stories to tell. They are stories of confusion, despair, loss, guilt, anger, invisibility, and of hope lost and sometimes recovered. They are stories of a search for explanations. They are stories of love. Researchers and clinicians have been slow to recognize the importance of these stories but gradually, it seems, more are beginning to 'get it'.

Researchers may want to explore new areas, such as the relatives of people who experience psychosis but who are not in the mental health system (the majority), and children growing up with a parent who is sometimes psychotic (Mordoch 2010). Another unexplored area is the experience of friends of people who experience psychosis, a most important group, especially in the teenage years when psychosis often emerges and when peers are so important (Brand *et al.* 2011).

Implications for practice

Hopefully, clinicians are also beginning to understand the importance of hearing the relatives' stories in order to gain a fuller picture of what is going on in the real world of the people they are trying to help. They too need to suspend their biases about the nature and causes of the problem(s) in front of them and about the possible solutions. Family members have, for far too long, been either ignored or, when included, fed a one-size-fits-all explanation and solution (Aderhold & Gottwalz 2004). Despite the common themes identified in this chapter, every family is different. Perhaps if clinicians listened a little more and 'educated' a little less everyone would end up a little wiser and more able to help.

References

Aderhold, V. and Gottwalz, E. (2004) Family therapy and schizophrenia: Replacing ideology with openness. In J. Read, L. Mosher & R. Bentall (eds) *Models of Madness: Psychological, Social and Biological Approaches to Schizophrenia*. London: Routledge.

Alivisatos, G. and Lykestos, G. (1964) A preliminary report of research concerning the attitude of the families of hospitalised mental patients, *International Journal of Social Psychiatry*, *10*: 37–44.

Angermeyer, M. and Matschinger, H. (1996) Relatives' beliefs about the causes of schizophrenia, *Acta Psychiatrica Scandinavica*, *93*: 199–204.

Angermeyer, M., Klusmann, D. and Walpuski, O. (1988) The causes of functional psychoses as seen by patients and their relatives. II: The relatives' point of view, *European Archives of Psychiatry and Neurological Sciences*, *238*: 55–61.

Bloch Thorsen, G.-R., Gronnestad, T. and Oxnevad, A. (2006) *Family and Multi-Family Work with Psychosis: A Guide for Professionals*. London: Routledge.

Boydell, K. M., Stasiulis, E., Volpe, T. and Gladstone, B. (2010) A descriptive review of qualitative studies in first episode psychosis, *Early Intervention in Psychiatry*, *4*: 7–24.

Brand, R., Harrop, C. and Ellett, L. (2011) What is it like to be friends with a young person with psychosis? A qualitative study, *Psychosis: Psychological, Social and Integrative Approaches*, *3*: 210–221.

Byrne, R., Davies, L. and Morrison, A. (2010) Priorities and preferences for the outcomes of treatment of psychosis: A service user perspective, *Psychosis: Psychological, Social and Integrative Approaches*, *2*: 235–244.

Corcoran, C., Davidson, L., Sills-Shahar, R., Nickou, C., Malaspina, D., Miller, T. and McGlashan, T. (2003) A Qualitative Research Study of the Evolution of Symptoms in Individuals Identified as Prodromal to Psychosis, *Psychiatric Quarterly*, *74*: 313–332.

Corcoran, C., Gerson, R., Sills-Shahar, R., Nickou, C., McGlashan, T., Malaspina, D. and Davidson, L. (2007) Trajectory to a first episode of psychosis: A qualitative research study with families, *Early Intervention in Psychiatry*, *1*: 308–315.

Esterberg, M. L. and Compton, M. T. (2006) Causes of schizophrenia reported by family members of urban African American hospitalized patients with schizophrenia, *Comprehensive Psychiatry*, *47*: 221–226.

Geekie, J. and Read, J. (2009) *Making Sense of Madness: Contesting the Meaning of Schizophrenia*. Hove, England: Routledge.

Gladstone, B. M., Volpe, T. and Boydell, K. M. (2007) Issues encountered in a qualitative secondary analysis of help-seeking in the prodrome to psychosis, *Journal of Behavioral Health Services & Research*, *34*: 431–442.

Grausgruber, A., Meise, U., Katschnig, H., Schony, W. and Fleischhacker, W. (2007) Patterns of social distance towards people suffering from schizophrenia in Austria: A comparison between the general public, relatives and mental health staff, *Acta Psychiatrica Scandinavica*, *115*: 310–319.

Hakansson, C. (2009) *Ordinary Life Therapy: Experiences From a Collaborative Systemic Practice*. Chagrin Falls, OH: Taos Institute Publications.

Hardcastle, M., Kennard, D., Grandison, S. and Fagin, L. (eds) (2007) *Experiences of Mental Health In-Patient Care*. London: Routledge.

Hawkins, M. (2010) *How We Got Barb Back: The Story of My Sister*. San Fancisco, CA: Red Wheel/Weisser.

Jaffe, P. (1992) First-Person Account: My Brother, *Schizophrenia Bulletin*, *18*: 155–156.

Kagigebi, A. (1995) First-person account: Living in a nightmare, *Schizophrenia Bulletin*, *21*(1): 155–159.

Karanci, A. N. (1995) Caregivers of Turkish schizophrenic patients: Causal attributions, burdens and attitudes to help from the health professions, *Social Psychiatry and Psychiatric Epidemiology*, *30*: 261–268.

Kawanashi, Y. (2006) *Families Coping with Mental Illness: Stories from the US and Japan*. London: Routledge.

Kermode, M., Bowen, K., Arole, S., Joag, K. and Jorm, A. (2009) Community beliefs about treatments and outcomes of mental disorders: A mental health literacy survey in a rural area of Maharashtra, India, *Public Health*, *123*: 476–483.

Kurihara, T., Kato, M., Reverger, R., and Tirta, I. (2006) Beliefs about causes of schizophrenia among family members: A community-based survey in Bali, *Psychiatric Services*, *57*: 1795–1799.

Lefley, H. (1985) Etiological and prevention views of clinicians with mentally ill relatives, *American Journal of Orthopsychiatry*, *55*: 363–370.

McGill, C. W., Falloon, I. R., Boyd, J. L. and Wood-Siverio, C. (1983) Family educational intervention in the treatment of schizophrenia, *Hospital & Community Psychiatry*, *34*: 934–938.

Magliano, L., Fadden, G., Economou, M., Xavier, M., Held, T., Guarneri, M. . . . Maj, M. (1998) Social and clinical factors influencing the choice of coping strategies in relatives of patients with schizophrenia: Results of the BIOMED I study, *Social Psychiatry and Psychiatric Epidemiology*, *33*: 413–419.

Magliano, L., Guarneri, M., Fiorillo, A., Marasco, C., Malangone, C. and Maj, M. (2001) A multicenter Italian study of patients' relatives' beliefs about schizophrenia, *Psychiatric Services*, *52*: 1528–1530.

Magliano, L., Fiorillo, A., De Rosa, C., Malangone, C. and Maj, M. (2004) Beliefs about schizophrenia in Italy: A comparative nationwide survey of the general public, mental health professionals, and patients' relatives, *Canadian Journal of Psychiatry*, *49*: 323–331.

Magliano, L., Fiorillo, A., De Rosa, C., Malangone, C. and Maj, M. (2005) Family burden in long-term diseases: A comparative study in schizophrenia vs. physical disorders, *Social Science & Medicine*, *61*: 313–322.

Magliano, L., Fiorillo, A., Malangone, C., Del Vecchio, H. and Maj, M. (2008) Views of persons with schizophrenia on their own disorder: An Italian participatory study, *Psychiatric Services*, *59*: 795–799.

Magliano, L., Fiorillo, A., Del Vecchio, H., Malangone, C., De Rosa, C., Bachelet, C. . . . Maj, M. (2009) What people with schizophrenia think about the causes of their disorder, *Epidemiologia e Psichiatria Sociale*, *18*: 48–53.

Monteiro, V. B., dos Santos, J. Q. and Martin, D. (2006) Patients' relatives' delayed help seeking after a first psychotic episode, *Revista Brasileira de Psiquiatria*, *28*: 104–110.

Mordoch, E. (2010) How children understand parental mental illness, *Journal of the Canadian Academy of Child and Adolescent Psychiatry, 19*: 19–25.

Neugeboren, J. (2001) *Transforming Madness: New Lives for People Living With Mental Illness.* Berkeley, CA: University of California Press.

Neugeboren, J. (2003) *Imagining Robert: My Brother, Madness, and Survival.* New Brunswick: Rutgers University Press.

Neugeboren, J. (2009) Not by genes alone: A brother's point of view, *Psychosis: Psychological, Social and Integrative Approaches, 1*: 93–94.

Penny, E., Newton, E. and Larkin, M. (2009) Whispering on the water: British Pakistani families' experiences of support from an early intervention service for first-episode psychosis, *Journal of Cross Cultural Psychology, 40*: 969–987.

Phillips, M. R., Li, Y., Stroup, T. and Xin, L. (2000) Causes of schizophrenia reported by patients' family members in China, *British Journal of Psychiatry, 177*: 20–25.

Piercey, B. (1985) First-person account: Making the best of it, *Schizophrenia Bulletin, 11*: 155–157.

Read, J., Haslam, N., Sayce, L. and Davies, E. (2006) Prejudice and schizophrenia: A review of the 'mental illness is an illness like any other' approach, *Acta Psychiatrica Scandinavica, 114*: 303–318.

Shibre, T., Negash, A., Kullgren, G., Kebede, D., Alem, A., Fekadu, D. . . . Jacobson, L. (2001) Perception of stigma among family members of individuals with schizophrenia and major affective disorders, *Social Psychiatry & Psychiatric Epidemiology, 36*: 299–303.

Sin, J., Moone, N. and Wellman, N. (2005) Developing services for the carers of young adults with early-onset psychosis: Listening to their experiences and needs, *Journal of Psychiatric and Mental Health Nursing, 12*: 589–597.

Sin, J., Moone, N. and Harris, P. (2008) Siblings of individuals with first-episode psychosis: Understanding their experiences and needs, *Journal of Psychosocial Nursing and Mental Health Services, 46*: 33–40.

Smith, E. (1991) First-person account: Living with schizophrenia, *Schizophrenia Bulletin, 17*: 689–691.

Srinivasan, T. N. and Thara, R. (2001) Beliefs about causation of schizophrenia: Do Indian families believe in supernatural causes?, *Social Psychiatry and Psychiatric Epidemiology, 36*: 134–140.

Sundquist, A. (1999) First-person account: Family psychoeducation can change lives, *Schizophrenia Bulletin, 25*: 619–621.

Thompson, A., Stuart, H., Bland, R., Arboledo-Florez, J., Warner, R. and Dickson, R. (2002) Attitudes about schizophrenia from the pilot site of the WPA worldwide campaign against the stigma of schizophrenia, *Social Psychiatry and Psychiatric Epidemiology, 37*: 475–482.

Van Dorn, R., Swanson, J., Elbogen, E. and Swartz, M. (2005) A comparison of stigmatizing attitudes toward persons with schizophrenia in four stakeholder groups: Perceived likelihood of violence and desire for social distance, *Psychiatry: Interpersonal and Biological Processes, 68*: 152–163.

Wasserman, S., de Mamani, A. W. and Mundy, P. (2010) Parents' criticisms and attributions about their adult children with high functioning autism or schizophrenia, *Autism, 14*: 127–137.

Whittle, P. (1996) Causal beliefs and acute psychiatric hospital admission, *British Journal of Medical Psychology, 69*: 355–370.

Chapter 23

Summary and concluding comments

Patte Randal, Jim Geekie, John Read and Debra Lampshire

> My soul is ill. My soul, not my mind. The doctors do not understand my illness.
> (Vaslav Nijinsky 1919/1973: 184)

> There is a great need to acknowledge, have respect for, and use in treatment, the patient's own experience.
> (Sims 1988: 445)

We have now come to the end of our book. In this chapter we will recap on some of the themes from the 22 preceding chapters and draw some conclusions from this rich array of stories and research findings. Although we grouped the chapters in pairs, it is evident that there is considerable overlap between many of the themes that emerge from the individual narratives. Each chapter ends with implications for understanding and implications for practice, and we see some important common themes in these. We have been reflecting, throughout, on the business of how we go about relating to, listening to, hearing and understanding the private experiences of people often deemed 'psychotic' or who may have been given diagnoses such as 'schizophrenia', 'schizoaffective disorder', 'bipolar disorder' or other such sometimes distressing labels. Diagnostic labels are generally given by those deemed experts in making psychiatric diagnoses: psychiatrists. When Patte Randal began training to become a psychiatrist back in 1985, 25 years ago, she remembers feeling distressed at the expectation that she had to learn to talk to people only in order to elicit 'symptoms' – to listen for the *form* of a person's speech rather than the *content*, to reach a conclusion about diagnosis, rather than to make a relationship with the person. Accurate diagnosis, particularly in relation to phenomena deemed 'psychotic', depended on eliciting the 'objective signs' of the 'disorder' and these 'signs' were embedded in the '*form*' of speech (such as 'flight of ideas', 'ideas of reference', 'thought disorder', 'delusions', 'hallucinations' and so on). Discriminating form and content was the start of learning the 'expert' practice of the profession of psychiatry. 'Diagnosis' and 'treatment' were (and still are) the *sine qua non* of the medical profession and, in this context in particular, of the psychiatric profession. Objectivity was reified. Subjectivity was shunned as 'anecdote'.

Perhaps, although it is troubling, it is not too surprising, then, to read in the pages of this book the repeated stories of how the vital, private, unique and meaningful subjective experiences of the authors (like those of research participants) have often been missed by those clinicians to whom they have turned for assistance. The consequences of this serious and repeated 'talking past each other' have been clearly described in these chapters, perhaps none more so than in the last but one chapter where Jay Neugeboren movingly describes his reflections on his brother's 40 years of interactions with mental health services. His concluding heart cry, like that of all the preceding authors, is for clinicians who offer services to have the capacity to *truly* listen, to know how to be with the person in ways that feel validating and caring, to believe in the person's ability to survive and to be prepared to build relationships that will be enduring and committed. In short, he is advocating a paradigm shift towards a recovery-oriented approach. This is a theme expressed in various ways by all contributors to this book.

In Chapter 2, David Roe and Paul Lysaker detail research demonstrating the importance of personal narratives in recovery from psychosis. They explicitly point out how, in our different professions, we are taught to attend to and value certain things. In psychology what is valued is different from what is valued in psychiatry, nursing, occupational therapy or social work. What is taught may not necessarily be the most beneficial approaches for the people we serve, and indeed may be inadvertently harmful. Roe and Lysaker assert that as professionals we need to learn how to attend to how people have made meaning of their experience. We need to learn to listen. They point out that recently published personal narratives demonstrate the profound capacity of people to express aspects of their lived experience that have been repeatedly missed – with huge negative consequences. They conclude that narratives have potential healing power – and the act of re-negotiating meaning and recognizing connections between past and present life events can lead to increased self-acceptance, and indeed may be a unique element of recovery. They present the beginnings of a new science of quantitative assessment of the coherence of personal narrative, which may eventually help us to understand what will help people who have lost the thread of their life story to develop richer and more helpful personal narratives. They also acknowledge that disconnected stories may serve a protective function in keeping at bay unbearable emotions. Recognizing this might lead to very different and potentially more healing interventions than the current focus on diagnoses.

In Chapter 3 Jacqui Dillon beautifully and poignantly describes how her childhood experiences of devastating trauma and abuse and the consequent extreme states that manifested after the birth of her first child, were confusingly interpreted as symptoms of biological illness. There are many similarities between her unique story and the unique stories of others in this book who describe a crazy-making world where psychiatric 'help' was in part experienced as causing further harm because the subjective meaning was not understood. Jacqui portrays her experience of the therapy which was ultimately healing. Her concluding recommendation is for clinicians to be able to see the world and human experience in new ways, and to provide empathic witness; to see and hear the suffering of those they serve.

The sister chapter by Larry Davidson, presenting qualitative research relating to recovery from psychosis, shows us how to 'hurry slowly'. He argues that small steps are necessary when the 'taken-for-granted' aspects of experience can no longer be taken for granted. He points out that 'just having a sense of coherence and predictability in one's daily life can represent a major accomplishment'. He details how repairing the damage to sense of self and rebuilding confidence in the world and one's ability to function in it are paramount. Like other contributors, he concludes that clinicians need to develop an understanding of how to assist in promoting an increased sense of self, and that training of staff in these new and vital capacities is needed.

Chapter 5 presents Egan Bidois' cultural understanding of 'why' he went through the experiences he so graphically and articulately describes. In sharing his story with us, Egan demonstrates how important the question of 'why' is and how the answer to this question may be found in indigenous knowledge and practice – in Egan's case, within Māori ways of thinking about and relating to the kinds of experiences he describes. Egan's story illustrates the importance of finding meaning in experience and how this meaning is located within specific cultural contexts. He stresses the need for cultural expertise to help recognize interventions that might be helpful when people present to services in extreme states including seeing and hearing things that are not apparent to others.

Continuing with the focus on culture, and also drawing on Māori contributions to this discussion, Lambrecht and Taitimu in Chapter 6 explore research illuminating culture, subjectivity and psychosis. The authors wish to give subjectivity its 'rightful place' – neither rarefied in importance nor sidelined as has been the norm. They point out that different cultural approaches have led to silencing, objectifying and empowering subjectivity, and state that the tools for understanding psychosis in one culture cannot be transposed to another without vital elements being lost in translation. They advocate that research needs to happen from within a given cultural group in order to benefit that group, and assert that integrating various cultural healing options that have been experientially validated would require a paradigm shift in clinical and educational practices. It is interesting to speculate what might emerge if enquiry were made into the subjective experiences of clinicians trained within the dominant paradigm of the biological understanding of psychosis. How many would express distress at the imposition of a system that does not 'allow' us to fully hear and understand the stories of the people we serve?

Chapter 7 presents Patte Randal's personal narrative of recovery, emphasizing the subjective experience of spirituality and psychosis, and brings forward the concept of 'spiritual emergency' as an explanatory model that takes better account of personal meaning-making, and can lead to victorious rather than vicious cycles in the recovery journey. In Chapter 8, David Lukoff details research evidence regarding subjective experience of spirituality and psychosis and concludes that subjective experience of spiritual support may form the core of the spirituality–health connection.

Chapters 9 and 10 explore the personal narrative of loss of sense of self and the research into the existential aspects of the subjective experience of psychosis. Arnhild Lauveng clearly describes how her experience of identity was lost – not her actual identity. 'In retrospect I can see that in fact "I" was there all the time – but I felt the "I" didn't exist any more.' She goes on to call for clinicians always to keep in mind that they treat individuals, rather than treating 'psychosis'. Jim Geekie in Chapter 10 asserts that existential concerns lie at the heart of human experience and need to be addressed in clinical practice. He describes research findings that demonstrate that disturbances in self-experiences are central to the subjectivity of those who experience 'psychosis', but that these concerns are often ignored. The resulting invalidation commonly causes increased suffering. Telling one's own story can help in the development of a more integral sense of self.

Chapters 11 and 12 deal with the 'at risk' state of developing psychosis. Rory Byrne masterfully describes his life traumas and their consequences with the unfolding of 'the difficult psychological experiences' that are eventually characterized as an 'at risk' state. His detailed description sheds a uniquely revealing light on the process of the development of psychotic phenomena and his concern that he was 'mad'. Like other authors, he describes how he did not initially tell anyone of his plight. He goes on to say that the establishment of a primarily normalizing rather than pathologizing paradigm could reduce the service-based stigma currently experienced by those with such difficulties. He advocates the inclusion of mental health professionals who can speak with service users from the perspective of their own lived experience of similar difficulties and recovery from these. Kate Hardy details research into the high level of awareness demonstrated by those in the 'at risk' period (contrary to what is generally believed by clinicians), and advocates for the importance of eliciting and respecting subjective narratives as a means to access a holistic understanding of individual clients' needs and priorities, and potentially intervening in a way that is healing.

Chapters 13 and 14 explore the lived experiences of trauma and the consequent dissociation of intense emotion and subsequent psychotic phenomena. Wilma Boevink's narrative echoes Roe and Lysaker's earlier suggestion that a coherent narrative can bring with it the previously dissociated pain that has been too unbearable to endure. Eliciting such stories therefore needs to be undertaken with great sensitivity and care. John Read details the growing body of research supporting the links between first-person accounts of adverse life events and psychosis. It is becoming increasingly clear that the content of psychotic experience echoes the life experience of the person – and a wealth of information emerges when people are given a chance to tell their stories (as the stories in this book demonstrate) – experiences of isolation, loneliness, loss, witnessing parental violence, neglect, bullying, sexual, physical and emotional abuse, and the use of substances in an attempt to manage the unwanted consequences of these. From this perspective, symptoms can be seen as essential survival techniques, and people must be given the opportunity to speak about the worst that life has thrown at them, because not asking conveys that it is not safe to tell.

Chapters 15 and 16 deal with the experience of voice hearing. Debra Lampshire exquisitely reminds us that the story she shares with us here relates only to certain 'moments' in her life, and that she is more – much more – than just these 'moments' (something we need to keep in mind when reading each of the personal accounts in this book). She advises us that 'madness can be an enticing siren', one which led her to believe for a while that she had the responsibility of saving the world. She goes on to explain how she changed her relationship with the voices, and how they revealed themselves as 'incompetent communicators distorting and misinterpreting situations, often over-reacting to perceived threats.' Soon she realized that her voices were impotent without her and yet she tells us that 'no one prepares you for the destruction of what has been a way of surviving. I may have lost a tormentor, but I also lost a way of being.' Debra details her journey to recovery, which includes the benefit of continued voice-hearing. Like Egan Bidois, she says: 'Coming to terms with the "whys" is very cathartic; recognizing the "whys" but not allowing them to determine or control your future; that is autonomy.' The 'whys' for Debra are different than for Egan (involving multiple experiences of invalidation and rejection as well as childhood trauma), but understanding them was equally empowering. Vanessa Beavan in Chapter 16 presents research evidence regarding voice hearing, emphasizing the fact that there is compelling evidence that it is more accurate and more helpful to view psychotic-like symptoms as occurring on a continuum of human experience, found within both clinical and non-clinical populations. She describes the evidence for positive and negative aspects of voice content (which is often linked to past trauma), and points out that the negative voices in clinical samples are often less distressing to the individual than other life difficulties, and distress can be exacerbated by stigma. She concludes that a non-pathological model of voice-hearing would promote normalization, reduce stigma and encourage recovery through meaning-making and integration of the experience into the person's life journey. She advocates asking who the voices are and what they are saying, and suggests that beliefs about voices may offer clues to helpful coping strategies including spiritual understandings.

Chapters 17 and 18 present the subjective experience of delusional beliefs. John Wraphire writes movingly and with intense, powerful insight into his early childhood, the ensuing social isolation, and the development of his own delusional beliefs about receiving messages from the actions of others, resulting in his almost complete withdrawal from daily life, and his eventual resolution and recovery. Much can be learned from his description that can only be revealed through subjective experience. His statement that he believed everyone thought in the same way he did is an important reminder to us all – which of us is not prone to making the same error? Like others, being told that he had 'schizophrenia' and being given medication are described as unhelpful interventions, leaving him mistrustful of most mental health services. The simplicity and profundity of his own conclusions speak his truth: 'I think the cause of my social difficulties was having few friends. My lack of communication caused my beliefs to become inaccurate.' He explains that the sessions with his psychologist allowed him to talk about and make sense of his delusions, and he goes on to say that 'over the years my various social, spiritual and intellectual achievements have given me greater confidence', bringing to mind the 'small steps' described in Chapter 4. Campbell and Morrison in Chapter 18 detail research illustrating that the content of delusions relates to aspects of the person's life and, concerns, and, as with most psychological distress, is associated with unmet human needs. They describe a pathway of experiences of paranoia, which can develop in clinical and non-clinical populations, from fear and vulnerability to confusion and uncertainty to self under attack to engaging in safety systems which may have a positive effect initially but are ultimately self-defeating. They propose that persecutory delusions can be viewed as a psychological defence mechanism aimed to protect the individual from harm (often at the cost of a restricted life). The feature that seems to distinguish clinical from non-clinical experiences is having a sense of control, and this seems to be related to past experiences of negative events. Achieving a sense of safety seems to lead to less paranoia, and this therefore needs to be an aim of the therapeutic relationship. It may be that developing a coherent recovery narrative can occur with an increase in the sense of control and safety.

Chapters 19 and 20 deal with subjective experiences of negative symptoms. Eleanor Longden masterfully depicts her desperate attempts to survive an experience of intense despair by shutting down emotionally for fear of being overwhelmed by powerful emotions. She illustrates clearly that the concept of 'negative symptoms', with its implication of loss of emotional experience, is a wholly inaccurate term, reflecting what the observer (such as the clinician) may see and entirely missing what the client may experience. James Le Lievre's research provides us with an example of how approaching the so-called 'negative symptoms' by prioritizing the individual's subjective experience can shed light on these experiences that may help to guide clinical approaches to working with individuals who have endured these extreme states. Once again, both these contributors call for an empathic approach by clinicians to encourage service users to tell their stories, make sense of their relational confusion, and hopefully discover the meaning within the hidden peak experiences (spiritual emergencies?) that have characterized aspects of their psychosis but often remain unspeakable and unheard.

We end our book with two important chapters exploring the subjective experience of families of those who have experienced psychosis. In Chapter 21, Jay Neugeboren shares with us a poignant and moving account of his relationship with his brother Robert, and the trials and tribulations of both his relationship with his brother and their relationship with mental health services. In Chapter 22, John Read and Lorenza Magliano provide us with an overview of research into the family's experience, pointing out that all too often the family's subjective experience, both of their loved one's difficulties and of their search for effective help, is overlooked by both clinicians and researchers, echoing a theme from many of the previous chapters where the subjective experience of those most intimately involved in the experience is overlooked and unheard.

To conclude, then, we hope it is obvious to the reader that each of the contributors to this book has shared something of themselves and that each is intimately involved in the story they relate to us. While this is most apparent for those who share their personal experience of what we have been referring to as 'psychosis', those who conduct research into subjective experience must, we believe, also have some personal involvement if their research is to shed light on the experience concerned. All the stories in this book speak eloquently for themselves, conveying a recurrent theme that we all share the human condition and that those experiences that are referred to as examples of 'psychoses' are as much part of the human condition as are experiences such as 'love', 'happiness' and 'despair'. Our stories inevitably embody the important elements of our experience, and human experience lies on a continuum. Stories change. Our narratives become more coherent as we learn to face the pain of our suffering. We re-cover the same old ground in our attempts to recover from the inevitable traumas of life. We can get caught in vicious cycles, repeating old patterns, and becoming increasingly vulnerable. But the opportunity is always present for each life crisis to become an opportunity to increase resilience, and to be a catalyst for victorious cycles instead, as these stories so clearly demonstrate

References

Nijinsky, V. (1919/1973) *The Diary of Vaslav Nijinksy* (3rd edition) (ed. by Romola Nijinsky). Berkeley: University of California Press.

Sims, A. C. P. (1988) *Symptoms in the Mind*. London: Bailliere Tindall.

Index